POWER-UP

How Japanese Video Games Gave the World an Extra Life

By Chris Kohler

//////BRADYGAMES®

To My Parents

CONTENTS

FOREWORD

Today, the games industry is shifting radically as production values, costs, and development teams are increasing substantially in size. Making video games today is nothing like it was five years ago—never mind fifteen years ago. Western games are now starting to dominate the charts, but no one can dispute the profound effect that Japanese game creators have had on our industry. In fact, one may argue that without the Japanese contribution, the games industry might not be around today.

The impact of working closely with Nintendo and Konami has had a profound impact on our game design philosophies. One of the goals at Silicon Knights is to try to bridge the gap between Eastern and Western game creation philosophies by creating a synthesis that pushes the game industry forward. We believe that the game industry will be the dominant art form of entertainment this century, and that these steps are necessary for its growth.

In May 1999, Shigeru Miyamoto gave the keynote address at the Game Developers Conference. Something he said there continues to resonate in my mind. "For me, game creation is a lot like expression through music or poetry." That ideal really struck me as particularly moving and insightful. Through my experiences working with him over the years it is clear that all his designs incorporate tempo, rhythm and harmony—just like music or poetry would. Examining his work, this attention to detail in design is clear.

In this book, Chris details the things that make the game designs from Japan so special. Everyone in the industry should take note, for there are many valuable lessons to be learned. In order to understand the way things are made in Japan, you have to understand Japan, and Chris's time spent in Japan, as well as his ability to speak the language, allow him to examine things that the average Westerner would not have the opportunity to do. Like no one else can, Chris provides insight into some of the thinking and history behind creating games in Japan.

Denis Dyack
President of Silicon Knights
Director of *Blood Omen: Legacy of Kain* and
Eternal Darkness: Sanity's Requiem
Co-Producer of *Metal Gear Solid: The Twin Snakes*

INTRODUCTION

VIDEO GAMES ARE GOOD FOR YOU

"If the reader examines my work too carefully, he may discover that I'm only a journalist. This means that when it comes to knowing what I'm talking about, I'm no different from the next person; I just get paid for the telling."

- P.J. O'Rourke

Like Nintendo's Mario, this book has had many lives. The first and oldest bits were written right around Christmas of 2001, the first chapters of my graduation thesis at Tufts University. I submitted it under the title *The Cinematic Japanese Video Game* that spring. It received highest honors and I graduated with a BA in Japanese. Months later I was off to Kyoto, Japan on a one-year Fulbright fellowship to turn *The Cinematic Japanese Video Game* into *Power-Up*.

That's the version I tell at parties. The truth is that I have been writing this book in my head since I was eleven years old in sixth grade, and I decided that I wanted to be a video game journalist when I grew up. (I still do.) I was born after video games, and I'm not exaggerating when I say that I don't remember a time in my life without them.

One of my earliest memories is of my father programming a Blackjack game on our then state-of-the-art TRS-80 home computer with its 4K of RAM and cassette tape drive storage. Two years later our whole family would gather around our Atari 800XE to play *Frogger*

> **I was born after video games, and I'm not exaggerating when I say that I don't remember a time in my life without them.**

and the hundreds of other games we had on floppy disk. At the same time, my father tooled around with an Atari VCS video game system at work and got it to play copies of games that they had burned onto rewriteable chips, just to see if they could do it.

And then came the Nintendo Entertainment System. We got it on Easter morning, 1988. The Action Set with the *Super Mario Bros.* and *Duck Hunt* cartridge, two controllers, and a Zapper light pistol. *Super Mario Bros.* filled our days until we'd saved the Princess. This was something we'd never experienced with any of our drawer full of Atari games. This was a symphony of colors and music. The game play control was sublime. The characters leapt off the screen.

At eight, then nine, then ten years old I was finally old enough to really start to appreciate what I was experiencing. By then, video games had outgrown the simple shooting and jumping contests that were popular in arcades when I was a toddler. They were vast, open-ended worlds like *The Legend of Zelda*, filled with exploration and storylines. What I loved about video games at that age was the same thing that I loved about books. At school, I would draw Mario and the rest of the characters from the games in my notebooks, first just pictures with a few words and then full-blown comics, first imitations of the ones I'd read in *Nintendo Power* magazine and then original stories.

And at some point, probably through 'behind-the-scenes' articles in *Nintendo Power*, I realized that all these games that I loved came from Japan. So my eyes opened to the other forms of Japanese popular culture that had begun to trickle into suburban Connecticut by the early nineties: *manga* comic books in translation, usually on a tiny out-of-the-way rack in the comic book store in the mall, and whatever *anime* was on television at the time, mostly heavily edited and English-dubbed shows like *Sailor Moon*.

I chose Tufts University in large part because of the school's wide selection of Japanese language and culture offerings. Immersing myself into innovative courses like Japanese Visual Culture and Japanese Film opened my eyes, because I was beginning to realize that so many of the theories about Japanese art that I was learning applied directly to video games. It started to become clear why Japanese video games had become so popular and commercially successful worldwide. My struggle to explain this phenomenon culminated in the chapters that follow.

I am pleased and humbled that you have decided to read this book. Before we begin, some brief words on the research and quotes. Since *Power-Up* began as a thesis paper long before I had any access to face-to-face interviews with developers, many of the quotes came from interviews published in other books, magazines, and websites. In general I have kept the best quotes obtained in this early research, sometimes because I was not granted a face-to-face interview with the designer and sometimes because my time with them was limited, and I did not wish to retread ground that had already been covered in interviews.

I was fortunate enough while living in Kyoto to come across many interviews with game designers published in Japanese. In the cases where I felt sure that I could preserve the original meaning of the designer's words, I have printed them in quotation form. In cases where I could not, I used the interviews as a basis for narrating a series of events in my own words. I have footnoted the texts accordingly, especially in cases where a fact might not be considered common knowledge or may indeed be in dispute.

In cases where the quote comes from an outside source, I have used the past tense (...he said). If the quote is from a personal interview, present tense (...he says) is used.

I have tried my best to avoid the use of the first person throughout except where absolutely necessary—for although I want to put *Power-Up* into context, I want the stories of the developers to come through with minimal editorializing by yours truly.

And yet, just as in previous books on video game culture, it is impossible to escape the fact that my own childhood, adolescent, and adult tastes, experiences, and preferences have highly influenced the format and content of this one. I would like to see more recent games like *Final Fantasy VII* dissected and analyzed as I have examined the earlier NES versions. But just as authors before me wrote their books about *Asteroids* and *Defender*, and I am writing mine about *Mario* and *Final Fantasy*, it is up to the next generation to analyze the games they grow up with.

With that out of the way,

"Let's-a-go."

CHAPTER 1

SUPER MARIO NATION

Games are popular art, collective, social reactions to the main drive or action of any culture. [They]...are extensions of social man and of the body politic...

As extensions of the popular response to the workaday stress, games become faithful models of a culture. They incorporate both the action and the reaction of whole populations in a single dynamic image... The games of a people reveal a great deal about them.

—Marshall McLuhan,
Understanding Media:
The Extensions of Man

The preceding quote served as the epigraph to David Sheff's seminal 1993 book *Game Over*, a riveting, novelesque portrait of the people behind the rise of Nintendo, the world's largest video game software publisher and, at the time, the dominant force in the video game industry. Ultimately, *Game Over* was a journalistic chronicle of international business intrigue and courtroom drama, but the choice of quote revealed that Sheff was thinking, too, about the cultural aspects of Nintendo video games—backed up by later admissions that it was his son's love for the games that initially drew him to the topic.

There's only one problem: Sheff was writing about video game culture solely as it pertained to America. And although there is much to say about Japanese video games in American culture, the fact is that the games Sheff was writing about *are not products or models of our culture*. They are products and models of *Japanese* culture, the "action and the reaction" of the Japanese population, presented nearly unaltered for our consumption.

And what consumers we are. Video game sales in the US have skyrocketed from a decade ago—3.2 billion dollars in 1995 to 6.9 billion in 2002, and Japanese-developed games have historically made up a large part of that sum. Many Japanese games, particularly those developed by Kyoto-based Nintendo Co., Ltd., top bestseller lists worldwide. Nintendo's *Super Mario Bros.* (1985) remains the single best-selling video game of all time, although other Nintendo titles like *The Legend of Zelda: The Ocarina of Time* and of course the various iterations of *Pokémon* have been no slouches.

Throughout the brief history of video games, Japanese-developed titles have set the world on fire—*Space Invaders* in the seventies, *Pac-Man* in the early eighties, *Super Mario Bros.* in 1985, *Street Fighter II* in 1991, *Final Fantasy VII* in 1997. And even when a non-Japanese game becomes a breakout hit in the US or elsewhere, it is often heavily based on elements pioneered in Japanese software and released for a Japanese-developed hardware system: *Tomb Raider* on the Sega Saturn in 1995, *Grand Theft Auto: Vice City* on the Sony PlayStation 2 in 2002.

So the question is, why? Why were Japanese video games so popular worldwide, from the earliest days, with little to no modification necessary? After all, the same thing has not been true for, say, Japanese films. And while Japanese animation and comics are quickly attaining mainstream popularity in the Western world, this is a very recent phenomenon. Only a handful of Americans knew about *manga* in 1980. Meanwhile, the rest of the country had *Pac-Man* Fever. And it was a fever brought on in part by the infectious, *manga*-style Japanese design sense of that video game.

Why, indeed? Well, to find the answer we should first ask: what separates the first video games from the video games of today? The immediate answer would seem to be that advances in computer processing power over the past four decades have produced video game hardware capable of superior graphics, and that the advent of the compact disc allows for more complex game designs thanks to its high memory storage capacity.

But this is not the entire answer. It is indeed true that the video games of today are far more technologically advanced than the first commercial home video game system. That was called Odyssey, which was released by the television company Magnavox in 1972 and sold for $99.99. Odyssey could, at

best, generate a white line running down the blank television screen and three white dots: two "paddles" and one "ball" that bounced between them, a television tennis game. Odyssey played other types of games as well, but all of them featured only a few small, monochrome dots appearing onscreen at once.

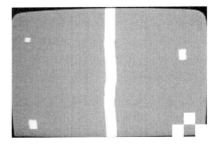

Odyssey and later home video games of the time were looked upon as disposable playthings and not permanent additions to one's home television set. This was, in part, because the earliest game systems were what are called *dedicated* hardware. New games could not be added to the system; only the games built into the hardware could be played. Furthermore, these games were simplistic, repetitive, and, after a short time, boring. This sort of mentality—that video game hardware would quickly become boring to the consumer—started to shift with the availability of *programmable* hardware, consoles that featured no built-in games but allowed the user to play new ones stored on separate media.

Programmable hardware helped begin the evolution of a video game machine from a simple plaything to a staple of the home entertainment center, the difference between a music box and a phonograph. Programmable systems also made it possible for game designers to create their work and sell software without having to supply the hardware as well.

Michael Katz, formerly of the video game company Sega, remembered this from the days when more and more video game publishers were starting to pop up in Silicon Valley: "There were so many cartridges already available to Atari players from Atari, that we couldn't imagine that any consumer needed more cartridges. Nobody thought that they [consumers] would perceive any kind of difference in the graphics…and we couldn't conceive of anyone paying $3 to $5 more at retail for cartridges from a company that no one had ever heard of."[1]

Imagine such a comment being applied to another medium: *There were so many books available to readers that we couldn't imagine that any reader needed more books. Nobody thought that readers would perceive any kind of difference in the words, and we couldn't conceive of anyone paying $3 to $5 more for books from a company that no one had ever heard of.*

Nonsense, right? But this made perfect sense when talking about the video games of the time, because *a game was a game was a game.* Most every video game being sold was a simple shooting or driving contest and there was little to differentiate, in the mind of the consumer, one cartridge from another. Games in the 1970s and early 1980s had no clear ending, but instead just continued with repetitive action for a few minutes until the player lost his last spaceship or crashed his tiny, monochrome car.

Today, game players spend hours immersed in role-playing games like *Dragon Quest* or *Final Fantasy*, puzzling over plot details, intricacies of the worlds they explore, the powers of their characters, and their relationships.

So it is not, in fact, simply that today's video games are larger and more graphically intricate: it is that the actual content and design—the very makeup of the games—has changed.

▓ ▒ ▓

Henry Jenkins, director of the Comparative Media Studies Program at the Massachusetts Institute of Technology, called today's video games "virtual play spaces which allow home-bound children…to extend their reach, to explore, manipulate, and interact with a more diverse range of imaginary places than constitute the often drab, predictable, and overly-familiar spaces of their everyday lives."[2] Jenkins elaborates, showing the various ways that modern-day video game play echoes nineteenth-century boy culture. He writes that nineteenth-century boys would draw on the adventure stories of the day as a template for their own play—reading a book about pirates and then playing as pirates, for example.[3]

Jenkins then noted that today's video games depend heavily on "fantasy role-playing, with different genres of games allowing children to imagine themselves in alternative…roles or situations."[4] This description is not restricted to the genre known as "role-playing games," which are elaborate story-based strategy games. Even today's simpler, action-oriented games feature specific characters and unique situations. The characters and scenarios in all of these video games are, therefore, serving the same imagination-igniting function as the adventure books.

Thus, perhaps the most important difference between the earliest video games and today's games is the insertion of what could be called *cinematic* elements. Rather than stick figures or spaceships representing the player, today's games star fully fleshed-out characters with backgrounds, motivation, and perhaps development throughout the story. Games incorporate narrative; they are built around a story line. And most games today include what are referred to as cut scenes or cinematics—sometimes non-interactive, often film-like sequences that set up or advance the story, which is typically a complex, lengthy affair.

Cinematic elements are appealing to game players because they can enhance the game experience. Game designers quickly learned the value of flashy reward screens for a job well done, of giving players concrete goals with set rewards to strive for. If a game has likeable characters, players can become attached to those characters and more deeply involved in the game. And if a game has a storyline, players have a concrete incentive to "beat" the game: they want to complete the story, to bring closure to the narrative.

This revolution came about as a result of Japanese influence on this American pastime: these cinematic game elements that are so common today originated in Japanese video games of the early eighties. In one of the first books ever written on video games, a 1982 volume called *Video Invaders*, author Steve Bloom wrote that "the Japanese have a 'comical sense,' and are great fans of comic books, sitcoms, and cartoons. Taito America's president, Jack Mittel, explained: 'They [the Japanese] want more of a story line, more of a Walter Mitty experience that's like a whole movie...'"[5]

Even the name of Bloom's book illustrates the huge impact that Japanese games had on American game culture from the first: the name Bloom chose for his volume, *Video Invaders*, is a play on the name of a video game developed by the Japanese company Taito, *Space Invaders*. Bloom goes on to describe the then-new Japanese game *Donkey Kong* (which would spawn the world-famous *Mario* series, although Bloom did not know it at the time) as "another bizarre cartoon game, courtesy of Japan."[6]

WHY JAPAN?

"Japan," wrote Alex Kerr in his provocative book *Dogs And Demons: The Fall Of Modern Japan*, "while maintaining a competent standard in many industries, and intellectual or artistic pursuits, does not lead the way in any single field."[7] This is not entirely the case. Though Kerr lays out a well-researched case on the decline of Japanese traditional art, architecture, cinema, and technology, perhaps the Japanese video game is the exception that proves the rule.

These "bizarre cartoon games" were coming from a country and a people in love with cartoons and comics. Frederik L. Schodt, who has written two books and countless articles on Japanese comics, wrote in 1983 that the Japanese consider them to be "an effective…way of transmitting information, and they use them everywhere… Aiding in this explosion in the use of cartoons is the fact that so many people learn how to draw them… For younger generations comics are *the* common language… [They] live in an age that emphasizes the image…[and] naturally have no bias against comics. They are, appropriately, referred to in Japan as the *shikaku sedai*, the 'visual generation.'"[8]

Not only that, but there were aspects of Japanese design sense that lent themselves specifically to the medium of the video game. Japanese *anime* characters, heavily influenced by the style of *manga* pioneer Osamu Tezuka, are cartoonish and unrealistically proportioned, even when the stories they tell are deadly serious. In his book *Understanding Comics*, Scott McCloud noted that Japanese *manga* artists prize abstract, iconic characters, and that abstraction in general is key to identification with the characters in a story. In the

book, which is presented in comic form, he draws himself, the narrator, in an abstract style for this very purpose of engaging the reader.[9]

Tetsuwan Atomu—"Mighty Atom" or "Astro Boy"—is the most well-known creation of "god of manga" Osamu Tezuka. Tezuka's style was inspired by Disney, and most modern anime and game characters are styled much like Tezuka's big-eyed, strangely proportioned hero.

"This way of drawing characters," noted J.C. Herz in her book *Joystick Nation*, "translated easily into early video games, which didn't have the graphic resolution to represent characters with adult proportions. Small, cute characters had fewer pixels per inch and were easier to use, and so video games borrowed, for reasons of expediency, what *manga* had developed as a matter of convention."[10]

The Japanese believe this style to be *mukokuseki*, a word that literally means "lacking nationality" but is used mainly to refer to the "erasure of racial or ethnic characteristics and contexts from a cultural product."[11] Indeed, though Japanese *anime* character designs lack any ethnically Japanese features, the style itself can hardly be said to "lack nationality" when it is a unique creation of Japanese artists, completely different from American or European comic artwork.*

★ Sometimes, of course, Japanese video games *do* have certain Japanese ethnic or cultural context. These are usually removed or replaced if the game comes to the US—see chapters 8 and 9.

More generally, the Japanese have a centuries-old tradition of visual culture. One might go so far as to say that the image, rather than the word, has always been at the forefront of Japanese culture. From the *ukiyo-e* woodblock prints of the "floating world" to the highly stylized visual experiences that comprise the traditional *Noh* and *kabuki* theater, from the sexually charged *shunga* prints that gave way to vivid and chilling *gekiga* "film books" that were the precursors to modern *manga* comics, in every era of Japanese history we find that the most popular art forms were *visual in nature*.

One might even say that *haiku*—short Japanese poems that present, in as few words as possible, a vivid image of a seasonal nature scene—are visually oriented. Even the Japanese written language is made up of pictographs that come from representational drawings.

The notion of the image grew up differently in the Western world, where picture books, comic books, and chapter books with illustrations are looked down upon as children's entertainment. A child who reads books without illustrations is said to be reading on an adult level; an adult who avidly reads comic books would be thought strange. But the *shikaku sedai* (a phrase that now describes even today's middle-aged Japanese) privilege the image as a method of communication and so have a love for comics and animation. "One result" of this outlook, wrote Schodt, "is that many talented young people—who in other times might have become novelists or painters—are becoming professional comic artists."[12] And in the early '80s, as Schodt was writing these words, many of these young people were becoming video game designers.

Their American contemporaries, meanwhile, seemed to have no idea what was going on. In *Video Invaders*, American game designer Tim Skelly, then of Cinematronics, attacked the Japanese game design philosophy, calling them "horrible copiers" and adding, "most of their games don't cut it here anyway. I foresee them losing a lot of business here in the States."[13] In less than one year's time, however, Cinematronics—and many companies like it—would be the ones losing a lot of business, as the video game market dried up in the United States. It was Japanese companies that would revive the US industry.

Wrote video game historian Leonard Herman, "At one time the United States had been the leader in all forms of manufacturing from automobiles to television and radios. As time passed, Japan…eventually took them over…[but] the only markets that they couldn't take over were computers and video games. Computers appeared to be the only true American product remaining. Because they were small scale computers, video games were also an American phenomenon…until 1978 when Taito released *Space Invaders* and Japan quickly took over with an attack all of its own."[14]

In 1983, the U.S. video game market crashed. Video games still thrived in Japan, but American companies like Atari, Coleco, and Mattel were not able to keep the industry afloat in the US. Many video game publishers went bankrupt by 1984. In 1985, Nintendo introduced its Famicom video game system in the United States, and along with it a full library of Japanese video games translated into English. In a year's time, Nintendo had resurrected the dead video game market. American companies like Atari tried to compete but American video games could not stand up to games like Nintendo's *Super Mario Bros.*

Even today, thanks mostly to the early influence of Japanese "bizarre cartoon games," a great many successful games in the US are Japanese. In their January 2002 issue, editors of the popular video game magazine *Electronic Gaming Monthly* voted for their favorite 100 games of all time. Of the 100 games listed:

86 had recognizable, distinct characters.

78 had a full story or story elements.

38 were role-playing games built entirely around a story progression.

93 were Japanese in origin.

WHY IT MATTERS:
VIDEO GAMES AS MULTICULTURAL GATEWAY

This book is intended to be a celebration of the art form of video games with an eye toward the positive aspects of the games. Other such books examining video games have not been so kind to the medium. Academic and journalistic books have attacked video games for being sexist, racist, violent, and ultimately harmful to children. The book that most typified this sense of hysteria was called *Video Kids: Making Sense of Nintendo,* written by University of Miami professor Eugene F. Provenzo, Jr. in 1991.

In his book, Provenzo concluded that society had to "eliminate the violence, destruction, xenophobia, racism, and sexism that are so much a part of the world of Nintendo."[15] At the 1993 joint Congressional hearings on video game violence, Provenzo was called upon to testify as an expert witness. He repeated his findings at the hearings, testifying, "video games are overwhelmingly violent, sexist, and racist."[16] After his presentation, Senator Joseph Lieberman (D-Conn.), the primary architect of the hearings, asked Provenzo to elaborate on his charge that Nintendo's video games were racist.

"In interviews with children," replied Provenzo, "what I found was that they talked about the ninjas [enemy characters in the *Teenage Mutant Ninja Turtles* games] as being bad. Then [I] asked them about who ninjas were, and they [said they were]...the Japs and the Chinese. It turns out that they perceive Asians, any Asians, as being extremely violent, as being dangerous, as being evil."[17]

Taken at face value, this provocative statement seems damning. But the text of his book tells a somewhat different story. In the chapter titled "Aggression and Video games," Provenzo described children's involvement with the *Teenage Mutant Ninja Turtles* video games:

> "One child presented a detailed description of weapons such as throwing stars and katangas [sic]. Significantly, despite detailed knowledge of Ninja weaponry, most of the children interviewed seemed to have little understanding of where the Ninja came from or what they signified. A fourth grade boy explained, for example, that he wasn't sure if the Ninja were Chinese or Japanese, but that the Chinese and Japanese were the enemies because "just because they are from Japan they might want to do something different from you. And they are dangerous because they might want to fight with you."[18]

Note that this one utterance from one fourth-grade child serves as *Video Kids'* prima facie evidence of racism; the only finding that Provenzo offered in the entire book to back up his conclusion that Nintendo games were *overwhelmingly racist*. Confusingly, Provenzo even noted in his book that for the most part the children he interviewed had "little understanding" of what race *ninja* are. What the children *did* know was that the Ninja Turtles were *turtles*, and the enemy ninja were *robots*. It's far-fetched to imagine that children might even consider robots and sea creatures to be of any particular race.

Regardless of the hysteria that earlier books typified, later research—on the growing *manga* and *anime* boom in the US—started to tell a very different story about the perceptions of Asians, and Japanese in particular, that are held by American youth. Dr. Antonia Levi wrote in 1996 that, due to the proliferation of *anime* in American popular culture, "America's Generation X and Japan's *shin jinrui* will never again be complete strangers to one another."[19] "There we were, happily debating whether to focus education on multiculturalism or Western Civilization, and the kids made their own choice with *anime* and *manga*."[20]

Academics like Levi and Susan J. Napier seem to be generally excited about the prospect of *anime* creating a generation of American young people who are culturally in tune with their Japanese counterparts. But do Japanese video games count? Napier explicitly made this connection in her book *Anime From Akira To Princess Mononoke*, stating in her chapter on American *anime* fans that many of them "often [first] come across *anime* in computer or video games" which would make an interest in *anime* "quite natural." She did not cite examples of video games with *anime* influences or those based on *anime* series, but many of them made their way to the United States long before the *manga* or *anime* did: a game based on the adult-oriented spy thriller *manga Golgo 13*, for example, was released for the Nintendo Entertainment System in the US in 1988, well before the *manga* or *anime*.

> "America's Generation X and Japan's *shin jinrui* will never again be complete strangers to one another."

Frederik Schodt predicted this in 1983: "In the years to come, the sheer size and momentum of Japanese comics culture will make itself felt around the world indirectly, through the commercial spin-offs of toys, animation, picture books, video games..."[21] *Super Mario Bros.* and *Final Fantasy* were not "spin-offs" of any particular *anime*, but the style of the games came out of a country whose booming comics and animation culture gave birth to them. So whether American children—or any of these researchers—knew it or not, *Super Mario* was a warm-up, an introduction to the unique visual style of the Japanese such that when a generation that had grown up on Nintendo was introduced to *Akira* or *Princess Mononoke*, there was something familiar about these cultural imports.

Or, as game designer Keiichi Yano puts it, "Video games were the big can-opener." Yano has a unique perspective on this phenomenon: born in Tokyo, he lived in Los Angeles until he was 20, moving back to his native Japan to design new and inventive video games like the critically-acclaimed music game *Gitaroo-Man*. (He is interviewed in Chapter 5 of this volume.) Comics were for kids, animation was for kids to drag their parents to see, but video games were high technology, an exciting new form of entertainment that Mom and Dad enjoyed too.

And there were no major barriers to the enjoyment of Japanese games by Americans. Early Japanese-developed games did not require language transla-tion beyond a few simple sentences. Sometimes they were written entirely in English to begin with. Video games in general were a contemporary American invention, and there was nothing that clearly labeled newcomer Nintendo as Japanese. Early video games themselves were not acquainting American chil-dren with the full scope of Japanese culture in any significant way, but they opened the doors.

The results are evident. Many of today's schoolchildren perceive Japan *not* as the anonymous enemy but as a great place to be; they want to live there, speak Japanese, and play the latest games without waiting for them to be released in the US. The younger ones love the *anime* version of the *Pokémon* video game, the older ones have moved up to Akira Toriyama's *Dragon Ball*, and every day another middle-schooler discovers the post-apocalyptic movie masterpiece *Akira*. Off to college, they enroll in courses on Japanese film and discover Kurosawa. And they want to understand what they're watching, so enrollment in Japanese language and culture courses has skyrocketed from pre-Nintendo levels.

"What exactly is the cultural status of a Nintendo game," asked Henry Jenkins, "based partially on American generic traditions or adopted from spe-cific Western texts, drawing some of its most compelling iconography from Japanese graphic art, licensed by Japanese corporations, manufactured and designed by corporations in both the Americas and Asia, and for sale to both Japanese and American marketplaces?"[22]

It is difficult to know if this question can ever be satisfactorily answered. In any case, the time is right to look at these games and the people who make them. For indeed, the games of a people reveal a great deal about them.

CHAPTER 2

AN EARLY HISTORY OF CINEMATIC ELEMENTS IN VIDEO GAMES

Until the serious study and recording of the history of video games began in the early 1990s, most people were under the impression that the first video game was *Pong*, the simple monochrome table tennis game that Atari released in late 1972. *Pong* was the simplest of games even by early-seventies standards. Its only moving graphics were two white vertical "paddles" that moved up and down on either side of the screen and a square "ball" that bounced between them, and its lone sound effect was the eponymous "pong" that sounded when a ball bounced off the paddle.

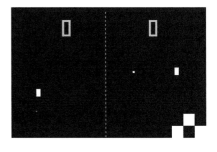

Pong's simplicity certainly made it *seem*, especially in hindsight, like it must have been the first video game. But it came chronologically after Magnavox's *Odyssey* system, which was available in May 1972. Its high price ($99.99) kept it from success, along with the fact that it was available only in Magnavox stores, where salespeople hoping to make an extra sale gave the impression that it only worked on Magnavox TV sets. As an arcade game that could be enjoyed by anyone for a quarter dollar, *Pong* was far better received. And in fact, it was greatly improved over the tennis game that *Odyssey* played; the graphics were higher-resolution, the sound was satisfying, the score was displayed onscreen, and the game play made more sense[*]. But it was still not the first video tennis game.

Nor was *Pong* the first coin-operated arcade game. That was called *Computer Space*, and Nutting Associates, the company where Atari founder Nolan Bushnell was originally employed, produced it in 1971. *Computer Space* was a game for two players: each controlled a spaceship on the screen and tried to shoot down the other player. Although it was first sold in 1971, it was in fact almost an exact copy of a game called *Spacewar* written by members of MIT's Tech Model Railroad Club in 1961 for the PDP-1 computer[1].

And although *Spacewar* and, later, *Computer Space* were popular with technology-savvy college students, the public shied away from the complexities of the game itself. Far from being simple and inviting, *Computer Space* featured complex physics and a lengthy instruction booklet attached to the machine,

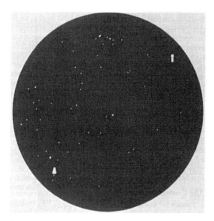

Screen rendering of Spacewar. Computer Space, the arcade version, looked similar but the graphics were drawn with dots.

which explained how to use the various buttons that filled the front of the futuristic-looking cabinet.*

This is all to say that the main reason *Pong* is often considered the first video game is because it was the first *successful* video game. Learning from his mistakes, Bushnell asked one of his first employees at Atari, an engineer named Al Alcorn, to create as simple a game as possible. Two paddles, one ball, one line of impeccably succinct directions printed on the cabinet: "Avoid missing ball for high score." The prototype *Pong* machine was placed in a Sunnyvale, California bar called Andy Capp's Tavern—which also had a handful of pinball machines, jukeboxes, and a *Computer Space*[2]—and was an instant success. By 1974, Atari-made *Pong* machines and many imitation versions could be found in bars and pool halls across the country, and home versions were popular Christmas gifts starting in 1975.

Pong crossed the Pacific to Japan as early as 1973. Bushnell attempted to open a Japanese office, but found—as most American companies do—that he could not make substantial inroads into the Japanese market without allying himself with an existing Japanese company. So he sold the Atari Japan operation to Masaya Nakamura, the head of a Tokyo-based amusement company called Nakamura Manufacturing Company, later shortened to Namco. Nakamura was a self-made businessman who started his company by operating and maintaining two coin-operated mechanical kiddie-horse rides that he had purchased second-hand. He set them up in one of the only locations he could, the roof of a Tokyo department store. By the time he was contacted by Bushnell, Nakamura was manufacturing and distributing his own rides and other amusement machines, and saw the acquisition of Atari Japan as the perfect way to expand his operations. His already-established connections gave Nakamura the distribution channels necessary to get arcade games into Japanese businesses.

Namco's Hideyuki Nakajima and Masaya Nakamura with Atari's Manny Gerard (center). Photo: RePlay Magazine

Still, though, Namco was lagging behind competitors like Taito. Taito, which is Japanese for "far east," was a company established in 1953 by Michael Kogan, a Russian Jew who had moved to Tokyo. Taito's original business was in importing coin-operated amusement machines like peanut vending devices. Later, Kogan began to brew and sell Japan's first domestic vodka. By 1954 Kogan was importing jukeboxes into the country; soon Taito was manufacturing its own. As *Pong* clones became big in America, the company started importing used Pong units, refurbishing them, and distributing them in Japan.

Taito engineer Tomohiro Nishikado was with the company since these early days, and recalled later Taito's first experience with imported games. "When we first started looking at these games, it was the opinion of management that it wouldn't work. The price was too high—for one unit, they wanted from six to eight hundred thousand yen. And to look at it, it was just a box with a television and a dial. But we wanted to see if it would actually sell like they said it would, and so for the time being we bought just one.[3]

"We set it up in a test location, and it was surprisingly popular. Instantly, we realized: 'This is going to be the era of video games.' Management told us that we should be able to make our own, original games. And since there was nobody else in the company with experience in electrical circuits, this job fell to me. Just like that."

The first "original" games that Nishikado designed were similar to the games that Nakamura was importing. Namco had *Pong* and the four-player *Pong Doubles*, Taito had *Soccer* and the four-player *Davis Cup*. In 1974 Taito released *Speed Race*, Japan's first driving video game, which used a realistic steering wheel as its controller instead the of off-the-shelf volume-control dials that were standard on *Pong* machines. *Speed Race* became the first Japanese game imported into the US when an American pinball and video game distributor called Midway licensed it. The same year, Atari released its own driving game called *Trak 10*, and driving became another important genre of arcade game.

▓ ▓ ▓

A few years later, as "the era of video games" was bringing forth new ideas one after another, two games that proved highly popular in both countries began to add tiny elements of **character** and **story** into the arcade game formula. *Breakout* (1976), developed by Atari, in which the player had to bounce a ball back to the top of the screen and "break" a wall of blocks one by one. *Western Gun* (1975), developed by Taito, featured two cowboys that shot at each other. These two games were still very limited by the technology of the time, which allowed only a few small, black-and-white images to be displayed. But *Breakout* and *Western Gun* illustrate the emerging difference between American and Japanese game design.

Breakout was originally conceived as a one-player *Pong* variant (*Pong* and all its clones were two-players only). It was designed by a twenty-year-old Atari employee named Steve Jobs, who at the time was building the proto-type of the Apple II personal com-puter in his garage with his partner Steve Wozniak, who worked for Hewlett-Packard but would come in to Atari to help his friend.

The game that Jobs and Wozniak built for Atari had graphics even more abstract than *Pong*. At least *Pong*'s graphics were supposed to represent tennis rackets; *Breakout*'s lines and blocks were simply lines and blocks. The cabinet artwork on the finished game showed a car-toonish drawing of a prison convict breaking through a brick wall, but neither the imagery within the game itself nor the game play action suggested a prison-break theme.

To illustrate how Japanese game designers, even ones with a background in engineering, were thinking about video games at the time, this is what Tomohiro Nishikado had to say about *Breakout*: "Even though *Breakout* had simple graphics, it was interesting. At the time when we were thinking about how to add characters to the games, they were going in the total opposite direction… The Taito management guys were half-jokingly saying, 'What is this? America's really losing, aren't they?', but in actuality, they were embarrassed."[4]

Breakout was perhaps even more successful in Japan than in the US. Atari had granted Masaya Nakamura an exclusive license to distribute *Breakout* in Japan under the name *Burokku-kuzushi* (literally, "block-busting"). But Atari insisted that they manufacture each system and send it to Nakamura. Unfortu-nately for Nakamura, the *yakuza*—Japanese organized crime gangs—began producing counterfeit *Burokku-kuzushi* machines by the truck full, and Naka-mura was stuck. Without telling Atari, he decided to start producing the machines himself, and they were huge sellers. Atari later sued and won.

Meanwhile, Nishikado at Taito was developing character-based games like *Western Gun*, which was released in the US, by Midway, as *Gunfight*. Few American players knew at the time that they were playing a Japanese game, but the difference was clear. Taito was adding characters and fragments of story. This is not to say that *Western Gun* had story sequences or fleshed-out character designs, but it had artwork of wild west cowboys on the cabinet, and the in-game graphics, with cacti, covered wagons, rocks, and player-characters that were identifiably human, matched the out-of-game artwork.

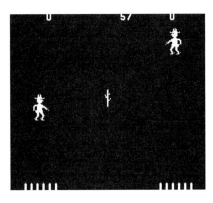

Gunfight became Midway's first major video game hit[5]. Its popularity could certainly be attributed to its originality amongst a field of identical games. What made it original was its use of human characters in a modern setting. Rather than miniature shapes that represented either spaceships or abstract blocks, *Gunfight* featured almost cartoonish humans. The original Japanese advertisement flyers for *Western Gun* showed that these were video game versions of Japanese *manga* characters. Of course, these *manga* style drawings were not used in the US, and even if they were, nobody would know they were Japanese—how could cowboys be Japanese, anyway?

And although *Gunfight* had no story sequences, nor its gunmen any personalities, besides yelling "GOT ME!" when they were shot, it at least drew upon the existing store of American 'western' films and cowboy stories. And its characters, should the player choose, could easily be given personalities, because people know what cowboys look like, act like, and the reasons for which they might start shooting at each other.

Gunfight was important for another reason: an engineer named Dave Nutting reprogrammed the version that Midway released. The reprogrammed version was the first arcade game to use a microprocessor. Taito's original version, like every other game prior, had used integrated circuits. The point was not lost on Nishikado: "As a game, I thought our version of *Western Gun* was more fun. But just from using a microprocessor, the walking animation became much smoother and prettier in Midway's version. As a technology person, I thought, 'I've got to use microprocessors from now on.' And so, I used a microprocessor for my very next game, *Space Invaders*."[6]

For a time, in 1978, 'video games' meant only one thing the whole world over: *Space Invaders* had shaken up a slumping industry to become "the first blockbuster video game."[7] By the end of its life cycle, there were more than one hundred thousand *Space Invaders* machines in Japan alone. Bowling alleys, pachinko parlors, and even small vegetable stores actually cleared away all of their inventory and devoted all of their store space to rows upon rows of sit-down, tabletop *Space Invaders* games. A severe shortage of the 100-yen coins required to play the game temporarily forced the Japanese government to *quadruple* its production. Within one year of its US release, an additional 60,000 machines had been sold. One arcade owner said of *Space Invaders* that it was the first arcade game whose intake "represented a significant portion of the cost of [buying] the game in any one week." That is, it was the first video game that paid for itself within about a month.[8]

As for game play, *Space Invaders* was like a more frantic version of *Breakout*. The player controlled a laser gun at the bottom of the screen and fired at a gauntlet of enemy alien creatures. But rather than standing still, the aliens moved left to right and dropped one row each time the group reached the end of the screen. As their numbers became smaller, the invaders moved faster, becoming much harder to shoot.

At this stage in his career as a game designer, Nishikado appreciated the game play formula that Atari pioneered with *Breakout*: the goal of 'clearing' one screen and proceeding to the next, which would be a crucial, almost reflexive game-design element from then on. In 1982, Taito import manager S. Ikawa described what Nishikado added to the game play as "a feeling of tension. A little neglect might breed great mischief."[9] The invaders' death march made the game singularly fast-paced and heart pounding, and *Space Invaders* was one of the first games where elaborate strategies and secret shooting methods became crucial to victory.

This exciting game play transcended any cultural boundaries, succeeding in Japan and the US, where the game industry was in a slump after Atari had released its first home system with interchangeable cartridges, the Atari Video Computer System, later known as the 2600 VCS. In his 1984 book *Zap!: The Rise And Fall of Atari*, Scott Cohen argued that the success of the VCS, and perhaps the US video game industry in general, was all thanks to *Space Invaders*:

> It wasn't until *Space Invaders* that video games began to utilize the full potential of the technology that went into creating them. *Pong* wasn't as exciting as Ping-Pong, but *Space Invaders* was more exciting than bowling, which is very much what *Space Invaders* was like, except *Space Invaders* was about twenty times faster... *Space Invaders* was a new form of entertainment... It also created a new craze in home video games. Atari VCS sales went through the roof.[10]

On a larger scale, *Space Invaders* represented the next step in the evolution of the cinematic Japanese video game. Again, although it had no story sequences, the outer space alien battle drew upon popular space action movies, books, and comics, such as the film *Star Wars* that Nishikado knew was popular in America at the time, but also *anime* films that had begun to gain popularity in Japan at that time, like *Uchuu Senkan Yamato* (*Space Battleship Yamato*).

What's more, when he decided to set his game in space with alien creatures, Nishikado first opened his sketchbook and filled a few pages with nearly professional-quality drawings of aliens that looked like squid and octopi. A member of the *shikaku sedai* 'visual generation,' it is evident from looking at Nishikado's sketchbook that he grew up practicing *manga* art. Even in the actual game, the little aliens that appeared on screen had decidedly cartoon-like qualities: animated faces with eyes and mouths, and tentacles that dangled below. Here, again, was the Japanese 'comical sense' invading video game design, and causing dramatic impact.

▨　▧　▨

And yet *Space Invaders'* phenomenal worldwide success turned out to be nothing compared to *Pac-Man's*. *Pac-Man* became the quintessential, iconic video game character. Even people who didn't know anything else about video games knew *Pac's* round, yellow face. The game itself was a huge moneymaker, selling over 100,000 machines in the US alone. Many publishers sold *Pac-Man* strategy guides, four of which appeared—simultaneously—on the *New York Times* bestseller list in 1981.[11] The *Pac-Man* character appeared on the cover of *Time*. The song "Pac-Man Fever" reached number nine on the Billboard charts in 1982.[12]

Pac-Man was the creation of Toru Iwatani, who graduated from Tokai University in 1977 with a degree in electrical engineering and entered Namco that same year. "I didn't want to make anything in particular. But after I entered the company, I thought, well, I like pinball, so I guess I could make pinball games… But when I told them, they said 'We do not make pinball.' I guess I really should have done my homework before I decided to work here."[13]

But Namco, fresh from its fallout with Atari over the *Breakout* machines, did want to begin making its own original arcade games. Iwatani mixed his favorite elements of pinball and *Breakout* to design the first, a 'video pinball' game called *Gee-Bee* (1978). The game play was essentially like *Breakout*, but there were far more things to do onscreen. You could hit bumpers and roll over lit-up markers to score points, like pinball tables. *Gee-Bee* had a black-and-white monitor, but a piece of multicolored cellophane, like those used in later editions of *Space Invaders*, was put over the monitor such that the playfield was separated into different colors. In 1979, Iwatani followed up with *Bomb-Bee* and *Cutie-Q*, two more video pinball games. *Bomb-Bee* featured similar simple graphics, this time with a full-color monitor. *Cutie-Q's* improvements were not technological but *stylistic*.

Improving on the first two games' simple, block-based graphics, *Cutie-Q* featured colorful targets in the shapes of smiling faces, animated monsters, and ghosts. One character that waddled around was called "Walk-Man." Iwatani did this to appeal to a more general audience, one that he hoped would include women. "If you went to the game centers [the Japanese term for video arcades] at that time, you'd see nothing but guys. I thought what would make the games more attractive to women would be cute character design. So I designed cute characters for *Cutie-Q*."[14]

Iwatani confessed to not being very skilled at drawing, but also that he filled up his school textbooks with scattered *manga*. In any case, in 1980 he began work on *Pac-Man* and inadvertently created one of the world's most instantly recognizable icons. In fact, however, "rather than develop the character first," said Iwatani, "I started out with the concept of *taberu*."[15] He set the Japanese word *taberu*— "eat"—as his key word and began to create a game around that concept. This choice of key word was tuned toward making a game that girls would enjoy as well: "Women seem to like eating," said Iwatani.[16] (Fun foods in Japan, like elaborate ice-cream desserts, frosted doughnuts, and crepes, would seem to be most popular with young women.)

* I asked video game historian Steven Kent about this via email, and he told me that in his first interview with Iwatani, he told the story as truth...but that in a later interview, his comments were translated as something like "I wish I could say that this is how it happened." And in Shida and Matsui, volume 1, page 43, he is quoted as saying: "It's already passed into legend, so I'm going to stick with this: I took one slice out of a pizza and saw Pac-Man" (my translation).

"The games of the time were mostly games where you shot and killed aliens, and I wanted to go in the opposite direction."[17] Before creating the rules of his new game, Iwatani came up with the main character. As the story goes, Iwatani was eating pizza for lunch, took one slice out of the pie, and saw below him the figure of Pac-Man. This story is probably mythical, but it has more or less passed into legend by this point.*

Pac-Man's game play was not, like most other games, a simulation of something that had come before, whether a table tennis match or a spaceship flight, a cowboy shootout or a pinball table. *Pac-Man*, in which players moved Iwatani's yellow, chomping face through a maze filled with energy pills and deadly (yet comical) ghosts, was an experience that was only possible in the world of video games—a completely original concept.

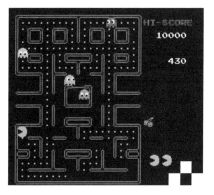

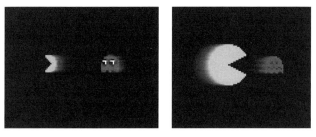

Pac-Man featured no real *narrative*, for neither the main character nor the ghosts had any sort of motivation or goals. But *Pac-Man* was the first game to make copious use of cinematic scenes. The game's introductory 'attract mode' featured a display like a theater marquee that introduced the four ghosts by name and gave some clues as to their personality, which showed through in the way they chased Pac-Man in the maze. And, upon clearing certain screens, the player was treated to some brief, humorous interludes "acted out" by Pac-Man and the characters. These served not only as a way of attracting new players over to the game machine, but also as a reward for skilled players.

Pac-Man was brought to the US by Midway, where it was just as popular, perhaps more so, than in Japan. But like most every other character-based game that was to follow, some textual changes were in order for the US market. One was to rework names of the ghosts, from *Oikake*, *Machibuse*, *Kimagure*, and *Otoboke* to *Shadow*, *Speedy*, *Bashful*, and *Pokey*, and their nicknames from *Akabei*, *Pinky*, *Aosuke*, and *Guzuta* to *Blinky*, *Pinky*, *Inky*, and *Clyde*.*

* As near as I can figure, the names of the ghosts mean *Pursue*, *Ambush*, *Capricious*, and *Slow*, and three of their nicknames play off of their colors; *aka* means red and *ao* is blue. *Guzuta* probably comes from *guzutsuku*—to linger or languish.

† *Not*, as far as I can discern, a reference to the hockey puck-like shape of the main character.

The name of the main character, or the Romanized version of that name anyway, also had to be changed. *Paku-paku taberu* is a Japanese expression meaning "to munch." So, similarly to "Walk-Man" from *Cutie-Q*, the character was called *pakku-man* after this onomatopoeic phrase.[†] The original Romanization of *pakku-man*, which was actually used on some arcade machines and merchandise in Japan, was Puck-Man. When Midway brought it to America, they asked to change the name to *Pac-Man* out of the (entirely rational) fear that vandals would erase a small part of the *P* so that it appeared to be an *F*.

No, it's not just an urban legend—Puck-Man machines were actually made! Picture credit: RePlay Magazine

Like they did with *Space Invaders*, Atari licensed *Pac-Man* for their VCS home video game system. But since the home system's computer processor was so weak compared to the arcade machine, and also because American Atari employee Tod Frye had hastily reprogrammed the game itself in a matter of weeks, VCS *Pac-Man* was a pale imitation of the real thing. The cut scenes were gone, the *paku-paku* sound effect was no more, and Iwatani's colorful, appealing graphic design was butchered. It was the beginning of the end for Pac-Mania, and the beginning of the crash that would cripple the American video game industry, making it ripe for takeover at the hands of Japanese companies.

But even in the earliest days, in an industry dominated by American companies, the huge, smash-success games in *both* countries were coming from Japan. Wherever you went, *Pac-Man* was a smash hit and a merchandising gold mine (*Pac-Man* lunchboxes, board games, figurines, etc.), and other video games followed in the wake of its popularity.

Pac-Man also became a hit Saturday morning cartoon show in America. In fact, the three video games that had thus far been turned into American Saturday morning cartoons were all Japanese in origin: *Pac-Man*, Sega's *Frogger*, and a game called *Donkey Kong*, which was designed by a young artist named Shigeru Miyamoto.

CHAPTER 3

THE PLAY CONTROL OF POWER FANTASIES: NINTENDO, SUPER MARIO AND SHIGERU MIYAMOTO

Genius is a word that should be kept behind glass, reserved for the truly exceptional. But no one who's ever been entranced by one of Shigeru Miyamoto's games can question his brilliance. Constantly imitated, but never equaled, he is without question the most inspirational video game designer in the world.

— "Why Are Shigeru Miyamoto's Games So Damn Good?"
Next Generation, February 1995

The development of the Japanese video game made a quantum leap the day that Shigeru Miyamoto began to design his first one. Born in 1953 in the town of Sonebe, on the outskirts of Kyoto, where his family had lived for three generations, young Shigeru's wild imagination was stimulated by comics and animation. The Miyamoto family had no car or television, but every few months they would take a train into the city to shop and see movies. Miyamoto especially remembers *Peter Pan* and *Snow White*. At home, he "lived in books, and he drew and painted and made elaborate puppets, which he presented in fanciful shows."[1]

"When I was a little boy, I liked to play pretend," said Miyamoto in a 1995 interview. "It was a lot like a computer simulation. When we played with friends, some games ended with a winner and a loser, and a friend played as a judge. When you have a friend play the judge, he can just change the rules as he likes. When I play through the computer, the computer judges very correctly... I found that difference interesting."[2]

In 1964, when Miyamoto was 11, his father Hideo brought home a television. Shigeru became "obsessed with animation" and "hooked on Japanese superheroes."[3] His favorites were some of the first animated shows on the NHK broadcasting network: *Chirorin-mura to kurumi no ki* ("Chirorin Village and the Walnut Tree") and *Hyokkori Hyoutan-jima* ("Accidental Gourd Island"). In middle school, his "eyes opened to manga" and he began to devour the popular artists of the day. "I liked gag manga, story manga—as long as it was manga, I liked it."[4]

Miyamoto loved to explore the countryside, "investigating hillsides and creek beds and small canyons," climbing through caves, wandering without a map and marveling at his discoveries[5]. He would take paper and pencils with him and draw the places he found. He "took cartoon-making seriously," inventing lives and personalities for his original characters and then making them into flipbooks. In high school he started a manga club.[6]

Miyamoto entered Kanazawa Municipal College of Industrial Arts and Crafts in 1970. He graduated five years later (he skipped class often)[7] with a degree in industrial design[8]. He didn't feel like he could cut it as a professional manga artist, which is why he decided to go to college. But by majoring in industrial design, he was able to continue drawing.[9] At school, he played the earliest video games and developed eclectic musical interests: The Nitty Gritty Dirt Band, Doc Watson,[10] The Beatles. He taught himself to play bluegrass on the guitar and banjo, and most of all he loved designing toys. [11]

AN INTERESTING COMPANY

Miyamoto envisioned himself perhaps designing telephones or other consumer goods. He wanted to work somewhere where he could "make a hit product."[12] But he knew he wasn't cut out for the rigid corporate world of Japan, and had no idea where to go. His father called an old family friend: Hiroshi Yamauchi, the president of Kyoto-based Nintendo Co., Ltd. As Miyamoto recalled, "At that time, Nintendo made not only amusement machines but also kiddie-cars and batting machines. I thought, what an interesting company. They'll let me do what I want to."[13]

Nintendo had been an "interesting company" long before Shigeru Miyamoto's father was born. Founded in 1889, the 22nd year of the Meiji era, by Kyoto businessman Fusajiro Yamauchi as Nintendo Koppai, the company was originally a small operation devoted to the manufacture of *hanafuda*, Japanese playing cards. *Hanafuda*, which Nintendo still manufactures today*, are small cards about the size of a cracker (or a Game Boy Advance cartridge) with beautiful seasonal imagery—nightingales, cherry blossoms. The forty-eight cards in the deck are printed on thick, high quality cardboard, so the deck is more than twice as tall as a standard deck of *toranpu* (Western playing cards) and about three times as expensive.

★ Although they represent an ever-shrinking side business, Nintendo's playing cards are still the high-quality gold standard in Japan. The hanafuda package is now made of strong plastic and features both kanji characters and the now-familiar English logo, but the designs of the cards and package are virtually identical. Nintendo is still so well-known as a card maker that the recent Xbox vs. PlayStation vs. GameCube console war is called "Bill vs. Aibo vs. Hanafuda-ya."

Nintendo's Daitoryou, or "President", brand of hanafuda featured a picture of Napoleon on the box.

The original Nintendo building, all of two stories high, stands near the intersection of Rokujou (6th St.) and Kiyamachi, near the Kamogawa River in Kyoto. The area is only a few minutes south of the hustle and bustle of downtown Kyoto, but it is drowsy today with a few small stores still open for business, a few nondescript bars and restaurants, and a virtually empty, nearly abandoned concrete building with wrought iron signs on the front that read, right-to-left in the pre-war style, *Yamauchi Nintendo Playing Cards*. Kiyamachi was and is a seedy part of town. In 1899 it was filled with gambling dens and brothels; today you find pachinko halls and "massage parlors."

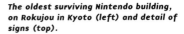

The oldest surviving Nintendo building, on Rokujou in Kyoto (left) and detail of signs (top).

Nintendo fit perfectly with this atmosphere, as *hanafuda* were used for very serious gambling. Yamauchi's cards, hand-pressed from the bark of mulberry trees, were unmatched. The high-rolling gamblers demanded the quality Nintendo cards, and Nintendo's *Daitoryou* (President) brand quickly became the most popular cards in Kyoto and neighboring Osaka. Profits surged when the *yakuza*, Japan's equivalent of the Mafia, operated high-stakes games of *hanafuda* in casino-like parlors. Nintendo profited handsomely, because professional players would begin each game with a fresh deck, discarding the old one."[14]

In 1907, Yamauchi began the manufacture of toranpu, making Nintendo and Nintendo became the first Japanese company to do so. The company grew and grew, but remained strictly in the playing-card business until 1949, when Hiroshi Yamauchi, Fusajiro's great-grandson, became the third president of Nintendo at all of twenty-one years old. Yamauchi fired every manager left over from his father's and grandfather's days. He had his cousin fired. He wanted it clear that he was the one in charge. He moved the plant and he modernized tech-

niques. In 1953 Nintendo became the first company in Japan to manufacture modern plastic-coated playing cards. In 1959 he licensed Disney characters and put them on the backs of his cards. Sales skyrocketed.[15]

Yamauchi took Nintendo public, listing his family's company on the Osaka Stock Exchange. He branched off new products and services: instant rice, a taxi company, love hotels that rented rooms by the hour. But by 1969 Yamauchi was unhappy with the performance of these ventures, and decided to play to Nintendo's strength, namely its reputation in the toys and games business. Two Kyoto natives were the heart and soul of his new Games department: Hiroshi Imanishi, who was the company's general affairs manager, and Gunpei Yokoi, an electronics graduate who was working as the maintenance man on the *hanafuda* printers.

Yokoi's inventions defined the new Games division and became the popular Ultra series of toys. The series included a plastic latticework hand that extended and grasped, a pitching machine that lobbed soft baseballs for safe indoor use, and a toy periscope. Nintendo's first major hit, however, was the Beam Gun series, created through a partnership with Sharp*, who was working with solar cell technology. Yokoi worked with a Sharp employee named Masayuki Uemura to develop a toy gun that "shot" a thin beam of light. If the player hit the tiny solar-cell target, it would trigger an electrical circuit and, for example, a plastic "beer bottle" held together by magnets would break into pieces. The two men worked well together, and Yokoi hired Uemura away from his sales position at Sharp.

★ This partnership continues to this day. Sharp designed and sold the Twin Famicom in the 1980s, a system that combined Nintendo's Famicom with the optional Disk System add-on; sold television sets with Famicom and Super Famicom systems built inside; and most recently in 2003 supplied the new LCD screens for Nintendo's handheld Game Boy Advance SP systems.

The Beam Gun series sold millions of units, which convinced Yamauchi and Yokoi to build the concept into a grander-scale operation. The bowling fad that took over Japan in the 1960's had died out, and Nintendo swooped in to convert old closed-down bowling alleys into Laser Clay Ranges. Players stood at one end of the alley holding large rifles with Beam Gun technology inside, firing at "clay pigeons" projected onto screens at the far end, where the bowling pins used to sit. The ranges were a big hit, but soon the economy slipped and the fad ended shortly afterward.*

★ Irony rating: five stars. The first bowling center for the Japanese public (the only other bowling alleys in Japan were for American military use) was an early project of a company called Service Games—or *Sega* for short.

Another invention of Yokoi's was marketed in 1973 as Ele-Conga. Capitalizing on the popularity of Latin music in Japan at that time, the Ele-Conga was really a high-quality drum synthesizer that let the user play electronic drum beats by pushing buttons. An optional attachment (shown right) used paper "records" with holes punched in them to play drum beats automatically.

Regardless, Nintendo was an established name in high-tech entertainment, with a brilliant staff that knew how to design and market hit products. Running with this image, Yamauchi moved to get in early on a growing trend: video games that were played on home television sets. In 1977, he licensed Magnavox's Odyssey video game hardware for sale in Japan. The systems that Nintendo released were not based on the original 1972 Odyssey system; they were based on the more refined hardware that Magnavox had developed in the wake of Pong's popularity. Atari's *Home Pong* was the runaway hit Christmas present of 1975, and by 1976 seventy-five companies, including Magnavox, had announced imitation versions.[16] A Japanese company called Epoch had already broken into the market with *TV Tennis*, a black-and-white tennis machine that was so primitive it could not even keep score on screen; players had to click plastic dials on the machine's front. At Yamauchi's insistence, Nintendo forged ahead technologically and licensed Magnavox's newer color Odyssey systems, releasing the Color TV Game 6 in 1977.

In sharp stylistic contrast to the futuristic, black- or metal-colored machines that other Japanese companies released, the CTVG6 was bright orange and had rounded edges. It had a toy-like design sensibility about it.

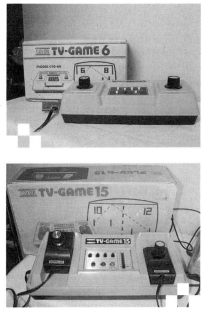

Inside the box, as the name implied, it featured full color graphics and six variations on the tennis game. At 9,800 yen, it was a pricey plaything, but the risk paid off. It was a smash hit, and a higher-end sequel released that year, the Color TV Game 15, which featured a few improvements: fifteen games, of course, and removable controllers.

CTVG6, like every other Japanese TV-tennis game at the time, had plastic dials that were permanently attached to the machine's face. These were used to move the paddles onscreen. But the CTVG15's controllers were attached to the back of the system by long wires, so players could sit comfortably away from each other and from the TV. When the system was not in use, the controllers sat in indentations on the face of the machine. Sleek and stylish, the CTVG15 was just as popular as its little brother. Nintendo sold over one million units between the two systems, and was beginning to carve out a nice place in the budding video game industry.

And then, Shigeru Miyamoto walked into Hiroshi Yamauchi's office for a job interview.

THE EARLY PERIOD

He was 24 years old with a goofy, freckled face and shaggy hair. He brought a recent invention of his to show Yamauchi. It was a clothes hanger designed for children, with soft edges and colorful animal designs—an elephant, a bird, a chicken. Miyamoto was hired as Nintendo's first staff artist[17] and assigned to the planning department. "I was hired as an apprentice planner," he recalled in a later interview, "but basically, I could do design, so I ended up doing a lot of design work."[18]

It is July 14, 2003, and we are sitting in an austere conference room on the first floor of Nintendo's new headquarters south of Kyoto station. This new compound is pure white and shaped almost like a cube. It is clearly visible from the roof of Kyoto Station, especially if you can read *kanji* characters that spell out *nin-ten-dou*; the company name means, approximately, "the place where luck is left in heaven's hands," appropriate for a company that got its start making cards used in gambling halls.

The meeting room's walls are as white as the building's exterior. Eight leather chairs sit low to the floor, around a long table. A gigantic widescreen TV and DVD player occupy one corner of the otherwise sparsely decorated room. Two young women, dressed identically in GameCube-blue, place iced green tea in front of us. I ask Shigeru Miyamoto what his very first job at Nintendo was, and he thinks silently for a long while before answering. It was a long time ago, after all. Finally, he speaks:

Nintendo's new headquarters, a shimmering white cubic structure, dominates the southern Kyoto skyline.

Miyamoto at the 2004 Electronic Entertainment Expo.

"The first thing they had me do, the first project I worked on, was to do the outer housing designs for two dedicated home game machines we were making, called Racing 112 and *Burokku-kuzushi*. The designers of the actual game hardware would tell me about the insides of the machine, and then from that I would design the outside."[19] This was actually quite close to what Miyamoto had originally envisioned, except that instead of designing comfortable telephones, it was video game consoles and controllers.

Immediately, Miyamoto knew that he wanted to improve on the designs of the CTVG6 and 15. "They were bad," he said, uncomfortable and difficult to understand. "I tried to make my designs more fun for the player to interface with. For example, with Blockbuster, I designed the console so you could play it either right-handed or left-handed. For Racing 112, I thought it was important that there be a gear shift handle, because it's fun to shift gears with a controller like that."

Comparing Miyamoto's designs to the earlier games, more differences emerge. *Blockbuster*'s casing was even more rounded and toy-like than those of the previous consoles*, and Racing 112 featured a large, comfortable steering wheel controller for the one-player mode *and* two removable paddle controllers for the two-player version.

★ It was also the first Nintendo game console to feature the Nintendo logo displayed prominently across the front of the machine. Nintendo had obviously built up a positive brand identity in the video game business by this time.

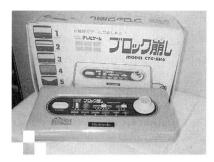

In fact, Racing 112 contained 112 possible variations on the game; switches on the front of the machine let the player control the speed and number of cars, the weave of the road, guardrails, slipperiness, and so on. These switches were typical of this type of console, but Miyamoto added picture labels for each switch in place of the text-only labels on the first two games. This was his design training coming into play; icon-based labels help users instantly comprehend the device's functions without having to read the instruction book or interpret cryptically short text labels.

This sort of design sense became so important to Miyamoto's creations at Nintendo that he eventually considered it his main job. "It's *ningen kougaku*," he says—"human engineering," the art and science of creating a smooth, natural interface between the machine and the user. From the first, Miyamoto's designs reflected this philosophy. Although the actual computer programs in Nintendo's machines were nearly identical to the many other video game consoles, the controller design set Nintendo's machines apart.

When Miyamoto was finally allowed to design the game programs themselves, things really took off for Nintendo.

But by 1978, he was still an assistant in the planning department, and so his next few jobs were relatively mundane. Having made a name in the home video game business, Nintendo turned to the emerging arcade-game market. This was more or less motivated by the huge success of *Space Invaders*. With demand for *Space Invaders* climbing higher and higher, and more potential spaces for machines than machines to fill them, numerous companies, Nintendo included, turned out *Invaders* clones by the roomful. Nintendo's entry was called *Space Fever*, and Miyamoto drew the in-game characters. Nintendo apparently liked his work;

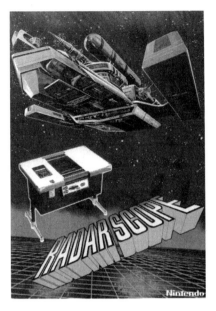

he went on to draw the characters for *Sheriff* (1979) and *Space Firebird* (1980), and he designed the cabinet and marquee artwork for *Sheriff* and another game called *Radarscope*.[20]

★ Yamauchi essentially stopped development of the home game consoles, but Nintendo released one more the same year as the Game and Watch. It was based on an arcade game that played a monochrome version of the game *go* (known as Othello in the US), with the white and black chips replaced by crosses and squares. The graphics of the arcade and home versions were extremely simplistic for 1980 (by this time, color games were the norm) but the rules of *go* are so complicated that the computer processors inside the machine

(cont.)

Nintendo was going through a few major changes during these years. Yamauchi, looking for a more innovative product, asked Gunpei Yokoi to develop a unique way of playing video games.★ Yokoi came up with the *Game and Watch* series, tiny hand-held games slightly larger than a credit card with screens that used liquid-crystal displays (LCDs). Other portable games had been released by companies like Epoch, but these mostly used light-emitting diode (LED) technology. LEDs were tiny red lights that could be turned on or off, so the "graphics" of these early games were, well, tiny red lights. LCD technology allowed screens to display relatively detailed cartoon pictures, although these graphics could only blink on or off to create the illusion of movement. Nintendo's designers were so adept, however, that the onscreen action looked quite good. The *Game and*

Watch series became incredibly popular.†

Another major change for Nintendo at this time was the establishment of an American branch. Yamauchi tapped his son-in-law, Minoru Arakawa, to head up the division in New York, with the sole initial intent of distributing Nintendo arcade games in the US. The first few games met with failure. The black-and-white *Sheriff* and *Space* Fever—imitation versions of *Western Gun* and *Space Invaders*, respectively—were old news by 1980. *Radarscope* also was very similar to all the other spaceship-shooting games in the American and Japanese arcades of 1980. But despite *Radarscope*'s unoriginal gameplay ("like *Galaxian* from Namco but more sophisticated," recalled Arakawa[21]), it became one of the most popular games in Tokyo.[22] It was, at the time, the second most popular game in Japan after *Pac-Man*.

Pac-Man was creating a sensation in America as well, and Arakawa believed that *Radarscope* would be Nintendo of America's big hit. He asked Japan for 3,000 units, which took up NOA's entire budget and took nearly four months to arrive by boat. By that time, *Radarscope*'s popularity in Tokyo had waned and the prototype units that had been set up in the United States were sitting idle, unplayed. Even more to their disadvantage, *Radarscope* was one of the most expensive arcade games on the market, and it came from a foreign country with a tiny American subsidiary. NOA was able to sell 1,000 games, but had 2,000 left over.[23] Arakawa needed a new game that he could insert into the *Radarscope* cabinets and sell, so he asked Yamauchi to have his staff create one. The only available designer was Shigeru Miyamoto.

had to be very powerful. The home version, called simply "Computer TV Game," cost a whopping ¥50,000 in 1980 and is an extremely rare collector's item today.

† The *Game and Watch* games were very simplistic contests, but a mascot character began to emerge in even the earliest ones: a stick figure with a Charlie-Brown-style round head and big nose called Mr. Game and Watch. The character is so recognized in Japan even today that a 2001 Nintendo GameCube title, *Dai-Rantou Smash Brothers DX* (Super Smash Bros. Melee in the US) featured Mr. Game and Watch as a hidden character. His fighting techniques were made up of the different actions from the early *Game and Watch* games, like *Fireman* and *Chef*.

DONKEY KONG

Video game design prior to Miyamoto's first effort had been a largely hit-and-miss process. Games were often designed and programmed by a single person. This meant that a successful game designer had to have a creative left brain from which he could pull new and interesting design concepts, *and* have a mathematically adept right brain that would allow him to translate his designs into a ones-and-zeroes computer program. Of course, at this time, the ability to program was far more important than the ability to design. A good program that ran an average design was sellable. An amazing design with a lousy program to back it up was useless.

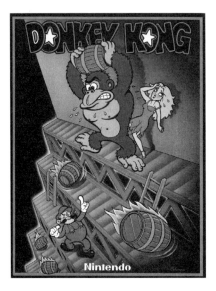

Nintendo

Giving the keynote speech at the 1999 Game Developers Conference in San Jose, Miyamoto displayed pictures of *Space Invaders* and said, "Until *Donkey Kong*, which I directed, programmers and engineers were responsible for game design. These were the days when the engineers were even drawing the pictures and composing the music themselves. They were terrible, weren't they?"[24]

This was especially true because the video screens of the time couldn't display sharp images. In fact, color screens had only come into wide use a year or two prior. The hottest game of 1978, *Space Invaders*, was black and white. And so even in 1980, as graphics got better, most games were still being developed around very simple, basic ideas: shoot asteroids, shoot bugs, shoot missiles. Games with standout design quality were the exceptions that proved Miyamoto's point.

Miyamoto was adept at design. But he had never designed a game before and did not know how to program a computer. He would never have been given a job designing games at Atari. So how did Yamauchi sense that Miyamoto would come up with such a revolutionary game?

Looking back on his childhood and college experiences, it seems that Miyamoto was always developing the two interests that would make him such an influential game designer. His love for exploration and fascination with new, unexplored territory extended into his college years: "When I went to the university at Kanazawa, it was a totally strange city for me. I liked walking very much, and whenever I did, something would happen. I would pass through a tunnel and the scene was quite changed when I came out."[25]

This sort of exploration and discovery would become a defining aspect of Miyamoto's games once the hardware became powerful enough to bring the worlds in his imagination to life. But his gift for character designs and his love for epic stories are the factors that made his first game a success. The story of *Donkey Kong* was a combination of *Beauty and the Beast* and *King Kong*, two of his favorites. He made it a point to note that his ape, Donkey Kong*, wasn't evil but simply misunderstood—"nothing too evil or repulsive." The gorilla's keeper was "a funny, hang-loose kind of guy" but, as Miyamoto made clear, he wasn't very kind to the gorilla. "It was humiliating! How miserable it was to belong to such a mean, small man!"[26] So Donkey Kong, mistreated and confused, escaped and took his keeper's girlfriend along.

Donkey Kong's master was drawn from a combination of Miyamoto's ingenuity and the technical constraints of the time. "I didn't know how to make a really cool character," said Miyamoto in 1993, "so I made Mario."[27] Mario, or Jump-Man, as Miyamoto originally called him, was "neither handsome nor heroic… someone anyone could relate to." Miyamoto described Mario as "a short, indomitable, mustached man in a red cap… a kind of Everyman who rises to heroism in the face of adversity" and whose "insignificance… makes him so appealing."[28]

★ Miyamoto wanted to title the game (and the ape) something that meant "stubborn monkey." The old English-Japanese dictionary yielded "donkey," as in a stubborn mule. "Kong" had been a generic Japanese word for "large, menacing ape" ever since the 1933 movie King Kong.

The idea of the unassuming guy who succeeds against the odds is a common theme in Japanese storytelling. To name a popular example from Miyamoto's day, take the main character Nobita from the ubiquitous *manga* and *anime* series Doraemon. Nobita is a middle school boy who is not any good at anything; he's not very smart or athletic or popular, but he wins in the face of adversity (with help from his alien robot cat). Mario doesn't have an alien robot cat, but the comparison is otherwise valid.

Other popular Japanese entertainment features a similar "neither handsome nor heroic" main character, but who is always "someone anyone could relate to." To illustrate this, Ian Buruma uses examples from *manga*, like the often-abused father figure from a popular strip *Dame Oyaji* ('Stupid Dad'), and from film, like the "most beloved character in the history of Japanese cinema," the lonely vagabond *Tora-san*, who is defined by his tragic failings and misadventures.[29]

This is not to say that Mario is a sad sack, an unlucky vagabond, or a fool. He is actually presented as hard working and heroic, but the Japanese preference for these sorts of characters is also clearly present in Mario's design. Mario is accessible—he is our father, or uncle or mailman, or little brother, or us—he is an average Joe. He's no superhero and yet we enjoy identifying with him.

To suggest this slightly dumpy, antihero image, Miyamoto drew a large nose and big, round eyes. Mario got a moustache because video game animation of the time couldn't render a defined mouth. He wore gloves and overalls to distinguish the movement of his arms when he walked. And his red cap was there so his hair wouldn't have to fly around when he jumped.

In other words, Mario was created to look as much like a vibrant, animated cartoon character as video game screens of the time would allow, and the effect was singularly impressive. Had anything been different about Mario—his arms frozen, his hair stiff, his face incomplete—he would have looked unnatural. Instead, he looked and moved more realistically, more like a human being than any video game character before him.

Donkey Kong was the first game project in which the design process began with a story. There were other games that had basic storylines, such as the jailbreak artwork from *Breakout*, but the stories were contrived to conform to the game after it was completed. With *Donkey Kong*, the original characters, their looks, and their motivations were created first, and the game play was crafted with them in mind.

In 1980, as in the early days of film, new video game genres were being invented constantly. "Block" games like *Pong* and *Breakout* gave way to "Space" games like *Asteroids* and *Space Invaders*. *Pac-Man* was the first "Maze Chase" game, spawning imitations from both countries. *Donkey Kong* was something entirely new, a genre that would consume the video game industry throughout the late eighties and early nineties: what Miyamoto called "running/jumping/climbing." Later on, this would be dubbed the "Platform" game, named after the platforms that the main character jumped and climbed.

Originally, Miyamoto recalled in a 2000 interview, the game he started to make wasn't a "running/jumping/climbing" game at all. "At first it was more of an athletic game—the character would ride up and down on a seesaw—it would be a game that used contrivances like that."[30] This was the invention of *Game and Watch* creator Gunpei Yokoi, but it didn't work with the technology of the time. "He wanted a game where you bounce on the seesaw and bounce up off of it. But," he laughs, "we couldn't figure out how to do it; it was really difficult. With a seesaw, if you get on one end, the other end goes up. If you hit one end real hard, the other end goes up just as hard. It was interesting to think about this, but we couldn't do it."

Another concept that didn't work out was *Popeye*. Originally, Miyamoto wasn't going to design characters at all for his first game. Instead, Nintendo was working on obtaining the *Popeye* license from King Features Syndicate. Miyamoto envisioned a game where Bluto took Olive Oyl away from Popeye, who made his way over obstacles, acquired his spinach—and BAM!—knocked Bluto out to end the round. But Nintendo was unable to get the license after all, and Miyamoto set to work on his original characters.

Since Gunpei Yokoi's seesaw idea wasn't working out, Miyamoto changed the design, instead creating a design prototype with barrels rolling down slopes, and the main character having to climb up and down ladders to avoid them. But looking at this design, Miyamoto felt it would be more fun to have a character that could jump on his own, and so "Jump-Man" (Mario's original name, drawing on Iwatani's "Walk-Man" and "Pac-Man") was born. The story fleshed out from there, and his characters were born. Miyamoto admits that he was still thinking about *Popeye* when he created his own characters, especially in the sense that Mario and Donkey Kong were not *truly* enemies.

"Even after the *Popeye* license fell through, I was still thinking about the relationship between Popeye, Bluto, and Olive Oyl. Their relationship is somewhat friendly. They're not enemies, they're friendly rivals.

> **Donkey Kong was the first game project in which the design process began with a story.**

"But I needed different characters. The main character, the big, strong guy, and the beautiful woman… well, uh, Olive really isn't a beautiful woman. I figured I'd make mine beautiful instead [laughs].

"What's kind of a mystery is, why did I title the game *Donkey Kong?* The main character, the player, was Mario. That much was decided. But Donkey Kong, his personality was the most fleshed-out of all of them. I think it's best to name the game after the strongest character."

Donkey Kong actually featured *more* gameplay than other games of the time. This also stemmed from Miyamoto's love of Japanese *manga*: "Thinking back, I would say that although it wasn't done consciously, I ended up designing *Donkey Kong* like a traditional Japanese four-panel *manga* comic strip. That way of telling a story in four distinct parts seemed natural to me, so I created four separate screens from the opening to the conclusion. The programmers were able to do this, but they told me at the time that I was essentially asking them to make four separate games!"

In the game's first stage (or perhaps "panel"), Mario starts at the bottom of an unfinished building site. Steel girders and ladders crisscross the screen, and Mario has to climb to the top, where Donkey Kong holds Mario's girlfriend Pauline imprisoned. Mario must jump rolling barrels, fire, and other obstacles that Donkey Kong throws at him. He can grab a hammer for temporary invincibility against the barrels (much like Popeye's spinach). In the final stage, Mario must remove all the rivets from a similar-looking structure, causing it to collapse, thus sending the monkey plummeting to his doom and reuniting Mario with his girlfriend.

The bright, animated cartoon characters and fresh game play alone would have been enough to make *Donkey Kong* stand out. But Miyamoto did something more with *Donkey Kong*. To understand what that was, first note that Miyamoto still calls the original *Pac-Man* his favorite game. In one interview, he said that *Pac-Man* was "the first game where I recognized an actual effort in design. You didn't have designers at the time, so most games didn't really have any design sense. When someone with a background in design like me saw that, I felt like this was my true calling in life."[31] "Back then, I would boast to myself that I was one of the five best game designers in the world. This is because there were very few artists involved in game design at that time."[32]

Pac-Man was innovative in its design and its use of cinematic cut-scenes, but there was no story being told. *Pac-Man*'s non-interactive, movie-like sequences simply showed humorous interludes featuring the game characters, but *Donkey Kong* was the very first game to tell a whole story, from beginning to end.

▪ ▫ ▪

Rather than take this for granted, perhaps we should ask, what *is* a narrative? And how, exactly, does *Donkey Kong* show it?

Film scholars David Bordwell and Kristin Thompson called narrative "a chain of events in cause-effect relationship occurring in time and space."[33] In her book <u>Art In Motion: Animation Aesthetics</u>, Maureen Furniss quotes Bordwell as explaining that in the classical model of cinema, this cause-and-effect relationship had to "lead toward a unified conclusion, or closure of the plot." Furniss then quotes Dwight V. Swain, who elaborates: "The *beginning* establishes your character within the framework of his predicament… The *middle* reveals the various steps of the character's struggle to defeat the danger that threatens him… The *end* sees the character win or lose the battle. Remember, in this regard, the story doesn't truly end until the struggle between desire and danger is resolved, with some kind of clear-cut triumph." Swain argued that every film story must have these three elements. These same principles, argues Furniss, can be applied to commercial animation.[34] You can see each of these elements beginning to emerge in the early "cartoon" video games, starting with *Donkey Kong*.

Most arcade games of the early 1980s not only lacked a story, they also had no cinematic scenes. When you dropped a quarter (or 100 yen) into *Space Invaders*, you weren't treated to a scene of the ship flying into battle or of the aliens departing their home planet. When you pressed the Start button, you were immediately thrust into the action with no buildup.

But *Donkey Kong* was different: upon pressing the Start button, we first see Donkey Kong ascend the building site on a pair of ladders, with Pauline slung over his shoulder (Fig. 1.1). Reaching the top, he places Pauline on the top girder and stomps up and down, causing the girders below him to bend and warp (Fig. 1.2). Reaching his final position in the top left of the playfield, he leers at the player (Fig. 1.3).

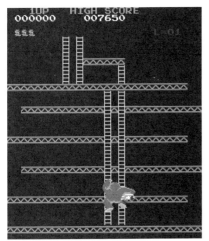

Fig. 1.1

Fig. 1.3

This scene of only a few seconds accomplishes several things all at once. First and foremost, it establishes the game's real-world setting: rather than the abstract star field of *Space Invaders* or the surreal maze of *Pac-Man*, this is an unfinished skyscraper. Much like the design of Mario himself, this setting is carefully chosen to show realism within the confines of technology. A finished office building would have required too much detail. But it was actually possible to display a series of girders, straight out of real life, on the game screen.

Another important aspect of this scene is that it gives the player time to reflect on the setting, on the graphics, and on the characters' mannerisms: Donkey Kong's maniacal grin suggests that he will be a tricky enemy. The player doesn't have time to look at the designs and think about the character traits while actually playing the game; the action is too involving.

After the introductory scene, an interstitial screen alerts the player that the game is about to start, and it also communicates the game's objective: get as high on the screen as possible (Fig. 1.4). The game begins, and although the large double ladders of the introduction are now split up into fragments, the game takes place in the same virtual space as the opening "movies" did.

Mario (bottom left) must fight his way up the girders, jumping over the barrels that Donkey Kong rolls down the structure (Fig. 1.5). While he does this, Pauline runs around the top girder, yelling "Help!" (Fig.

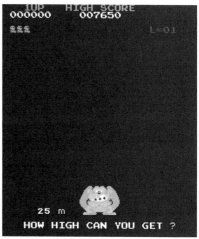

Fig. 1.4

1.6). To look away from Mario means death, complete with a halo (Fig. 17), so the player probably cannot concentrate on these background elements. But anyone watching another person play the game has the luxury of observing the various animations of the three distinct "actors" in the "scene": Donkey Kong's grin when Mario dies, Mario's determined face, Pauline's exclamations.

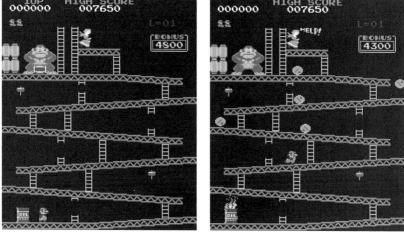

Fig. 1.5   *Fig. 1.6*

Fig. 1.7

When the player reaches the top, he is rewarded when Mario and Pauline are reunited, complete with a Valentine's heart above them (Fig. 1.8). But Donkey Kong is not yet defeated, and with a look of dismay, he snatches Pauline and carries her further up the structure as the heart breaks (Fig. 1.9). There is another interstitial screen before the second and final stage (Fig. 1.10), a set of straight blue girders that forms the skyscraper's top (Fig. 1.11). Mario must avoid fireballs; the barrels that Donkey Kong threw in the first stage would turn into fireballs that actively pursued Mario if he dawdled, and these are probably ones that managed to climb to the top of the structure. The player soon learns that climbing to the top is no longer the goal: Mario must traverse the entire structure to pull out the yellow rivets (by walking or jumping over them). Pauline runs back and forth atop the structure (Fig. 1.12), and Mario can collect her umbrella, hat, and purse for extra points in this stage. When Mario pulls the last rivet, the entire structure gives way (Fig. 1.13) and Donkey Kong falls to the bottom (Fig. 1.14) and lands on his head, his face contorted (Fig. 1.15). Mario and Pauline are finally reunited at the top of the screen as the final music plays (Fig. 1.16). This short scene is the *denouement*, the ending, the reward for a job well done, and it's the completion of the narrative.

Fig. 1.8

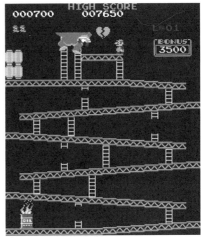

Fig. 1.9

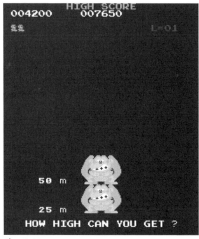

Fig. 1.10

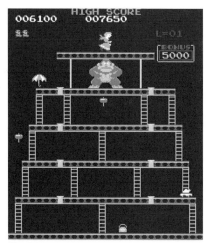

Fig. 1.11

Fig. 1.12

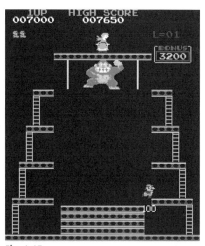

Fig. 1.13

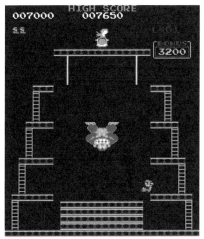

Fig. 1.14

Fig. 1.15

Fig. 1.16

■ ▪ ▩

Playing the game for the first time, Nintendo's American staff was incredulous. They thought the game played well but was ultimately too foreign; they expected a game in the established shooting or maze genres. Some, thinking the company would surely go under, began looking for new jobs. But still, it was the only game they had, so they decided to prepare the game for a US release, with a simple English-language translation of the game's story to be printed on the arcade cabinet. Because they felt "Jump-Man" wasn't catchy enough in English, they were wondering what to call the main character. Just then, their landlord came in, demanding the back rent payments. His name was Mario Segali.

Ultimately, Miyamoto's unique action and narrative development made *Donkey Kong* a massive hit in both the US and Japan, eventually outselling *Pac-Man* and *Space Invaders*. Nintendo of America was in business, raking in millions, helped by the fact that the game was too distinctive and story-dependent to duplicate successfully. And Shigeru Miyamoto was given the green light to produce more games.

His second, *Donkey Kong Junior*, was released one year later in 1982 and follows a similar beginning/middle/end narrative structure. *DK Junior's* story actually inverts the good/evil balance of the original, which helps to illustrate Miyamoto's assertion that neither Mario nor Donkey Kong were entirely good nor evil characters. After the player inserts a coin and presses Start, he immediately sees two Marios (the other one is probably an early version of Mario's brother character, Luigi) hauling the captured Donkey Kong up by ropes (Figs 2.1, 2.2). They push Donkey Kong to the top left of the screen as ominous music plays and the main character, Junior, appears. The player is instructed to get to the Key to "save your Papa!" (Figs. 2.3, 2.4). By this time, as you can see, even in Japan the main character had acquired the name Mario.

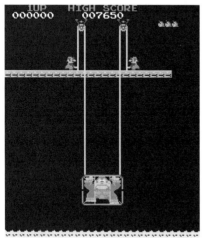

Fig. 2.1

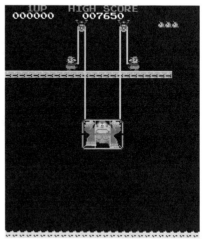

Fig. 2.2

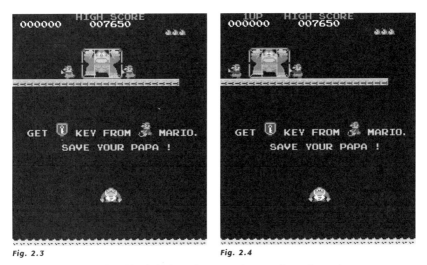

Fig. 2.3   Fig. 2.4

The screen flashes black before the game begins, but when play commences Mario and the caged Donkey Kong are in the same place, again establishing continuity between the non-interactive opening and the interactive game play sequence (Fig 2.5). Junior, who begins at the bottom left of the screen, is in fact a far more vibrant and animated character than Mario was—note his open-mouthed smile as he climbs the vine (Fig 2.6) and his charming death grimace (Fig 2.7). Avoiding the enemies that Mario continually releases and obtaining the Key, Junior is momentarily victorious but Mario is nonplussed; he pushes Donkey Kong off the screen (Fig. 2.8) to Junior's puzzlement, represented by animated question marks above his head (Fig. 2.9).

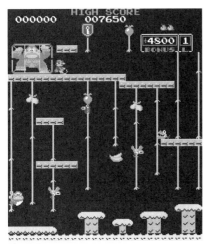

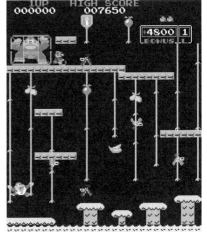

Fig. 2.5   Fig. 2.6

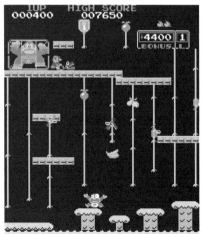

Fig. 2.7

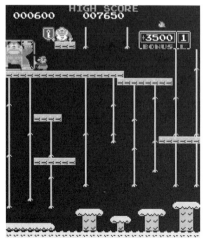

Fig. 2.8

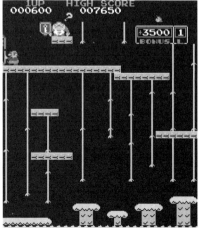

Fig. 2.9

On the next screen, Junior must push all of the Keys up into the locks to finally free his Papa, who is angrily stomping at the top of the screen (Fig 2.10). If the player accomplishes this difficult feat, he is rewarded with the story's end: Donkey Kong and Mario plummet to the ground (Figs. 2.11, 2.12). Junior, the smiling son, catches Donkey Kong, but Mario hits the ground (Fig. 2.13). As the two escape, Mario gives chase (Figs. 2.14, 2.15) but soon finds himself the recipient of a Donkey Kong boot to the face (Figs 2.16, 2.17).

Fig. 2.10

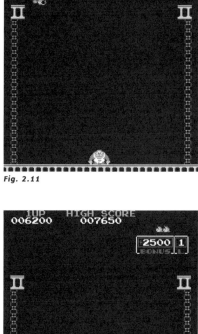
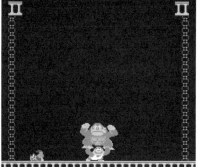

Fig. 2.11

Fig. 2.12

Fig. 2.13

Fig. 2.14

Fig. 2.15

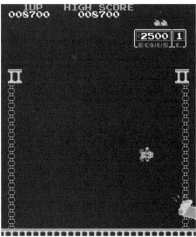

Fig. 2.16

Fig. 2.17

After the stories of *Donkey Kong* and *DK Jr.* are complete, each game starts again from the beginning, and new stages are inserted between the two main ones. These extra stages serve to make the quests longer and more difficult, but there are no additional cinematic scenes in the longer version of the game. The game continues until the player loses all of his Marios or Juniors. With every arcade game since *Space Invaders*, the player's goal has been to get the high score on the machine and enter his initials for all future players to try to beat. This is the eventual goal of *Donkey Kong* players. But an important distinction is that the *beginning Donkey Kong* player starts out with a very different goal: to complete the story. Score is a secondary concern; more important is finding out what happens when you rescue the girl and clear the second screen. The final fanfare (and the appealing image of Donkey Kong's goofy, defeated face or Mario's prostrate body) is a better reward than a series of numbers.

The cut-scenes were also nearly fully integrated into the game. Only the brief interstitial screens to alert players that they were about to take control broke the continuity between the cinematics and game play. Otherwise, the non-interactive scenes occurred on the same screen as the game—this was not the case for *Pac-Man's* cut-scenes. So, players watched these miniature, lifelike cartoon characters play out a story, and then had the privilege of controlling them for the middle of the narrative. This was important because it appealed to the consumer's desire to own the character.

In a 1997 book titled *Kids' Stuff*, Pennsylvania State University professor Gary Cross discussed the appeal of licensed character toys, which began to appear en masse in the 1930s. "Customers bought more than a plaything with their purchase [of a licensed toy]. They won entry into a special community of the initiated and of fantasy as embodied in the celebrity image… the toy made the owner a player in the world of the character."[35]

In the same way, the player of *Donkey Kong* became an active participant in the story. Even during the Depression, noted Cross, parents would pay a premium price to own a Mickey Mouse lunchbox rather than a cheaper, generic brand. So it's not surprising that this same sort of character association for *Donkey Kong* still translated directly into sales. *Donkey Kong* is still one of the biggest-selling arcade games of all time.

This comparison to toy marketing is important because video games have long been a children's pastime. But this was not always the case. The first successful arcade games—*Pong*, *Breakout*—were usually placed in over-21 establishments like bars and pool halls, and they turned fine profits from adult players. The early arcade game advertisements reproduced in Van Burnham's book <u>Supercade</u> all show adult or late-teen players crowded around the game cabinets. Meanwhile, advertisements for *home* video game systems showed parents and their young children (apparently 7 or 8 years old) gathered around the television.

It is clear that children were attracted to video games and that home games were being marketed to them—and to their parents, who ultimately decided on the $100+ purchase of a game console. Children also spent a lot of time in the arcades, as evidenced by the public-awareness campaigns led by concerned parents, who complained that their children were spending time in seedy public places like bars and pool halls just to play video games. The problems inherent to this sort of atmosphere led Atari founder Nolan Bushnell to envision a combination pizza parlor/arcade, decorated in bright colors and inviting to

children. This became the restaurant chain "Chuck E. Cheese" in 1977. This safe and inviting environment led to a preliminary stamp of approval on video games as children's entertainment.

Miyamoto contends that he makes video games for people of all ages, but it was in this new atmosphere of games-for-kids that *Donkey Kong* was released. *Donkey Kong*'s appeal to children had a lot to do with the vibrant graphics and cartoonish presentation. After all, the game's soundtrack and animation made it look quite like a cartoon television show. But the fact that the child could *control* the character—to have total control over a person and over a small system, something that few children have in their daily lives—was another big attraction. Psychologist Marsha Kinder wrote in 1991 about Nintendo's games as oedipal fantasies, noting that the most popular Nintendo games of the time (*Punch-Out*, *The Legend of Zelda*, and *Super Mario Bros.*) all starred a small, "insignificant" character who went up against a giant with far greater powers and toppled him, sometimes even saving the woman in his grasp.[36]

Children have always loved these sorts of child-beats-giant stories; Kinder points to David and Goliath, Jack and the Beanstalk, *The Karate Kid*, and the immensely popular *Home Alone* movies. But video games, beginning with *Donkey Kong*, added the element of control. In a study based on the Teenage Mutant Ninja Turtles properties, one six-year-old boy said that he liked the video game more because "you can move the guys yourself and in [the Turtles cartoon] you can just see them."[37]

In his book <u>Reinventing Comics</u>, Scott McCloud noted again the importance of control over the video game narrative by comparing them to superhero comics: "Superheroes are first and foremost about role-playing, becoming the character... comics have a great untapped potential for audience participation... but [the video game] already kicks comics' butt, and it's only going to gain strength in the coming years."[38] McCloud, as you might imagine, is also quick to praise the Japanese comics culture.

It is impossible to exaggerate how crucial the element of control has been to the success of Nintendo, to video games as an industry, and to the games as a popular recreation. "Video games constitute virtual play spaces,"[39] wrote Henry Jenkins. Miyamoto agrees. When he tells me that his main job is *ningen kougaku*, he means it; if the interface—the means by which the player interacts with the character—is not intuitive and fun, then the game isn't any good.

This assertion that control is the most important addition to video game narratives is backed up again and again, from Kinder to Jenkins, to no less a person as revered film scholar Donald Richie. In a recent interview with *Kyoto Journal*, Richie reinforced the connection between *manga*, *anime*, and video games:

> "...[A]nime, like the TV games that spawned them, gives the impression of control. One could, you will remember, starve the *tamagotchi* to death if one so chose. These gadgets give the power-deprived young the impression that they are in the driver's seat. So do manga. So do anime—the ultimate presentational (every frame hand-digitaled) narrative."[40]

After all, how else could one explain why children were able to identify with and wish that they could become Mario, *a thirty-something, overweight Italian plumber?* The best illustration of how much children of both cultures recognized and liked the character comes from a 1997 Japanese middle-school introductory English-language textbook. The lesson is titled, "How old is Mario?" and the main model conversation features two Japanese and two *gaijin* middle-schoolers playing a Nintendo Super Famicom and talking about Mario:

Ken: Sarah, do you know Mario?

Sarah: Yes, I do. He's very popular in the United States.

Yumi: Oh, really?

Paulo: Mario is not so young, but he's very cute.

Yumi: Oh? How old is he, Ken?

Ken: I don't know. Maybe about thirty-five.[41]

Miyamoto not only understood the importance of control, he was also superb at its execution. Note his addition of the jumping feature; he knew that in making the simple act of moving the character enjoyable, it would be even more fun for the player to completely control Mario's jumps. This became a defining characteristic of his games when Nintendo decided to release a programmable home video game system in 1983.

COMING HOME: *SUPER MARIO BROS.*

Looking at Marsha Kinder's study, it is clear that by 1990 "Nintendo" had become synonymous with "video games" in American parlance. "Nintendo game" meant all video game software, regardless of whether or not it was played on a Nintendo system, although it probably was. But this had not always been the case. In fact, up until 1984 the word was "Atari."

The Atari 2600 Video Computer System was the home video game console in millions of American homes, and it played the home versions of nearly every arcade hit: *Pac-Man*, *Space Invaders*—even *Donkey Kong*. Nintendo had licensed *Donkey Kong*'s home-system rights to a Hartford, Connecticut company called Coleco*, who published the game on the three leading video game consoles of the time: the Atari 2600, the Mattel Intellivision, and their own Colecovision console. To save precious space on the storage media of the time, none of the home versions contained the cinematic sequences—only the main game play was programmed onto the cartridges.†)

By 1983, most of the American programmable systems were being imported into Japan. The VCS was being sold as the Atari 2800; the Magnavox Odyssey[2] could be found as well; and Japanese toy mainstay Bandai, after releasing a line of dedicated and programmable systems called "TV JACK," had imported and sold three different American systems: Mattel's

* Stands for "Connecticut Leather Company"—based in Hartford, they had started out producing leather goods, then moved into children's toys, and then video games.

† Even more than that, the Atari 2600 and Intellivision versions looked and played absolutely terribly. The Intellivision version was so poorly rendered that Donkey Kong was colored green and resembled nothing more than an amorphous blob. There was speculation that Coleco only produced these games to show that the Colecovision, with its nearly perfect version of the game, was the best system to own. This probably isn't true, because the Atari version of *Pac-Man*, programmed by Atari themselves, was just as poor.

Intellivision, Emerson's Arcadia, and Milton Bradley's Vectrex.*

* The Vectrex contained a built-in vector graphics monitor, which allowed it to display finely detailed (but black-and-white) vector graphics, as in the *Asteroids* arcade machines. The Japanese name of the system was *Kousokusen*, or "light-speed vessel."

What's more, no less than five other Japanese companies, including Tomy, Takara, Epoch, and Sega, had released their own programmable video game consoles. What most of the systems on the market in Japan had in common was that they were very expensive. Commodore Japan's Max Machine sold for ¥34,800. Bandai's version of the Intellivision was ¥49,800, Tomy's Pyu-Ta was ¥59,800. Sega's SG-1000 (¥15,000) and Epoch's Cassette Vision (¥13,500) were much cheaper, but they were primitive by comparison.[42]

In short, the Japanese market was incredibly crowded, consumers were undoubtedly confused, and no clear leader had emerged. Nintendo president Hiroshi Yamauchi, having seen great success with Nintendo's first forays into the home video game market, wanted to take the lead by producing a cheaper and far more powerful programmable system than the dozen or so machines then fighting for shelf space.

That system was the Family Computer, or Famicom, which was released in Japan on July 15, 1983 and cost ¥14,800. It was an instant success; Nintendo sold more than 500,000 Famicoms in two months, and the strong sales continued. Released on the same day were Famicom versions of *Donkey Kong*, *Donkey Kong Jr.* and *Popeye*— Nintendo had finally acquired the Popeye license, but Miyamoto did not design the game. A translation of Miyamoto's latest arcade game, *Mario Bros.*, followed that September. *Mario Bros.* featured another version of the second Mario from *Donkey Kong Jr.*, but

★ MARIO BROS., BATTLE THE PESTS! TWO PLAYERS MAKE IT EASIER.

now he was clad in green and called Luigi. *Mario Bros.* was a running/jumping/climbing game in which two players could participate simultaneously. They could either try to attack each other and be the last man standing, or cooperate to reach higher levels. *Mario Bros.* was a step back in terms of narrative, as there were no cut-scenes, no girl to save, and no final monster to defeat. The creatures just kept coming until Mario and Luigi died. But, importantly, the Marios and their enemies were even larger and more cartoon-like in their animated movements.

Mario Bros. is also where Mario and Luigi acquired much of their character back-story. Miyamoto had already decided that Mario was a manual laborer who worked very hard, but because the game was set underground in a large network of giant green pipes, Miyamoto and team rationalized that Mario and Luigi should specifically be plumbers. And when they thought about what sort of place would have that kind of labyrinthine subterranean network of sewage pipes, New York immediately came to mind.

They knew from the first that they wanted to have Mario and Luigi attacking enemies directly rather than simply avoiding obstacles as in *Donkey Kong.* Turtles were used as the main enemy because Miyamoto wanted a creature that could be flipped onto its back and made helpless. Other enemies included crabs and giant flies. They wanted Mario to be able to jump on top of the enemy to defeat it, but this proved impossible to program; it would have required the program to distinguish between Mario touching the turtle from its top or its side, which would have required an algorithm too complex for the hardware to handle.[43] Instead, Mario and Luigi could jump up and hit overhead platforms from underneath, causing enemies atop these platforms to flip over. With an enemy harmless on its back, the player could then maneuver Mario directly beside it to kick it off the screen, thus defeating it.

The Famicom titles featured only the bare essentials, which means the few cinematic scenes from the arcade versions had to be cut. But the otherwise high quality of these translations, coupled with the system's low price, made the Famicom a moderate success in its first few years. A light gun that looked like a cowboy's six-shooter, complete with holster, hooked up to the Famicom and played home versions of Nintendo's arcade gun games, which themselves were themed on the Beam Gun toys and Laser Clay Ranges: *Wild Gunman, Duck Hunt, Hogan's Alley.* The latter two of these titles were directed by Miyamoto. Two more of Miyamoto's games, a motorbike racing/stunt game called *Excitebike* and a *Pac-Man* styled maze game called *Devil World**, were also quite popular.

* *Devil World* was the only one of Miyamoto's games that was never released in America. See Chapter 8.

But the "Famicom boom" that would ensnare Japan (and the world) in its colorfully animated grasp did not come until 1985 when *Super Mario Bros.* was released for the Famicom. *Super Mario Bros.* was Miyamoto's longest and most complex game to date, merging the cinematic, story-oriented *Donkey Kong* with the depth of play that *Mario Bros.* provided. *Super Mario Bros.* was so complicated that an extra processor chip called the MMC-1 had to be included on the game cartridge. And as a home game, it had something arcade games lacked: a lengthy, detailed instruction booklet. Although there was no opening story sequence in the game program itself, the first page of the *Super Mario Bros.* booklet spelled out the beginning of the story:

> One day the kingdom of the peaceful mushroom people was invaded by the Koopa, a tribe of turtles famous for their black magic. The quiet, peace-loving Mushroom People were turned into mere stones, bricks, and even field horsehair plants, and the Mushroom Kingdom fell into ruin.
>
> The only one who can undo the magic spell on the Mushroom People and return them to their normal selves is the Princess Toadstool, the daughter of the Mushroom King. Unfortunately, she is presently in the hands of the great Koopa turtle king.
>
> Mario, the hero of this story (maybe) hears about the Mushroom People's plight and sets out on a quest to free the Mushroom Princess from the evil Koopa and restore the fallen kingdom of the Mushroom People.
>
> You are Mario! It's up to you to save the Mushroom People from the black magic of the Koopa!*

* Taken from the US version's instruction booklet, which was an exact translation of the Japanese. See Chapter 8.

Donkey Kong was the first game that asked a player to accomplish the concrete goal of completing the narrative, but even a mediocre player could save Mario's girlfriend in a few minutes of play. The *actual* challenge of *Donkey Kong* was to get a high score by playing the same levels over and over again. Many other running/jumping/climbing games with a similar challenge followed *Donkey Kong*, but *Super Mario Bros.* was the first game in which simply completing the story was the *actual* goal of the player, and so the exhortations of this introductory text were to be taken seriously. *Super Mario Bros.* kept score, but nobody cared; the idea was to find out what happened when you saved the princess!

This sort of introductory text was common in home games before *Super Mario Bros.*, but none of them ever added so much to the game's story. Whereas the entire story of *Donkey Kong* had to be told in pantomime by the onscreen characters, the instruction booklet fleshed out the characters in far greater detail.

And because there were very few cut-scenes in the game program itself, this introduction was necessary. Later pages in the instruction booklet describe each enemy character in turn and reveal a bit about their personalities. Character introductions were not unprecedented either, but since the *Super Mario Bros.* stories and characters were turned into successful comic books, movies, television shows, and children's novels, there must have been something more appealing about the Koopa Troopas and Buzzy Beetles that populated Miyamoto's world.

The unassuming Mario gained some new powers and abilities in the world of *Super Mario Bros.* Some, like the ability to jump on turtles and kick the shells, were ideas from earlier games, and some were brand-new concepts taken from more of Miyamoto's favorite stories. From *Alice In Wonderland*, he took the Magic Mushroom, which would turn Mario into the giant Super Mario. And drawing on *Star Trek*, Miyamoto created secret "warp zones" that would allow players to instantly skip ahead to the game's final levels.

Finding and using the warp zones was crucial to Mario's victory, because in its time *Super Mario Bros.* was the longest and most complicated video game ever designed. Whereas most prior video games, including *Donkey Kong*, had taken place on a single screen or a succession of repeating screens, *Super Mario Bros.'* playfield was larger than the size of the display screen. As the player moved his character to the screen's right edge, the playfield would shift smoothly to the right to reveal portions of the playfield that were previously off-screen. This approach allowed each "level" to be dozens of screens long. *Super Mario Bros.* was not the first 'side-scrolling' game, but it looked smoother than any other and exploited the technique much more effectively.

Although *Super Mario Bros.* was a great step forward in graphics, characters, and game play, it lacked the beginning/middle/end narrative structure of *Donkey Kong*. The game begins with Mario on the title screen (Fig. 3-1). One can watch a demonstration of the game or press the Start button to begin. The terrain Mario must travel (always left-to-right) is impressively diverse: from the bricks-and-pipes level 1-1 to the giant platform trees of 5-3 (Fig. 3-2) to underwater levels through which Mario must swim (Fig. 3-3). This variety of terrain and color, not to mention the game's sheer scope, made Mario's world leaps ahead of previous video games. The fourth level of each world is a castle filled with fireballs and pools of lava. At the end, Mario encounters the giant lizard Koopa, also known as Bowser (Fig. 3-4).

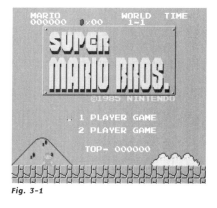

Fig. 3-1

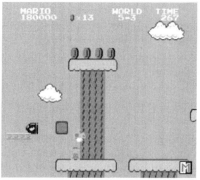

Fig. 3-2

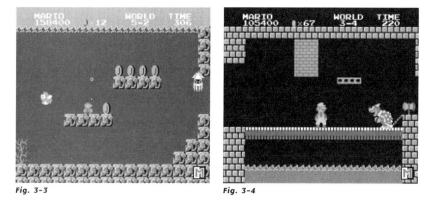

Fig. 3-3

Fig. 3-4

At this point, a gamer accustomed to the brief Atari games of the era would assume that the game is nearly over and that he is moments away

Fig. 3-5

from rescuing the Princess. But this is far from true. In fact, there are seven more "worlds" of four levels each to traverse before the Princess is found. All of the Koopas (Bowsers) save the one in level 8-4 are fake; after Mario defeats them he advances to the right to find not the Princess Toadstool (*Piichi hime*, or Princess Peach, in Japan) but instead one of her Mushroom Retainers (*kinopio*), who informs Mario that the Princess is, in fact, in another castle (Fig. 3-5).

Mario continues to hear this until the final level, 8-4, the most difficult in the game. While most other levels are rather straightforward paths, some with difficult enemies and most with hidden surprises (accessed by going down pipes and climbing up vines: Fig 3-6), level 8-4 is a devious maze. Following the wrong path sends Mario back to an earlier part of the level. If Mario makes it through this ordeal via trial and error, he goes up against the final gauntlet of enemies, ending with the real Koopa (Figs. 3-7 ~ 3-10). Mario can either kill Koopa (Bowser) with fireballs (Fig. 3-11) or cut the drawbridge by grabbing the axe (Fig. 3-12). If he does the latter, the player enjoys a comical sequence in which Koopa remains briefly suspended in midair, wiggling his toes as he discovers that his drawbridge has been cut from beneath him, at which point he plunges into the lava. In context, Koopa's maniacal, open-mouthed grin changes from leering to pathetic.

Fig. 3-6

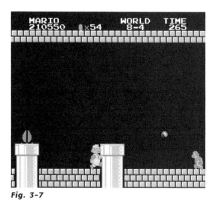

Fig. 3-7

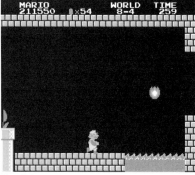

Fig. 3-8

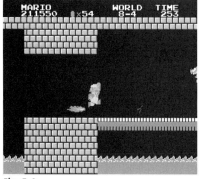

Fig. 3-9

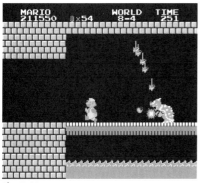

Fig. 3-10

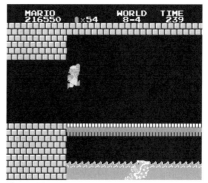

Fig. 3-11

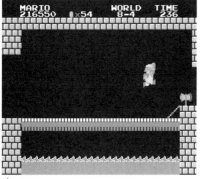

Fig. 3-12

Super Mario Bros. was, like the original Mario Bros., a step back in terms of narrative compared to the movie-like Donkey Kong games. Even Super Mario Bros.' ending simply consisted of a flat, motionless Princess congratulating Mario curtly (Fig. 3-13) before sending him on "another quest," a harder version of the original game (Fig. 3-14). Even so, Super Mario Bros. was novel enough to become the best-selling video game of all time, a record that it is in no danger of losing even today.*

* Super Mario Bros. sold approximately 6,810,000 copies in Japan alone. Worldwide sales figures are unavailable but would easily bring the total well past twenty million copies, not counting the millions and millions of bootleg copies that sold in China, Taiwan, Hong Kong, and elsewhere. The next highest game on the list is Nintendo's Tetris for the Game Boy, which sold 4,230,000 copies. [Data from 2002 CESA Games White paper, published by the Computer Entertainment Software Association in Tokyo.]

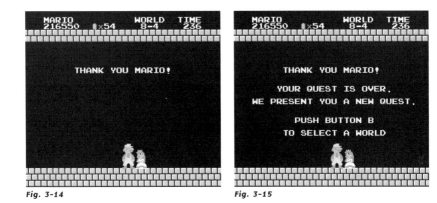

Fig. 3-14   Fig. 3-15

* For a detailed, informative, and entertaining account of Nintendo's success in the US, I heartily recommend David Sheff's Game Over.

The US version of the Famicom, renamed the Nintendo Entertainment System, launched in New York City for Christmas 1985 with games like *Duck Hunt*, *Wild Gunman*, and *Donkey Kong*, but not *Super Mario Bros.*, which arrived in 1986. As in Japan, it was Super Mario that launched "Nintendomania" in the US—it was so unlike any game that had come before that everyone had to have it.*

In Japan, a book that contained detailed maps of *Super Mario Bros.'* worlds, which plotted out all of the enemy locations, hidden warps, and power-up items, such as the Magic Mushroom, quickly became a certified best-seller. There were Mario *manga* serials, and finally an animated feature film, *Suupaa mario burazaasu: Piichi hime kyuushutsu daisakusen* (*Super Mario Bros: The Great Battle Plan To Save Princess Peach!*) was released to theaters in 1986. The film opens with Mario playing a Famicom late at night, suddenly finding that the characters have started to come out of the game screen. He attempts to save Princess Peach from Koopa but fails. Later that morning, Luigi convinces him it was all a dream. The next day, at the general store that the Mario Bros. run, Mario is lost in daydreams over the lovely Princess Peach when suddenly, a strange dog-like creature appears and summons the Mario Bros. to the Mushroom Kingdom.

Other plot elements added to the movie include the Mushroom King, who sends Mario, Luigi, and the dog-like creature on their way through the kingdom, and of course the final plot twist at the end, in which the dog is revealed to be Princess Peach's fiancé (he had fallen under Koopa's curse) and Mario's crush on the Princess comes to an unrequited end. Because that is the extent of the plot, the bulk of the film consists of repetitive 'choreographed' musical scenes depicting Mario and Luigi (the second player's character) running through the Mushroom kingdom stomping on enemies—very much like the bulk of the game.

Licensed Mario properties of this type took a while longer to reach America, but they did in spades: a live-action movie, a syndicated television show called *Super Mario Bros. Super Show* that featured live-action segments and animation, and a comic book series called Nintendo Comics System. The characters and plots for these generally came from the later games in the Mario series. As one might imagine, the later games not only expanded Mario's abilities but also greatly expanded the number of cinematic sequences and featured more refined character roles.

SUPER SEQUELS

> [Celebrated filmmaker] Jean Renoir, in a famous saying, pointed out that a director essentially makes only one film, has only one story to tell. A number of unarguable auteurs give clear credence to this notion [by remaking earlier films]… Such practice is perhaps even more common in Japan… That these men were in essence (and often in fact) their own producers when they remade their own films convinces us of their own overt desires to redo an earlier film, even beyond the manner in which all of these directors continually rework, repeat, and refer to motifs found in earlier films. That they were in a sense allowed to remake an earlier film within the commercial context in which they all worked is also not surprising… We also note something else: that in most of these instances (and others throughout film history to which one could point), the remakes add another dimension to the film, typically color cinematography.[44]

It is interesting that film critic David Desser finds the practice of remaking films "even more common" among Japanese auteur/directors, because we also find this to be true of Miyamoto and other Japanese game creators. *Donkey Kong Jr.* is the only game in the Mario series that could be called a true sequel in terms of storyline, a *continuation* rather than a *remake*. For the rest of the Super Mario Bros. games, the basic plot of the original—Mario defeats Bowser, saves Princess Peach—is retained, but there are more cinematic scenes and sometimes plot twists over the course of the game.

We find another parallel in the notion of advancing technology. New computer hardware technology from Nintendo is *always* accompanied by a new Mario game, even today. *Super Mario Bros. 2* (1986) launched with the Famicom Disk System, a floppy disk drive add-on only released in Japan. *Super Mario Bros. 3* (1988) was on a standard cartridge but contained

Nintendo's new MMC3 computer chip, which allowed for more complex graphics. The Nintendo Game Boy's launch in 1989 was accompanied by a scaled-down, portable Mario adventure called *Super Mario Land*. *Super Mario World* (1990) and *Super Mario 64* (1996) were the first games for Nintendo's Super Famicom and Nintendo64 hardware, respectively. *Mario Clash*, a 3-D version of the first *Mario Bros.*, launched with Nintendo's ill-fated 3-D platform, the Virtual Boy, in 1995. The one time that a new Mario game was *not* available at the launch of a Nintendo system was with *Super Mario Sunshine* on the Nintendo GameCube. In that case, the Mario game launched a little less than a year after the system, but *Luigi's Mansion*, a *Ghostbusters*-style haunted house adventure starring Luigi, was available on launch day.

In general, then, it is only when new technology makes it possible to truly upgrade the game that Miyamoto remakes his titles. There are, of course, many more games bearing the Super Mario name, from sports games like *Mario Golf* to puzzles like *Mario's Picross*. But the ones with which Miyamoto—who by the early 1990s had been promoted to "producer," overseeing the development of dozens of titles at once—had the most direct involvement are the ones that remake the original story.

Super Mario Bros. 2

The New Hardware: In 1986, the Famicom was riding high on the *Super Mario Bros.* Boom, and Japanese gamers eagerly anticipated Nintendo's next big move. It turned out to be a floppy-disk drive called the Famicom Disk System. The games came on small magnetic disks encased in hard yellow plastic, slightly smaller than the 3.5" floppies that would much later become standard on home PCs. The disks were double-sided and held more data than the standard cartridges for a cheaper price, about ¥4000 for a disk game versus ¥6000 and up for a cartridge. Even better, the disks were rewriteable. A video game store equipped with a Disk Writer kiosk could erase old, unwanted games and give the player a new game, with a new instruction book and stickers for the disk, for between ¥500 and ¥1000.

The Game: *Super Mario Bros. 2* was subtitled "For Super Players," and it was not a top-to-bottom remake, but rather a new and blisteringly difficult set of levels. Besides the different world maps and a few new enemy characters, the game's graphics, sounds, and story were entirely identical to the original.

Miyamoto was not very involved with the production of *Super Mario Bros.*
2. At a 2003 lecture at Tokyo University, he admitted as much: "Once we all
got a little bolder and hired on apprentice-type people, around the time of
Super Mario Bros., I could just bring out the original design and leave the rest
to apprentices. That ended up being the best way of all to make games. So by
that time I was a director—. I started work on Mario and Zelda sequels at the
same time. I was the director on both projects and I really thought I was
going to die."[45] Feeling pressure, Miyamoto focused his energy on Zelda and
left most of *Super Mario Bros.* 2 to a designer named Takashi Tezuka. "He
directed the project, and I contributed about ten percent."[46] Tezuka would go
on to work closely with Miyamoto throughout the Mario series.

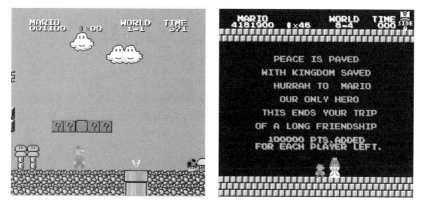

*Super Mario Bros. 2 looked superficially similar to the original game, although the levels were
much harder (top). A special reward awaited players who made it all the way to the Princess:
she was redrawn to look much prettier, and she recited a poem (in English) while a remixed,
lengthier version of the ending theme song played (above).*

Super Mario Bros. 3

The New Hardware: The Famicom turned five years old in 1988, and
that is *ancient* for a piece of video game hardware. These days, all but the
most popular video game systems are pulled from production before their
fifth birthday. But the Famicom, as perhaps the most popular video game
platform in history, had remarkably long legs. And Nintendo, as a conservative business loathe to do anything that might jeopardize their reign over the
Japanese and American game industries, were not about to shake things up
by introducing a new video game system. This despite the fact that hardware
technology had evolved considerably in five years and soon-to-be rivals NEC
and Sega were gearing up to release new machines with advanced processing

* But the Famicom Disk System could do *neither*, because the disk format did not allow for it. Nintendo realized this failure and pulled Disk System support, releasing nearly all its post-1986 titles on cartridge.

power. Of course, if Nintendo continued to produce 1983-era games like *Donkey Kong*, they'd quickly lose that number-one spot. There were two ways to produce more complex games on the Famicom: add extra memory to the cartridge ROMs, or add a coprocessor chip into the cartridge. *Super Mario Bros. 3* did both.*

The Game: *Super Mario Bros. 3* was Miyamoto's first complete, bottom-to-top remake of the Mario adventure. It is even today considered one of the finest video games ever made. While its graphics might not compare to today's games, the expansive world of Mario 3 (which most players never fully explore) let Mario *backtrack* through stages, climb *up and down* instead of left and right, and gave Mario several new powers, not the least of which was the ability to fly.

Each time Miyamoto remakes the Mario adventure, he refines and adds to the game play mechanics in this manner, but he also remakes the story. By examining the ending sequences of the latter Mario games—each of which includes Mario in the final showdown with Koopa, the rescue of the Princess, and some form of credits sequence—we can see how each game's ending became more and more like a film's.

In *Super Mario 3*, the fight against Koopa becomes even more epic and lengthy. First, in place of eight identical Koopa stand-ins, Mario squares off against one of Bowser's seven children at the end of each world (Fig. 4-1). When he finally eludes the traps and dangers of Koopa's castle, the player finds that he cannot simply run past Koopa or jump on his head to defeat him. Rather, he must trick Koopa into breaking his way through the blocks beneath him into the bottomless pit (Figs. 4-2, 4-3).* It is more of a *fight*, as the player must spend minutes evading and luring Koopa to his doom, rather than simply running underneath him, as in the first game. This accomplished, Mario can enter the door to the right, into the Princess' chamber (Fig. 4-4).

* One of Miyamoto's new ideas for the game play of *Super Mario Bros. 3* was that Mario could put on a variety of 'suits' that gave him new powers. The suit shown in this picture is in fact a *tanuki*, and one of the things that *tanuki* Mario could do was turn into a statue. This is another example of how the games were being created specifically for a Japanese audience.

Fig. 4-1

Fig. 4-2

Fig. 4-3

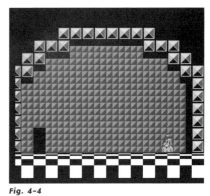

Fig. 4-4

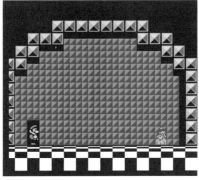

Fig. 4-5

The meeting-the-Princess scene is entirely refined. First, we see the Princess crouched in a corner of the darkened room (Fig. 4-5). Mario then appears in the door and turns on the lights (Fig. 4-6). The two meet each other in the center of the room (Fig. 4-7), and the Princess delivers a short, congratulatory message (Fig. 4-8). In the Japanese version (left), the Princess' comments are rather subdued: "Thank you! Peace has returned to the Mushroom world. The End!" The English translators had a bit of fun with the Princess' comment for the American version of the game (right): "Thank you! But our Princess is in another castle! ...Just kidding. Ha ha ha! Bye bye."

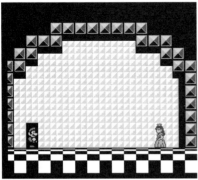

Fig. 4-6

Fig. 4-7

Fig. 4-8

With this, the same curtain that rises at the very beginning to reveal the game's title screen now drops (Fig. 4-9), and we see a series of drawings representing the game's eight worlds (Fig. 4-10) before the curtain finally falls and we see the "The End" title (Fig. 4-11). The rising and falling curtain adds a theatrical element and reinforces the beginning/middle/end structure. Due to the game's length and difficulty, the player has probably seen the curtain rise far more often than he has seen it fall, which makes the final curtain fall even more gratifying.

Fig. 4-9

Fig. 4-10

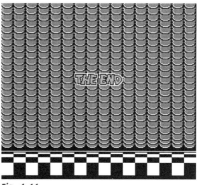

Fig. 4-11

Super Mario Bros. 4: Super Mario World*

The New Hardware: *Super Mario Bros. 3* started the Famicom boom all over again in Japan and the US, but by the time it was released, Sega's Mega Drive and NEC's PC Engine had been released worldwide, and the Famicom was starting to show its age. By 1990, Nintendo could hold out no longer and released

* The "Super Mario Bros. 4" portion of this game's title was dropped in the United States. Nintendo quite often changes the names of its games for different territories.

the 16-bit processor-powered Super Famicom. Only two games launched with the system, but one of them was Miyamoto's *Super Mario World*. Game and system sold out immediately, with demand vastly outpacing supply.

The Game: With *Super Mario World*, Miyamoto and the Mario team (which had by then expanded to sixteen people) had a far more advanced game console to work with. This meant that there could be more detailed, colorful artwork and expansive play areas, and cinematic sequences could be longer and more fanciful. Mario could revisit any world he had previously completed; and indeed, he had to, because most levels had multiple "exits" that would lead to new and sometimes super-secret areas.

The final fight against Koopa is also more intricate and lengthy (Fig. 5-1). This time Mario must pick up the little, robotic Mecha-Koopas that Koopa throws from his Clown Copter and hit Koopa in the head with them. Each time Mario knocks out Koopa, he disappears and the Princess emerges from the copter for a second to throw Mario a Super Mushroom as she screams for

help (represented, as in *Donkey Kong*, with the text, "Help!" above her head). When Koopa is defeated, the Princess is dumped from the copter, which spins into the horizon with Koopa still inside. The Princess walks over to Mario and gives him a congratulatory kiss (Fig. 5-2). A short text message confirms that Mario's adventure is over (Fig. 5-3), but the ending sequence has only just begun.

Fig. 5-1

Fig. 5-2

Mario's adventure is over.
Mario,the Princess,Yoshi,
and his friends are going
to take a vacation.

Fig. 5-3

First, we see celebratory fireworks (Fig. 5-4), end-ing with a large, heart-shaped one (Fig. 5-5)—have Mario and the Princess fallen in love? A movie-like credits sequence follows, underneath which we see Mario, his dinosaur friend Yoshi, and the Princess rid-ing back to Yoshi's house, followed by the eggs that Mario has collected along the way (again, by defeat-ing Koopa's seven children) (Fig. 5-6). When they arrive back, we see a colorful, vibrant scene showing the eggs hatching, and Mario and the Princess wave good-bye to the player (Fig. 5-7). But the endgame continues: a lengthy 'cast' sequence presents all of the enemy characters in the game and names them, ending with Koopa and his children (Fig. 5-8). At last, the "THE END" screen appears, accompanied by a detailed, *manga*-like portrait of Mario, Luigi, and the Princess (Fig. 5-9).*

★ This *amazed* me as a child—absolutely *amazed* me. I was so in awe of what the hardware could do, of course, but beyond that I was just stunned at how much this illustration added to the characters and to the world behind the games. Looking back, this picture was probably what inspired me to draw comics based on the world of the Mario games.

Fig. 5-4

Fig. 5-5

Fig. 5-6

Fig. 5-7

Fig. 5-8   Fig. 5-9

This ending sequence, like that of *Super Mario Bros. 3*, calls attention to the beginning of the game. When Mario starts his adventure, the first place he enters is Yoshi's House, where he finds that Yoshi has gone out on a quest to rescue his friends (the unhatched eggs). By bringing the action back to the beginning of the game, Miyamoto again sets up a definite sense of completion, of the player having come full circle.

Super Mario 64

The New Hardware: By 1996, Nintendo was, for the first time, in trouble in its home country.[*] The 16-bit era was ending and Nintendo faced real competition in the "next-generation" hardware front from, of all companies, Sony. Their PlayStation was running neck-and-neck with the Sega Saturn in Japan, and it was making inroads in the US. The PlayStation and the Saturn were CD-ROM game systems, but Nintendo decided to stick with cartridges for its Nintendo 64, named after the machine's 64-bit graphics processor. This riled game developers and caused quite a few of them to take their popular Famicom and Super Famicom game series to the PlayStation and Saturn. That left the Nintendo 64 standing only on the quality of Miyamoto's games—which were consistently brilliant.

[*] The Super Famicom was the system of choice in Japan, but clever marketing and a successful lineup of sports games gave Sega's Mega Drive (Genesis) an early lead in the US.

The Game: *Super Mario 64* took advantage of the Nintendo 64's advanced graphics processing power and was one of the first 3-D adventure games. Hailed by one magazine as "The Best Game Ever Created," *Super Mario 64* was truly a quantum leap in game design. *Super Mario Bros. 3* and *Super Mario World* added elements of non-linearity to Mario's adventures, but with its 3-D freedom of movement, *Super Mario 64* was like no adventure Mario had ever encountered. Just running through levels to find the 'exit' was no longer the goal. Mario had to explore the worlds around him and accomplish many, varied tasks to find 120 secret stars scattered to the four corners of the Mushroom Castle.

After earning at least 70 stars, Mario could face Koopa, this time by running *around* him, grabbing his tail, spinning him around, and throwing him far away, into a spiked bomb on the edge of the playfield. After the final battle, Mario is transported outside the Mushroom castle, where he began his adventure. The giant stained glass portrait of the Princess, visible from the game's opening, is revealed as the Princess' magical imprisonment. She floats down from the sky, thanks and kisses Mario, and brings him back inside the castle to bake him a cake—the Mushroom retainers are again present. The scene is "acted" with recorded voiceovers for Mario and Princess Peach, and the "camera" captures the action from many different angles. As one of the first 3-D games in which such "camera work" could be done, this scene showed how far film-like video games had come and offered a glimpse of the future. Again, a lengthy credits sequence follows, and an intricate "THE END" title screen closes the game.

Super Mario Sunshine

The New Hardware: Having given up their first-place position to the Sony PlayStation, Nintendo cut its losses as soon as possible, pulling Nintendo 64 support in early 2001 to concentrate on launching the Nintendo GameCube, the company's first optical disc-based system*, starting in the fall of that year. Nintendo built the GameCube from the ground up to connect to its newest portable system, the Game Boy Advance—Nintendo had never lost its commanding lead in the portable market.

The GameCube launched a week prior to the Microsoft Xbox but a year behind the PlayStation 2, and even this was too early for Nintendo to supply a Mario game at launch time. Nearly a year later, *Super Mario Sunshine* was released worldwide.

* Specifically, the GameCube uses 3.5 inch optical disks, which are much smaller than the standard DVDs used by the PS2 and Xbox. Those two systems can play DVD movies, DVD audio, and audio CDs, but the GameCube cannot. In 2002, Panasonic released the Q, a combination GameCube and DVD player, in Japan only. Sales were low because most GameCube owners already had a DVD player, whether standalone or built into another game system.

The Game: *Super Mario Sunshine* represents yet another location change for Mario's adventures. Now, instead of taking place inside Mushroom Castle or Dinosaur Land, the crew travels to the tropical Isle Delfino. The story is told in lengthy cinematic sequences that depict Mario, Peach, and friends traveling by plane to the island. Other such sequences are sprinkled throughout the game, telling a similar story to the earlier titles but now more fleshed out with character dialogue and vibrant animation. Interestingly enough, the dialogue is spoken in English even in the *Japanese* version of the game, subtitled in Japanese.

The tropical, water-covered setting was necessary for Mario's newest game play innovation, a water-shooting backpack called F.L.U.D.D. Mario could use this to spray a jet of water at enemies or rocket skyward with a powerful blast, but its main function, the reason why Miyamoto and team built the game around the device, is that it let Mario hover in the air for brief periods. This was done in an attempt to solve the difficulties of jumping in a 3-D game. One of the chief complaints about *Mario 64* and, indeed, most other 3-D platform games, was that it was too difficult to accurately judge jumping distance. Having the ability to hover and change direction in midair allowed more accurate jumping and made *Sunshine* easier to play, although the learning curve for using the water pack was a bit steeper.

So it is not only the story that changes throughout each Mario game, but also the elements of control: the new moves and abilities given to Mario, and the changes in the actual game controller. *Donkey Kong Junior* added a new dimension to the avoid-all-enemies game play by allowing Junior to increase his speed by climbing up two adjacent vines at the same time—of course, doing this would make him twice as vulnerable to enemy attack, since enemies slid down only one vine. This was a choice that *Donkey Kong* players didn't have to make. With *Mario Bros.* the core game play changed completely, from avoid to conquer; by knocking the enemies out from the lower levels and then kicking them straight on, they were defeated. Also, *Mario Bros.* was the first and last game in the main series to offer simultaneous two-player game play. Mario and Luigi shared the same screen and could either help or hinder each other; the players could cooperate or compete.

Super Mario Bros. introduced dozens of new moves for Mario, the most important being the power-ups that made him grow taller, shoot fireballs, or be temporarily invincible; collecting coins for extra lives; jumping on enemies' heads; breaking bricks; entering pipes to subterranean secret worlds; climbing beanstalks to find *heavenly* secret worlds; finding bricks with hidden coins; kicking turtle shells to defeat more enemies…and on and on. *Super Mario Bros. 2* introduced upside-down pipes and strong winds that blew Mario back; warp zones that worked backwards; and a differentiated Luigi who jumped higher and ran faster than Mario but was more likely to go careening into a waiting enemy or trap.

Super Mario Bros. 3 introduced worlds that could scroll up and down as well as back and forth, allowing Mario to retrace his steps to find more hidden secrets. This added an element of non-linearity; similar was the map screen that gave Mario a limited choice as to which area to tackle next. Between rounds he could play card games for extra powers or visit Toad's house for free gifts. Mario had a stock of extra items on the map screen to use before entering difficult levels...and on and on.

Super Mario World gave Mario even more freedom. He could revisit any level he had previously conquered. Many of them had a hidden goal that would lead to a brand new level, which itself might have two exits; he could ride on Yoshi the dinosaur, who could eat enemies with his long tongue...and on and on. Super Mario World was so vast, so sprawling that Miyamoto and team included a lithium battery in the cartridge that would save the player's game in progress. This concept was pioneered with Nintendo's role-playing adventure Legend of Zelda but became standard fare for nearly all genres soon after the release of Super Mario World.

With Super Mario 64 came a brand new controller. The controller for the Super Famicom featured unique "shoulder buttons" where the index fingers rested on top of the unit. These L and R buttons, for Super Mario World, let Mario advance the screen to the left and right to see what was up next: an interesting if impractical concept. The main controller for the Nintendo 64, however, featured something revolutionary for a console game system: an analog joystick.

Arcade joysticks and the Famicom D-pad were digital; when you pressed the pad or stick to the right, the signal was only "on" or "off," regardless of how hard you pressed the buttons. But the analog joystick measured how far you pushed it. For Super Mario 64, pushing the joystick a tiny bit would make Mario tiptoe, pushing it halfway would make him walk at normal speed, and all the way would make him run at full speed.*

★ Nintendo kept the controller secret for a very long time, fearful that rivals would copy the analog stick if they knew about it. Their fears were well founded; once the Nintendo 64 debuted, Sega and Sony immediately started work on their own analog joysticks. (Sega actually made it to market first with theirs.)

With the Nintendo GameCube, Nintendo refined their controller even more, using a unique button layout, a more comfortable stick, and analog L and R buttons. These triggers worked with the water-shooting pack in Mario Sunshine, enabling Mario to shoot just a little water or a firehose-style blast that knocked enemies (and sometimes Mario) backwards.

An in-depth discussion of the new moves, abilities, and secrets found in each new Mario game and the controller innovations that worked in tandem with them would literally fill a book on its own. And because we don't want to do that just yet, perhaps we should take a brief look at Miyamoto's other world-famous, consistently groundbreaking game series.

THE LEGEND OF ZELDA

Zeruda no Densetsu (*The Legend of Zelda*) is only slightly less internationally recognized than the Super Mario games. The original *Legend of Zelda* was released on the Famicom Disk System in 1986 and was unlike any Famicom game before it. For *Zelda*, Miyamoto drew on his store of childhood memories and created a vast world called Hyrule, filled with green forests, stony mountains, and dark, labyrinthine dungeons. Rather than being on the forced, straight-line path of a Super Mario game, the player was able to move around the world of Hyrule at will, going from place to place in any of the four compass directions. The player had to find important items and solve puzzles to conquer the nine dungeons and finish the adventure.

Not only was *Zelda* the largest game that had ever been created for the Famicom, it was one of the first Famicom games that did not end when the player died. When a player ran out of Marios, he had to start again from the beginning. Not so with *Zelda*—the player could save the game to the writeable portion of the Disk Card and start again where he left off. *Zelda*'s world was so expansive that the player *needed* to save the game and start again; it simply couldn't be completed in one sitting.

Zelda "was so different that we were afraid that people couldn't figure out how to play," recalled Nintendo of America president Minoru Arakawa. Nintendo's own testers needed ten hours or more to truly start enjoying the game, and even then they needed to be guided through the process by Nintendo's Japanese employees. Nintendo of America gave America's young (and not-so-young) adventurers the next best thing: a 1-800 telephone hotline that they could call to obtain advice. By 1990, the number of people staffing those phone lines had grown from four to two hundred.[47]

Still, Zelda's plot and characters were only slightly more refined than Donkey Kong's. The player's character was named Link, a small elven boy charged with

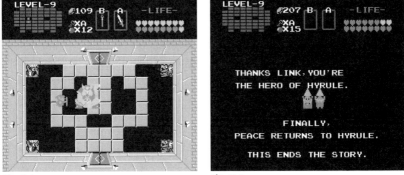

Fig. 7-1   Fig. 7-2

finding the eight pieces of the Triforce—a mystical item of unknown power—and rescuing Princess Zelda from the evil Ganon. The story was conveyed, as in the first Super Mario games, via sparse text boxes and limited character animation. After the decisive battle with Ganon (Fig. 7-1)—which could be won only if Link searched out the Silver Arrows in the game's final dungeon—a nearly motionless Princess Zelda thanked Link and told him that "this ends the story" (Fig. 7-2).

A brief credits sequence (Fig. 7-3) then followed, something that very few games had in 1986. Even well into the 1990s, it was rare to see a video game with a full credits sequence featur-
ing the real names of the designers. This was because video game com- pany management didn't want their designers' names known lest they get hired away by competitors. This was less of a problem in Japan because most employees stay at the same company for life. Even so, Miyamoto and his co-designer were referred to by pseudonyms; Miyamoto was referred to as S. MIYAHON—the *kanji* for *moto* can also be pronounced *hon*.

Fig. 7-3

The *Zelda* sequels and remakes progressed in much the same way as the Mario games did. The basic *story* hardly changed, but the *plot* was always embellished upon with new characters, plot twists, and expanded cinema scenes.* The Super Famicom game, *The Legend of Zelda: A Link To The Past* (directed by Kensuke Tanabe) didn't just start in the middle of the action, with the only back-story in the game's instruction booklet. Instead, it began with a lengthy story introduction in which Link gets out of bed on a stormy night and sneaks into Hyrule Castle. This is not played out automatically, the player *controls* Link during these scenes.

★ A quick film-studies lesson: the story is the events of the narrative (Using an array of weapons, a boy rescues a princess from the clutches of a horde of demons.). The plot is exactly what happens and the order in which it happens (boy enters cave, is given magical sword, kills monster, finds money...).

Similar story scenes abound throughout the game. The most impressive was the ending, which began with a lengthy story scene featuring Link and a rotating, three-dimensional Triforce, juiced up with the new game system's processing power (Fig. 7-4). This was followed by a succession of brief story scenes showing the various ways that peace had returned to Hyrule (Fig. 7-

5). Finally, a credits sequence listed the full names of all involved (Fig. 7-6). Said credits sequence also featured a moving, orchestral-sounding score that was, at the time, a giant leap for videogame soundtracks.

Zelda II: The Adventure of Link is the black sheep of the series, abandoning the original game's top-down action for side-scrolling sword fighting mixed with RPG game play. No other Zelda games using this style have ever been produced.

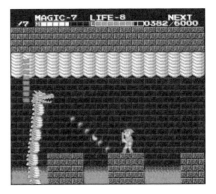

Fig. 7-4

Fig. 7-5

Fig. 7-6

Much like *Super Mario 64*, the first N64 incarnation of Zelda, *The Ocarina of Time*, introduced a full 3-D world. Of course, because *Zelda* was more of an RPG-style adventure game and less of an acrobatic, athletic action game, the move to 3-D had less of an impact. Futhermore, previous Zelda games already featured non-linear worlds, which meant that Link already had the freedom to roam about, unlike Mario. *Ocarina* featured numerous cinematic scenes, all rendered in 3-D graphics and thus they were more movie-like than practically any Nintendo game before it.

Having already accomplished a masterpiece *Zelda* game with *Ocarina*, *Majora's Mask*, the second N64 Zelda game, took the series for a drastic turn. Miyamoto had handed over the director's chair to his right-hand man on the series, Eiji Aonuma, who concocted a brilliant game play system. Like the movie *Groundhog Day*, the world of the game was caught in a constant three-day loop. Every three days, which took about an hour and a half of game play time, the game world would reset, forcing Link to lose all of his progress. He had to steadily accomplish small tasks before the world ended again.

Although it had its happy and silly moments, *Majora's Mask* was a remarkably dark and sometimes depressing game. The world's inhabitants started each day not knowing what was to come, but by the end of the third day the entire city had descended into chaos—people's true natures began to come out, families and friends ripped apart. And even when Link could solve their problems, there was, until the very end of the game, nothing he could do about it; at the end of the third day, everyone died. (See Chapter 10 for more.)

After *Majora's Mask*, Aonuma moved on to direct the first GameCube installment of the series, *Kaze no Takuto* (Baton of the Wind, called *Wind Waker* in the US). In sharp contrast to the realistically-designed scenery and characters of the Nintendo 64 games, *Wind Waker* used a graphical style known as cel-shading ('toon-shade' in Japan). This made the game look remarkably like an *anime* film. But although the new Link looked happy and childlike, the places he explored were still dark and dangerous, creating an artistically brilliant contrast.

Then, just as series fans were getting used to the cel-shaded look and anticipating that it would be used again for the next installment in the series, Aonuma and Miyamoto threw yet another curveball. They showed off the new *Zelda* game for the first time in the spring of 2004, and it was not cel-shaded nor cartoonish. It was a dark, violent, gritty, and realistic world inspired more by *Lord of the Rings* than *Astro Boy*. A grown-up Link galloped on his horse, slashing the heads of grotesque monsters. The series was again about to take a drastic turn.

When asked in a 1995 interview if he thought his games were "humorous," Miyamoto attributed it to "us Kansaiites. Kansai is the area covering Osaka, Kyoto, and several other cities. The Kansaiites make much of wits, explicit jokes, and are proud of making people laugh. The Kansaiites feel like cracking a joke or two even during a very serious talk."[71] Although *Zelda* games featured a few humorous scenes and characters, the tone of the games was much more serious than that of the Mario games. The opening and closing screens of the *Zelda* games tended to feature towering titles and somber music, or, once the technology allowed it, sweeping orchestral scores. If the Mario games followed from and expanded upon the comedic aspects of Miyamoto's *Donkey Kong* story, then the Zelda series was the serious, dark battle between good and evil.

That his work could even in 1986 be classified into serious, lighthearted comedies, and dark, intense adventures shows just how much Miyamoto changed video games.

FUTURE GAMES

Time marches on, and things change. Miyamoto is still recognized as one of the world's leading game designers, garnering a nomination, but not a win, for Best Game Designer in WIRED magazine's 2002 Rave Awards. New Mario and Zelda games are still the highlights of Nintendo's game lineup, but their release dates are no longer the earth-shattering events they were in the company's prime. *Super Mario Sunshine* was barely a whisper in the US compared to the tornado that was *Grand Theft Auto: Vice City* for the Sony PlayStation 2, which racked up millions of dollars in *pre-sales* before its October release.

The *Grand Theft Auto* series, developed in Scotland by Rockstar Games, is a far cry from Miyamoto's colorful wonderlands. My young cousins (then 14 and 10) introduced me to GTA3 one summer and showed me how your character, a gangster-in-training, regains his health in critical situations. Super Mario collects golden coins to fill his health meter; Grand Theft Auto's main character has to do a little more legwork. As I watched, the boys hijacked a car, killed the driver, sped immediately toward the red light district, solicited a prostitute, pulled into a dark alley—"the car has to be totally hidden or she won't do it with you," they tell me—then watched the car bounce up and down as the girl moaned and the player's health replenished.

Fully restored, the characters exited the car. As the younger yelled, "Kill the hooker!" his older brother guided the character to beat the girl to death with a baseball bat. Blood pooled around her slinky red dress. Then, a distinctly video-game-like thing occurred: a wad of bills popped up and rotated on the ground, gleaming like a 1-Up Mushroom—it was the fee that the character had just paid for her services. The kids then directed the character to take the cash and dash off, hijacking a different car now, to throw the police off the trail.

"I am not sure whether that sort of extreme subject matter is always appropriate," said Miyamoto in a WIRED interview. Nonetheless, *Vice City* designer Leslie Benzies won the WIRED award that Miyamoto lost. There was little argument that he deserved it; critics maintained that it wasn't the extreme violence and sexual situations that made the GTA series fun. Rather, it was the polished game play interface. Not to mention the fact that, as one American game designer put it in the same article, "*Grand Theft Auto* is basically a rip-off of *Zelda*, because *Zelda* invented massive-world games that let players explore freely, rather than following a linear path. Miyamoto innovates, so he's pushing the form. End of story."[49]

Miyamoto has always been thinking far ahead of his time. Many of his ideas for the original *Donkey Kong* had to be scrapped because they simply couldn't be done yet. In a 1991 interview, when *Super Mario World* was released in the United States, Miyamoto revealed that he wanted to have Mario ride a dinosaur like Yoshi ever since the first game in the series, but the technology wouldn't allow it. In the same interview, Miyamoto conjectured, "Who knows what Mario will look like in the future. Maybe he'll wear metallic clothes!"[50] Five years later, in *Super Mario 64*, Mario could in fact wear metal clothes that let him walk on the bottom of pools of water.

Shigeru Miyamoto relaxes with SimCity creator Will Wright, circa 1989. Photo credit: Jeff Braun.

And those who had seen the 1986 anime *The Great Plan To Save Princess Peach* knew that Mario defeated Koopa at the end of that film by grabbing him by his tail, swinging him in a circle, and letting go. This preceded the identical Koopa fights in *Super Mario 64* by an entire decade. One wonders how many *new* ideas Miyamoto has had recently, and how many of the features in every new Mario adventure have been in Miyamoto's head long before technology allowed him to implement them in a game. When Miyamoto closes our interview by talking about wanting Nintendo to go into the robotics field so that he can create a giant robotic Donkey Kong suit and stomp around in it as "some kind of a part-time job," it is hard to know if he is joking.

Said Miyamoto at the 1999 GDC, "Many people have said that I should make movies. But I don't feel like a moviemaker, I feel like a creator of fun. For me, game design is like expression through music or poetry—while I'm always trying to hit on new ideas, I place a lot of importance on tempo and sound effects. The designers that use rhythm are successful—when I hold the controller and set the tempo, I feel like I'm making my own personal game…

We use cinematic sequences to stimulate players' emotions— But we position these sequences as only one part of development. We opt not to use our limited time and energy on pre-rendered cinematics."

Indeed, although Miyamoto pioneered the use of narrative in video games, the games he directs do not put the focus on telling lengthy, in-depth stories. So many of his games follow the same man-loses-princess, man-finds-princess story with little variation. Miyamoto has said that he would rather concentrate on producing games with unique and deep game play. Of course, Miyamoto is head and shoulders above every other game designer in this area. Miyamoto's contribution to cinematic gaming is most profoundly felt in his earliest titles, because he was the first to create games with beginning/middle/end narrative structures and non-interactive cinematic scenes, and he was one of the first to create original, if simple, cartoon characters for his game worlds.

To see the later development of the cinematic Japanese video game, we turn our eye to the Japanese RPG.

▓ ▒ ▓

CHAPTER 4

QUESTS AND FANTASIES: THE JAPANESE RPG

On April 1, 2003, an event occurred that shook up Japanese video games culture with the force of a minor earthquake. Two longtime rivals merged, as the video game publishers Square and Enix became one company called Square Enix. Enix was a financially healthy publisher with its fingers in a few different pies; the Enix logo could be seen on games as well as *manga* weeklies. Square was not so healthy; a financially disastrous movie project and the startup costs involved with setting up an online version of their hit game had brought the balance sheet down from the heights it had recently begun to enjoy. To trace the history of these two companies is to trace the meteoric rise, first in Japan and later in the rest of the world, of a genre known as the role-playing game, or RPG.

DRAGON QUEST

The video game fan culture, like other such groups, has its own group of famous names and revered masters. As in other subcultures, some of these names are well known, but only to those in the circle, while some names are household words. In America, Steven Spielberg is known as a movie director even outside the circles of film buffs, while a name like Federico Fellini, though known to every film enthusiast, would draw a blank with someone outside of that group.

Yuji Horii.

Is there a name like Steven Spielberg in video games? In America, the simple answer is "no"—not even Miyamoto is well known here outside the video game fan culture. How about in Japan? The simple answer in this case is "yes"—but it is not Miyamoto. In terms of name recognition, the Steven Spielberg of video games is Yuji Horii, who designed an RPG called *Dragon Quest* for a video game publisher known as Enix.

Yasuhiro Fukushima started the company in 1975 as, of all things, a publisher of tabloid magazines that advertised real estate. This was the company's focus until 1982, when, after a failed attempt to spin off a nationwide chain of stores, Fukushima decided to take the money he had made from publishing and enter the computer software market. He changed the company name to Enix. (The name came from a combination of "Eniac," the first computer, and the immortal bird, the phoenix.[1]) To find game designers for his company, Fukushima took a cue from the *manga* industry.

By and large, writes Sharon Kinsella in her book *Adult Manga, manga* publishers "make initial contact with new artists through a system of *manga* competitions… High-circulation magazines, put out by large publishing companies, offer the winners large cash prizes."[2] Fukushima launched a similar contest and his choice of venue illustrates again the difference between early American game design and early Japanese game design. Where American game designers were culled from a group of computer hobbyists, Japan searched for computer tinkerers but also *manga* fans.

Fukushima advertised his *Enix Game Hobby Program Contest* in computer-enthusiast and manga magazines, with million-yen prizes for three winners.

Those winners were Kazuro Morita, Koichi Nakamura, and Yuji Horii, a writer for the popular *manga* magazine *Shonen Jump,* who submitted a PC tennis game called *Love Match Tennis.* One of the things that motivated Horii to design a game for the competition was that *Jump*'s editor loved computer games and often ran Horii's computer game articles in the magazine.[3]

Love Match Tennis became one of Enix's first releases in 1983. "You moved the player with the cursor keys and swung the racket with a button. It was like the simple arcade games of the time," said Horii in a 2000 interview.[4]

Horii didn't think he would win the contest, nor imagine that he would place first over Nakamura's entry, since Nakamura was already known in computer enthusiast magazines as an up-and-coming hobbyist programmer. When Enix expanded into Famicom games, it was Nakamura's cartoonish and creative contest entry, *Door Door,* which became their first release.

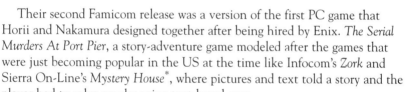

Their second Famicom release was a version of the first PC game that Horii and Nakamura designed together after being hired by Enix. *The Serial Murders At Port Pier,* a story-adventure game modeled after the games that were just becoming popular in the US at the time like Infocom's *Zork* and Sierra On-Line's *Mystery House*[*], where pictures and text told a story and the player had to solve puzzles using text-based commands. *Port Pier* cast the player as a detective trying to catch a serial murderer. He had to follow up leads and investigate the various game characters.

[*] The first game designed by Roberta Williams, whose next game would be the groundbreaking PC adventure title *King's Quest.*

Reprogramming the game for a Famicom version in 1985, Horii and Nakamura had begun to be influenced by computer role-playing games like *Wizardry* and *Ultima,* which were based on pen-and-paper RPGs like *Dungeons and Dragons.* Mimicking the game play of *Wizardry,* Horii added underground dens of monsters for the police officer to tackle as he solved the mystery. (Horii even went so far as to use the phrase "Monster surprised you!", lifted

directly from *Wizardry*, in the Famicom version.) Horii wrote an article in *Shonen Jump* introducing readers to the adventure game genre and to *Port Pier*. The game caught on with Famicom owners; gamers sent in the registration cards included in the software with written letters of praise.

Horii and Nakamura, as computer hackers, enjoyed the complex dungeon crawling and statistics managing of *Wizardry*. But they realized that RPGs were too complicated for the mass audience. This had not been a real concern before 1985, because tech-savvy computer enthusiasts were practically the only people who owned the computers to play the software. But after the 1985 Famicom boom caused by *Super Mario Bros.*, the Famicom was in millions of Japanese homes and Enix had a much wider potential audience.

To create his game *Dragon Quest*, Horii decided first to make the game system easier to understand. He needed to introduce players to the concept

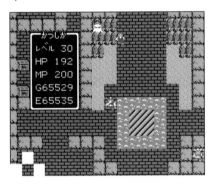

of *becoming* the main character, to gain experience and gold through fighting monsters and acquire new powers, greater strength, and better weapons. Thus, by the end of the game, the player-character would grow from a weak fighter-in-training to a powerful knight. This stood in contrast to games like *Super Mario Bros.*, because Mario was always the same Mario throughout the game.

Another way to ingratiate *Dragon Quest* with the mainstream, *Shonen Jump*-reading audience was to have *Shonen Jump*'s superstar *manga* artist Akira Toriyama (who had risen to fame with a comedy *manga* called *Dr. Slump* and was now drawing his martial-arts masterpiece *Dragon Ball*) do the illustrations for the game, to give it an authentic *manga* feel and instant consumer recognition. This was all arranged by *Shonen Jump*'s game-crazy editor, recalls Horii, not by Toriyama himself.

Dragon Quest's music composer, meanwhile, had been the one to express interest in Enix. Koichi Sugiyama was a classically trained composer already known for his television program scores. A game enthusiast, he was one of the Famicom users who sent in the questionnaire-postcards from an Enix *shogi*, or Japanese chess, PC game. Upon seeing the postcard, an Enix producer contacted him to find out if he was *the* Sugiyama from television. When it turned out that he was, he asked him if he would like to compose the score for Enix's next Famicom game. Sugiyama readily agreed, adding more star power to the project.

Toriyama's and Sugiyama's contributions made *Dragon Quest* as visually and aurally exciting as the game play was unique and sophisticated. But when *Dragon Quest* was released in May 1986, sales were so low that Enix stood to lose a lot of money on the project. Luckily, a string of articles written by Horii in (you guessed it) *Shonen Jump*, introducing players to the idea of an RPG, did the trick. Kids and adults alike were captivated by Toriyama's artwork and brought the game home, where they found that Sugiyama's music was richer and more exciting than any game music had ever sounded. *Dragon Quest* sold over two million copies, and *Shonen Jump* saw its already high 4.5 million-copies-per-week circulation jump to 6 million, in great part because of the *Dragon Quest* tie-ins.[5]

Since Horii's name was inextricably tied to the game through his Shonen Jump articles, his personal fame increased along with *Dragon Quest's*. *Super Mario Bros.* and *The Legend of Zelda's* creator, by contrast, was nearly anonymous.

A sequel released the next year, *Dragon Quest II*, sold out immediately. The next year, it was clear that *Dragon Quest*–mania had taken over Japan. *Dragon Quest III* was released on February 10, 1988—a Wednesday. School-children across the country called in sick to line up outside stores for their precious cartridges. Some high school students skipped school and mugged smaller children on the way home from the game store, taking their copy of *Dragon Quest III*. These problems were so widespread that they were brought to the attention of the Japanese Parliament, who decreed that henceforth *Dragon Quest* games were to be released on Sundays or national holidays only.

This media attention only further cemented the name "Dragon Quest", or *dorakue*, as the Japanese abbreviated it, in the public mind. Like American kids and parents in the early 1980s called all arcade games "Ataris" and later, all side-scrolling action games "Mario" whether or not they were actually Mario games, Japanese parents would say "My kid plays too much *dorakue*" to mean the new genre of RPG games.[6] Ask a Japanese person who grew up in the eighties to draw "slime" and they will draw you Dragon Quest's adorable onion-shaped monster. And it was not only the Japanese public, but also other game designers, who were catching the *dorakue* bug. Soon, the RPG—patterned

largely after the mainstream, *anime*-inspired worlds of *Dragon Quest*, not Dungeons and Dragons—would become one of the mainstay genres of Japanese video games.

At Square Enix headquarters in Tokyo, a small sign marks the most important office in the building—the *dorakuebu* or Dragon Quest Section.

MOTHER

Starting with *Donkey Kong*, we saw stories accompanying game play, and writing stories became the work of game designers. This trend continued for about 10 years as we saw many artists enter the industry as game designers. Then, particularly due to the success of *Dragon Quest* in Japan, we saw a new trend in which scenario writers were figuring heavily into game design. It was as this time that I was inundated with thick scenario drafts from hopeful writers. Many famous writers and musicians wanted to make a video game, just for the sake of business.

— from Shigeru Miyamoto's keynote speech at the 1999 Game Developers' Conference

There was at least one game designer who wasn't particularly fond of *Dragon Quest*'s game play. "I personally have a fundamental dislike of the RPG system," says Shigeru Miyamoto. "I think that in RPGs, you are completely bound hand and foot and can't move. Only gradually, as your character gains powers, do you become able to move your hands, your feet... you come untied slowly. And in the end, you feel powerful. So what you can get out of an RPG is a feeling of happiness, but I don't think that is a game that is *fundamentally* fun to play.

"But," he admits, "with Mario's games, if you're not good at them you may never get good. Anyone can become really good at an RPG, though, and if you still want to play a Mario title... in those cases it's a good system. There are many people who like it, and there are certain types of games for which that system is perfectly suited. The RPG system works best for games with lots of dialogue, to help bring about a writer's voice, to bring a book to life."

One person who was better at *Dragon Quest* than he was at *Super Mario Bros.*[*] was a writer named Shigesato Itoi, who came to Nintendo a few years later with the hopes of creating his own video game. Born in 1948, Itoi had dropped out of Hosei University after a year, but had become remarkably successful even without a college degree (a rarity in Japan). Itoi was one of the most sought-after freelance copywriters in Japan, writing mainly for high-profile clients. He wrote the lyrics to hit songs like the chart-topping "Tokio" by Kenji Sawada[7], and later wrote copy for Studio Ghibli, the animation studio of acclaimed director Hayao Miyazaki. In 1988, Itoi's name became a household word when he lent his distinctive voice to the role of the caring dad in Miyazaki's masterpiece *Tonari no Totoro* (*My Neighbor Totoro*).

★ Itoi admitted as much in an interview published in the Famicom Tokyo museum exhibition guidebook: "...it is impossible for me to get good at [Mario]," he said, but he was "hooked" on *Dragon Quest*.

When the now-famous Itoi came to Nintendo that year with an idea for an RPG, Miyamoto was far from starstruck. "My policy is that we don't make games with a famous person's name stuck onto it, if that person has only done a little something. And I said to him, 'if you think that just a little bit of effort is going to make a really great game, you're wrong.' And I think that upset him a little. But after thinking about it carefully, he made up his mind and said that even if he had to stop working on other projects, he would like to dedicate himself to a video game. And so I agreed to do it, and from that point on, we shared the same goals."

With Miyamoto's help on the game play, Itoi set to work on the creative aspects of an RPG that subverted the traditional *Dragon Quest* world design. "I was wondering why all RPGs were set in medieval Europe," said Itoi in a 2003 interview.[8] "Of course, the origin of RPGs is *The Lord of the Rings*, and then they made a [pen-and-paper] game called *Dungeons and Dragons*, but those are not the indispensable elements." Itoi's game *Mother* took place in a fractured-fairy-tales version of small-town America. Instead of medieval-sounding town names, the places were named after American holidays. The main character fought with a baseball bat rather than a sword. Rather than pulling healing herbs from treasure chests in castles, the player found hamburgers in trashcans behind ranch-style homes. And the first enemy was not a Slime but an angry neighborhood dog.

Still, Itoi's writing style made *Mother* more avant-garde than *Dragon Quest*. "It was like haiku," he said. Because the cartridge size of Famicom games was too small to store the two thousand Chinese *kanji* characters used in Japanese writing, RPG text, including *Mother*'s, was written only with the 50-character phonetic Hiragana script. (This was convenient since the children playing the games couldn't read all two thousand *kanji* yet anyway.) Rather than lament this limitation, however, Itoi embraced it. "Since the lines were only written with the basic Japanese alphabet, I wanted them to "speak" to you. I would actually say them aloud, re-digest them, and try to listen to them with my heart."[9]

Haiku, as well, were traditionally only written in *hiragana*. Itoi uses the most famous haiku of all to explain *Mother*'s use of ambiguous dialogue: *An old pond/A frog jumps in/The sound of water*. "So what?" asks Itoi. "But that is the part where the readers' take jumps in. *Mother* had quite a few of those lines; it would ask you 'are you so-and-so?' but then, the only answer you would get would be '*sou ka*' ('really')… Those three characters trigger your imagination by making you go, '"Really?" What the hell does that mean?'"[10]

★ In 2003, *Mother 1* and *2* were re-released on one cartridge for Nintendo's Game Boy Advance system in Japan. Accompanying this game's release was the announcement that *Mother 3*, a nearly-completed but cancelled project for Nintendo's 64DD disk-drive add-on for its Nintendo 64 system, would be released later on the Game Boy Advance.

It's clear just how intriguing *Mother*'s questions were to the Japanese—*Mother* is considered the "third RPG series," ranked high in the Japanese consciousness alongside *Dragon Quest* and *Final Fantasy* despite having only had one sequel released thus far[13]—*Mother 2* on the Super Famicom, released as *Earthbound* in the United States—where, it must be said, failed to perform up to Miyamoto's expectations despite a massive advertising campaign. The *Dragon Quest* games fared little better across the Pacific. But one Japanese RPG series set the world on fire.

FINAL FANTASY

There is no one name in video games that is as well known in America as Yuji Horii's is in Japan. But that's not to say that there are no Japanese video game creators who enjoy some level of mainstream recognition in America. Consider the following:

Composer Nobuo Uematsu was profiled as an "Innovator" in a Time Magazine feature titled "Time 100—The Next Wave: Music." The article, noting his "substantial U.S. following," said that Uematsu's "supple, heartfelt tunes" imbue video games "with grandeur and depth, the way John Williams' score helped propel *Star Wars* into hyperspace."[11]

Painter Yoshitaka Amano's 1997 exhibition "Think Like Amano" displayed in noted art galleries from New York City to Tokyo, leading to a much-publicized collaboration with American author Neil Gaiman called *Sandman: The Dream Hunters*.

Director Hironobu Sakaguchi's first feature film, *Final Fantasy: The Spirits Within*, was a $137 million project backed by Columbia Pictures and released to great fanfare in theaters across the United States in the summer of 2001.

The level of international recognition that these artists share—and it is perhaps more than any other Japanese painters, composers, or directors save Kurosawa—all came about because these three men came together to work on a Famicom title called *Final Fantasy*.

In 1987, just as *Dragon Quest*'s popularity was beginning to skyrocket, Hironobu Sakaguchi, Square Co., Ltd.'s senior game designer, was ready to leave the company. But first, he wanted to make one last game. Sakaguchi had joined Square in 1984 while on spring break from Yokohama National University, where he was a computer science major. At Yokohama, he became friends with another young student named Hiromichi Tanaka, who was a computer *otaku* who often went to the Akihabara district of Tokyo to buy computer parts and new games.[12]

Sakaguchi fell in love with RPG games playing *Wizardry* on Tanaka's Apple II computer. "It was totally different from the arcade games of the time—there was a story and you could play them for a long time. So I fell into this thing called role-playing games, and after that I hardly ever went to class. I would just pull all-nighters with *Wizardry*."[13]

In the spring of 1983, toward the end of their third year, Tanaka and Sakaguchi decided to find a part-time job programming computer games. It just so happened that a PC software application company called Denyu was looking to establish a games division that they were going to call Square. The two students were hired, along with three other programmers. Their workplace—a tiny two-bedroom apartment in Yokohama.

With Sakaguchi serving as the creative director, the five young men set about making their first game—*Deathtrap*, a PC adventure game in which the player took the role of the last person left alive on a deserted island. Released in 1984 and taking up three five-inch disks, it was a massive work. It was a hit, and Sakaguchi and Tanaka decided to take a leave of absence from their schoolwork.

A sequel released later that same year, *Will: Deathtrap II*, was an even bigger hit. In 1985, Sakaguchi directed an action shooter game called *Cruise Chaser Blasty*, which featured character designs and animation from Studio Sunrise, the creators of the popular *Mobile Suit Gundam*. As the Square division grew in popularity, the teams of people working on each title grew larger, and Sakaguchi began to concentrate less on programming and more on creative design and scenario writing.

* Actually, perhaps *Thexder* is notable for a few other reasons. *Thexder* was one of the first games developed by a company called Game Arts, who would later develop role-playing games, such as *LUNAR: The Silver Star* and *Grandia*, that were heavily influenced by the *Final Fantasy* series. In addition, *Thexder* was also released for personal computers in the United States by a company called Sierra, who was by then well on its way to becoming a premier computer games company with its *King's Quest* adventure game series. This may have marked the first collaboration between an American PC games company and a Japanese one.

† Sakaguchi's schoolmate Tanaka was still with Square. In fact, he would go on to direct such legendary games as *Seiken Densetsu* for the Game Boy (*Final Fantasy Adventure* in the US). Koichi Ishii would direct the game's sequels, released as the *Mana* series in the US.

Square eventually grew so important that it was spun off as its own separate company in May 1986, just as development was beginning to switch from personal computers to Nintendo's Famicom. (One Famicom game was produced with the Denyu name on it—a space-shooter called *Thexder*, notable only for being Square's first Famicom game.*) As a separate entity, Square Co., Ltd. released no fewer than 11 titles for the Famicom and Famicom Disk System by October 1987. For its disk games, Square had established a separate brand called DOG, or Disk Original Group, which partnered with other PC software companies to port their PC games, like *Little Computer People* or *Deep Dungeon*, to the Famicom Disk System. It was a much lower-risk endeavor than publishing cartridge games, although since less than 50% of Famicom owners owned a Disk System, their potential audience was vastly smaller.

Meanwhile, Sakaguchi was the leader of a small group called Square A Team, responsible for original cartridge-based games. Despite the name, Square A Team was thought of as less important; as a company with its origins in PC software, the Famicom Disk System business was thought to be the future of the company. Still, since Sakaguchi was the senior man, with Square since its beginning, he ran the A Team, consisting of himself; Iran-born, Cal State-educated programmer Nasir Gebelli (who was legendary in Apple II circles as being able to turn out a new game every five weeks); and Koichi Ishii among a handful of other programmers.†

Square A Team's early cartridge games garnered some measure of attention. *King's Knight* (1986) may have been styled like a medieval RPG, with wizards and knights and dragons, but played like a straightforward action shooter. *Highway Star* (1987) made great use of Gebelli's skill at 3D graphics programming; it was an exceptional 3D auto racing game that used a pair of motorized 3D glasses that Nintendo sold for the Famicom. That same year, Sakaguchi and Gebelli designed an original Disk System game called *Tobidase! Daisakusen*, which was a Mario-styled run-and-jump action game but in 3D—the "camera" was *behind* the little man on the screen, and the enemies and bottomless pits scrolled toward him. An optional pair of traditional red-and-blue 3D glasses was sold separately.*

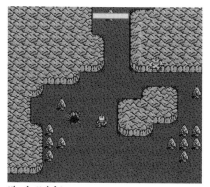

King's Knight

Highway Star

Tobidase! Daisakusen

★ Sakaguchi's games were the only Square games to be released on the NES. Square released *King's Knight*, Nintendo published *Highway Star* as *Rad Racer* (and featured it prominently in the 1989 movie *The Wizard*), and Acclaim published *Tobidase! Daisakusen* in cartridge format as *3-D World Runner*.

When both these games sold a respectable 500,000 copies, Square management encouraged Sakaguchi and Gebelli to continue to create 3D action games.[14] But Sakaguchi hated these kinds of games. He wanted to combine the role-playing genre of *Wizardry* with the colorful graphics and sophisticated sound effects that were possible on the Famicom. So he went to the president of Square with his idea, and got the approval to create his game. He called it *Final Fantasy*, because he planned on quitting Square after he finished it and return to school.

By this time, *Dragon Quest* was beginning to become popular, but Sakaguchi wanted to create something different. First, although Horii's game featured a large world, with many enemy-filled dungeons and towns filled with villagers to talk to and stores selling any number of weapons, magic spells, and healing items, *Dragon Quest's* plot was shallow and formulaic. Like many Famicom games, it was quite similar to Super Mario's story—the hero had to defeat the evil Dragon Lord and save the Princess. Sakaguchi wanted a plot larger than this, with supporting characters, plot twists, and many individual story threads that tied together into one epic storyline.

As far as graphics and sound, Sakaguchi wanted something less childish than *Dragon Quest*. Akira Toriyama's colorful *manga*-style drawings of short, bright-eyed characters were in the same style as most other Famicom games, embodying the nature of *kawaisa*—cuteness—that Japanese consumers were and continue to be drawn to. And Koichi Sugiyama's soundtrack was like a cross between John Williams' *Star Wars* scores and Koji Kondo's *Super Mario Bros.* music—upbeat, exciting marching-band tunes with plenty of horns and drums. After having been assigned to create a succession of Famicom-cute games in which he had no personal interest, Sakaguchi had no interest in this style. He decided that *Final Fantasy* would have a serious, adult, *sabishii* (lonely) look.

To this end, he sought out freelance artist Yoshitaka Amano. Amano had already achieved modest critical and cult recognition in Japan—he joined the Tatsunoko animation studio (known best for *Mach Go Go Go*, known in the West as *Speed Racer*) in 1967 at the age of fifteen and within a year was designing characters for Tatsunoko's top shows like *Gatchaman* and *Hutch The Honeybee*. After 15 years with Tatsunoko, he left to pursue a freelance-illustrating career. *Anime* films like *Vampire Hunter D* and *Tenshi no Tamago* (Angel's Egg) won him mainstream success in the early eighties, and he then brought his unique visual style to *Final Fantasy*, creating the concept art for the characters, monsters, world, and scenery.[15]

Nobuo Uematsu, meanwhile, was another Yokohama resident who had been Square's full-time composer since 1985 and had composed the music for games like *King's Knight Special* and *Highway Star*. For *Final Fantasy*, he remembered being specifically told to "make a contrast to the *Dragon Quest* series."[16] Uematsu incorporated his own *sabishii* style of music, using mostly synthesized versions of stringed instruments and woodwinds to create moving orchestral arrangements.

Meanwhile, Sakaguchi fleshed out his story and world. "The basic concept was really a mythical concept of the whole earth, with fire and water representing everything on Earth. I took that concept and represented those elements [with crystals], and that… became the core theme for *Final Fantasy*. I took a preexisting idea—the four or five basic elements of the world; sort of an orthodox and mythical concept—then molded it into an original fantasy story."[17]

Final Fantasy was nothing if not original; it was different from any other Famicom title by far. The difference was first seen on the game's cardboard box, which featured Amano's ethereal, lifelike watercolor of the game's main character and not a cartoony montage. There were even more differences once the game was turned on.

Final Fantasy, unlike practically every other Famicom game, *did not* begin with a title screen. The first image you see is the opening lines of the game's story, being painted in white cursive characters down a blue screen[*] (Fig. 8-1), reminiscent of the famous openings to the *Star Wars* movies, as gentle harp arpeggios play in the background. The next screen (Fig. 8-2) still doesn't show the game's title, just three options: *tsuzuku* (continue a saved game), *yarinaoshi* (start a new game), and *messêgi supîdo* (speed of the in-game text messages). Choosing *yarinaoshi* brings the player to a screen where he is asked to create four characters by choosing the character "job" (general class divisions like sword fighter, martial artist, mage) and giving him a four-character name (Fig. 8-3). The game then opens to find your four warriors (represented on the map by the first character you created) standing outside a walled castle town (Fig. 8-4). Entering the town or castle and speaking to the citizens or guards reveals that your party is the *hikari no senshi* (Light Warriors), and that the king would like to speak to you (Fig. 8-5).

> [*] It might seem like I am embellishing with this description, but the use of *hiragana* cursive script instead of broken English written in capital letters is a deliberate stylistic choice—it added to the "Japaneseness" of the game, making it much more Japanese than *Super Mario*, for example.

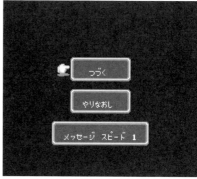

Fig. 8-1.   *Fig. 8-2.*

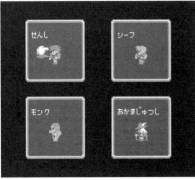

Fig. 8-3.

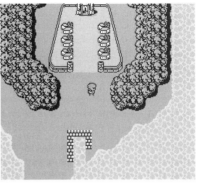

Fig. 8-4.

Fig. 8-5.

The player controls the four Light Warriors throughout the game. The Light Warriors are never individually referred to by name, nor does the group ever split up. The player is in control of all four party characters, but for purposes of the story they are one unit, with no separate personalities. This stands in contrast to almost all future games in the *Final Fantasy* series, so it is important to note now. Although the player is technically developing four separate characters, in terms of the story the player is only developing one *unit*—the same as in *Dragon Quest*.

The king mentions that the sage Lukhan (as yet unseen) has predicted the coming of the Light Warriors, and exhorts them to save the Princess from the evil Garland (Fig. 8-6). After buying weapons, armor, and magic spells in the town and perhaps fighting monsters in the surrounding forest for experience, the player makes his way to the temple located just north of the town (this information is derived from brief conversations with the townspeople; Fig. 8-7). Walking directly north leads you to the chamber where Garland and his bats are holding the Princess captive (Fig. 8-8). After some taunts, the Light Warriors and Garland battle (Fig. 8-9). Victorious, the Light Warriors can speak to the Princess and are automatically returned to the castle (Fig. 8-10), where the King states that he has ordered a bridge built to the "continent" (providing access to the rest of the game world) to aid you in your quest—which is to visit the four elemental Temples (air, water, earth, fire) located throughout the world and bring light back to the four Orbs that the Warriors each hold.

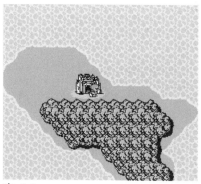

Fig. 8-6.

Fig. 8-7.

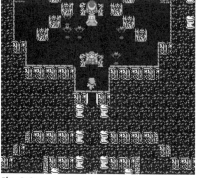

Fig. 8-8.

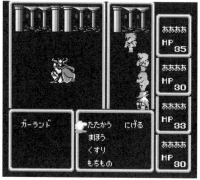

Fig. 8-9.

Fig. 8-10.

As soon as the Warriors leave the castle and step onto the bridge (Fig. 8-11), the game shifts to the title screen, and we see, for the first time, *FINAL FANTASY* (Fig. 8-12). The words are set in English lettering over a silhouette of the Light Warriors looking at the Temple in the distance, across the river. The main musical theme of the game, a slow, melodic piece titled "Final Fantasy," plays as a short story sequence ("And so, their journey begins...") appears. The credits roll (Fig. 8-13) and the music swells to a climax as the game play screen (the world map) reappears.

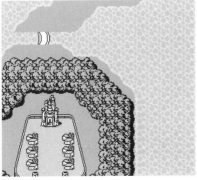

Fig. 8-11.

Fig. 8-12.

Fig. 8-13.

Let us take some time to analyze this opening sequence, from the story scenes to the fight with Garland, as it is remarkably telling of what the *Final Fantasy* series would become, and how it differed dramatically from other video games. First, Sakaguchi uses a number of movie-like techniques to direct the action. We begin *in medias res*, "in the thick of things," with the player dropped into the world and left to find for himself what the quest entails, much like a movie audience is asked to fill in the gaps in the narrative themselves during the film's opening. The delay of the title screen is key, since one classic cinematic "hook" is to show the film's title after a few minutes of film have already gone by, or even after an initial story sequence.[*] Credits, as well, are often shown before the film, during the title sequence. To do this in a video game was revolutionary, since the message was "We, the individual creators, are important enough to be recognized."

[*] The same approximate effect can be seen in, to name one familiar example, Disney's *The Lion King*, as the title is displayed on screen only after an elaborate musical number that sets up the story.

But perhaps even more importantly, this opening sequence is removed from the rest of the game in many specific ways. First, it is set on an island, physically removed from where the rest of the game will take place. Second, the entire episode occurs before the title screen appears and the text says, "And so, their journey *begins*." It is not a coincidence that this first quest has the Light Warriors, at the behest of a nameless King, save the Princess from an evil fiend (who, later in the game, reveals himself to have very dragon-like features). This is sending a not-so-subliminal message to the player: "*Final Fantasy* is about much more than saving the princess. Compared to the adventure that is about to take place, saving a princess is merely child's play and prologue." The message was not lost on a group of game players who had literally all been exposed to *Super Mario* and *Dragon Quest*.

For the world of *Final Fantasy*, Sakaguchi drew on other fantasy works, most notably Tolkien: the three different non-human races in the game were, as in *The Hobbit* and the *Lord of the Rings* trilogy, Elves skilled at archery, Dwarves who lived and mined the underground, and Dragons who asked the Light Warriors to complete tests of bravery and skill. (By *Final Fantasy IV* in 1991, Hobbit-inspired Halflings would be added to the world.) Words like *mithril* (a mythical blend of silver and steel from the *Rings* books) were freely borrowed as well. While the primary mission of the game was to find the four Temples and defeat the elemental Fiends, other quests that had to be completed to advance the story were about helping people in need: restoring sight to a blind witch, reviving the sleeping Elf prince, defeating a group of pirates to liberate an occupied town.

There was little development of the main story until the very end of the game, when the Warriors, with all four Orbs lit, return to the first temple and find Garland. He reveals himself to be Chaos, the dragon-like lord of time (Fig. 8-14). Defeating him, the player is treated to one final screen on which the story scrolls by (Fig 8-15). The end of the story is somewhat twisted and rather convoluted in translation, although the text does take pains to point out that the hero of the story is "YOU," —an important reminder of the control the player has over the story. A detailed "The End" screen finishes the game (Fig 8-16).

Fig. 8-14. Note that these final three pictures are from the English-language version of the game.

Fig. 8-15.

Fig. 8-16.

The story of the 2000-year time loop is the subject of much ridicule by *Final Fantasy* fans today, not only because it didn't make much sense but also because most of it seemed to be tacked on at the end of the game—told, not shown, in a series of rapid-fire text screens. This took some of the feeling of exploration and discovery away from the player, but at the same time it was clear that Sakaguchi was attempting something above and beyond the traditional video game stories. And it worked: *Final Fantasy* was enough of a success that Sakaguchi stayed a game designer.

SEQUELS

Final Fantasy was released in December of 1987 and became a breakout success. With their newfound popularity, Square was able to transfer their business over to cartridge titles almost exclusively. Two more cartridge games were released in 1988: a strategy RPG called *Hanjuku Hero* and an RPG called *Deep Dungeon III*, the sequel to two of their FDS games. And their final two Famicom Disk System titles, a shooter called *Raijin* and a pinball game called *Moon Ball Magic*, were released on July 12th of that year, although they weren't available in the same deluxe packaging as their earlier releases. (In fact, they were *only* available through the Disk Writer kiosks that stood in video game and toy stores of the time; customers gave their old disks to the shopkeeper, who would write a new game to it for 500 yen or about $5.*) But Sakaguchi had nothing to do with any of these titles; in fact, until nearly a decade later, the games he worked on would be *Final Fantasy* titles only.

★ This makes collecting a complete set of Square releases nearly impossible.

Square released *Final Fantasy II* that December. *Final Fantasy II* still retained the elements of fantasy from the first game—talking creatures, magic spells, evil demons, haunted temples, and swordfighting. What was different about *Final Fantasy II* is that the focus of the story had been changed: instead of a game in which four faceless fighters were merely the vehicle by which the player experienced a contrived time-travel plot, *Final Fantasy II*'s story was about human beings, and their personalities, relationships, and hardships.

More specifically, it was inspired by *Star Wars*—a group of young people get involved with a secret rebel alliance who are rising up against the evil empire. (Sakaguchi had just seen *The Empire Strikes Back* and was inspired.) They fight, aided by friends, turncoats and advisors, and eventually overthrow the emperor. These characters have distinct physical features and personalities.

After a title screen (in English) and the story screen (in Japanese; Figs. 9-1, 9-2), the player is asked to give the characters names. (The instruction booklet says that their names are Frionel, Maria, Guy, and Leonheart.) Immediately after deciding on the last name, the game starts—in the middle of a battle (Fig. 9-3). A group of four enemies called *kurokishi* (who we later find out are black knights of the empire, like *Star Wars*' Stormtroopers) wipe out our four heroes in seconds. Although the player has control over the party, they die as soon as the *kurokishi* attack (Fig. 9-4). After the battle, we see two people dressed in white standing around a character in red. From the conversation we determine that they are healing Frionel's wounds (Fig. 9-5). They leave and Frionel stands up, leaving the room while calling out for his comrades (Fig. 9-6).

FINAL FANTASY II
(c) 1988 SQUARE
PROGRAMED BY NASIR
CHARACTER BY YOSHITAKA AMANO
SCENARIO BY KENJI TERADA

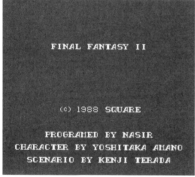

Fig. 9-1.

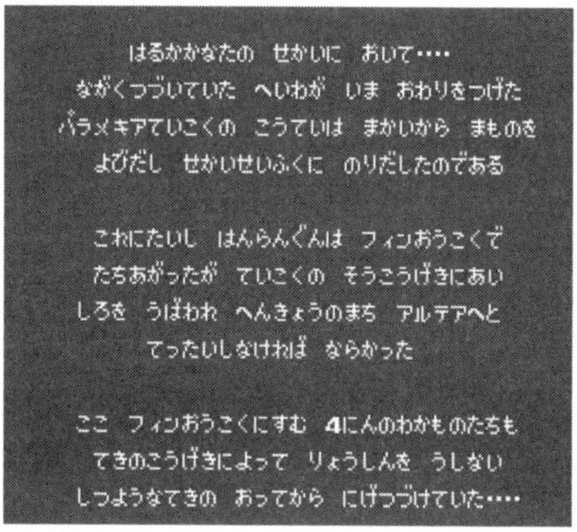

はるかかなたの せかいに おいて‥‥
ながくつづいていた へいわが いま おわりをつげた
パラメキアていこくの こうていは まかいから まものを
よびだし せかいせいふくに のりだしたのである
これにたいし はんらんぐんは フィンおうこくで
たちあがったが ていこくの そうこうげきにあい
しろを うばわれ へんきょうのまち アルテアへと
てったいしなければ ならかった
ここ フィンおうこくにすむ 4にんのわかものたちも
てきのこうげきによって りょうしんを うしない
しつようなてきの おってから にげつづけていた‥‥

Fig. 9-2.

HP MP
フリオニール 30/ 30 5
マリア 20/ 20 5
レオンハルト 40/ 40 5
ガイ 30/ 30 5
たたかう
にげる
まほう
もちもの

Fig. 9-3.

くろきし
6かいヒット
マリア
900ダメージ
クリティカルヒット!!
HP MP
0/ しぼう 5
20/ 20 5
0/ しぼう 5
0/ しぼう 5

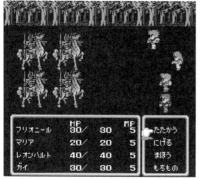

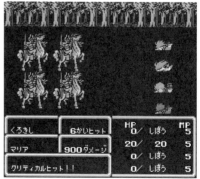

Fig. 9-4.

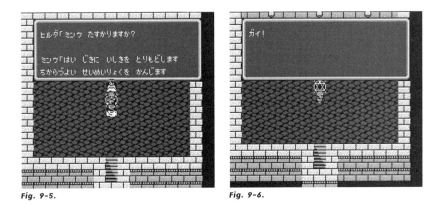

Fig. 9-5.   Fig. 9-6.

Outside the room, he meets Maria and Guy (Fig. 9-7). None of them knows where Leonheart is. They enter a chamber and speak to the rebel leader Hilda and her assistant Minh, who send them on their first mission (Fig. 9-8). Thus far, the characters have moved around and interacted without the player's control; something that never happened in *Final Fantasy*. But soon, the player finally is given control of his group of three, and can walk them around the secret rebel base (Fig. 9-9), out into the surrounding town (Fig. 9-10), and finally out onto the main world map (Fig. 9-11). Now, as in the first game, the player needs to buy weapons, armor, and magic spells, gain experience by fighting monsters around the town, and finally begin the first trek up to the northern castle.

Fig. 9-7

Fig. 9-8.

Fig. 9-9.

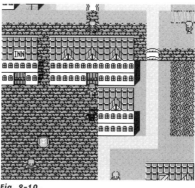

Fig. 9-10.

Fig. 9-11.

Final Fantasy II, then, begins similarly to *Final Fantasy* from a game play standpoint, but quite differently in terms of storytelling. It again begins *in medias res*, but now even more so—the player is probably shocked to find himself in the middle of a battle. Sakaguchi did not *need* to show this battle, but doing so—and forcing the player to attack and perhaps even attempt to defeat the *kurokishi*, even though it is soon revealed to be impossible—demonstrates without words the near-futility of the rebels' fight against the empire in their current, untrained condition. Moreover, the player might feel an attack of nerves upon being thrown into a combat situation with no preparation—even better to entice the player, to involve him in the game.

What's more, this helps to blur the line between battles and storyline. In the first game, battles were entirely separate from story exposition—the player watched the story take place, then fought the enemy. Now, story was being told *through* battles. In later games, dialogue and story twists would even take place in the middle of battle scenes.

Although the player has given names to four characters, the fourth, Leonheart, is missing after that first battle. He does eventually turn up again to fight the final battles with his comrades, but until then the player's party has an "open" fourth slot. At various points in the story, other characters will join your party—the female pirate Layla, who at first attempts to rob the others but fails; Gordon, the cowardly imperial prince who defects to the rebel side; and Josef, an older, powerful martial artist and mayor of the town of Salamando, among others. Layla and Gordon are weak characters who need training before they will be effective in battle, but Josef turns out to be far more powerful than your group. In one scene, Josef leads your party to an abandoned snow mine, but a trap set by the Empire sends a huge boulder rolling toward your party. Josef bravely stops the boulder, but is crushed by it and dies.

As the stage direction required for these cinematic scenes became more and more involved and important to each game's story, Sakaguchi started to use the art program MacPaint to sketch out rough storyboards and give them to his programmers. He plotted out this scene carefully, because this was the scene in which Josef would become the first *Final Fantasy* character to die. Other story-games had shown the deaths of minor, non-player characters, but this was the first time that a vital player-character, who the player had spent time nurturing, equipping, and training, actually died during the course of the story. All of that work was essentially lost, and just to twist the knife a little more, so was any expensive armor or weapons that character may have been wielding.

This death scene and later ones like it, in the words of one writer who was interviewing Nobuo Uematsu for the Japanese games magazine *Famitsu*, was meant to "irritate" players, but is "why *Final Fantasy* succeeded and established its reputation." Uematsu's response was that although he is "rather opposed to all those deaths and tragedies" and "often argue[s] with Mr. Sakaguchi about it," he confesses that he is by now "rather good" at creating moving music to accentuate these scenes. "The contrast to other games," noted the writer, "makes *Final Fantasy* stand alone."[18]

Final Fantasy II also stood apart from other games for its ending scene. Instead of a lengthy, text-based ending, after the three main characters defeat the emperor, we see them return to the rebel base, where they speak with the supporting cast and we see the closure of their personal stories (Fig. 9-12). After this brief scene, we fade to the final bit of the story, which echoes the white-on-blue opening but this time with a black background (Fig. 9-13). This is followed by the game's final sequence in which, unlike nearly every other Famicom game of the time, each person who worked on the game is given full credit and listed by his full name (Figs. 9-14).[19] Other popular games released around this time either had no credits sequence (*Super Mario*) or listed pseudonyms (*Zeruda no Densetsu*), so this was not only a big step toward recognition of game designers, but also made the game even more like a film.

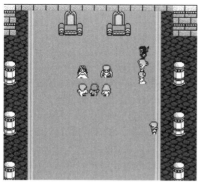

Fig. 9-12.

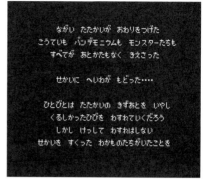

Fig. 9-13.

ながい たたかいが おわりをつげた
こうてい'も パンデモニウムも モンスターたちも
すべてが あとかたもなく きえさった

せかいに へいわが もどった‥‥

ひとびとは たたかいの きずあとを いやし
くるしかったひびを わすれていくだろう
しかし けっして わすれはしない
せかいを すくった わかものたちがいたことを

An even larger step was taken with *Final Fantasy III*, released in April 1990. As Square's final original Famicom title, *Final Fantasy III* represented all that they had learned about maximizing the Famicom hardware.* The graphics and sounds were still primitive by today's standards, but they were light years ahead of earlier Famicom games— the characters were more animated, the music more pleasing to the ears.

MUSIC COMPOSE
NOBUO UEMATSU

Fig. 9-14.

Even so, the character-building model reverted back to that of original *Final Fantasy*. The player began with four identical-looking youths and gave them not only names but jobs (like the original game's character classes —Fighter, Mage, Ninja, etc.). But in *Final Fantasy III*, the player could change his character's jobs whenever he wanted. In this way, by giving his characters skills across a variety of disciplines, he could (and indeed, *had* to) build all-powerful warriors by game's end.

Although *Final Fantasy II*'s character-based player party had been scrapped, *Final Fantasy III* was certainly not any less of a cinematic, story- and character-centric game. Indeed, Nobuo Uematsu has commented that the push to make the *Final Fantasy* series into movie-games started with *Final Fantasy III*. "We have

* Years later, as the popularity of the series was skyrocketing and the original games, produced in more conservative numbers, became harder to find, Square released *Final Fantasy I+II*, the first two games on one cartridge, as its final Famicom title. This was in February 1994, and despite the fact that CD-ROM video game systems like the SegaSaturn and the Sony PlayStation were just months away from being released, *Final Fantasy I+II* sold like hotcakes and is now a high-priced collector's item.

a lot of people [on the *Final Fantasy* team] who love movies, so maybe that's why we're trying to recreate a movie in a game. Still, we often discuss that we will never be able to catch up to movies just by trying to mimic them."[20]

So, what was it that Sakaguchi and team did to create a more movie-like atmosphere with *Final Fantasy III*? First, after the now-traditional white-on-blue story scene that begins as soon as the power to the Famicom is turned on (accompanied by the now-traditional harp arpeggios; Fig. 10-1), and after the player names the four youths, the first thing we see are the four youths falling down a pit (Fig. 10-2). Actually, what we *see* is the small sprite representing the party's lead character being rotated against a black background. We *know* that the four kids have just fallen into a pit because of the falling sound, reminiscent of a Doppler effect: *beeeeeyoooooop*. The next screen erases all doubt, as we see the youths talking to each other: "Ow!… We've fallen into a pit!… That stinks." (Fig. 10-3)

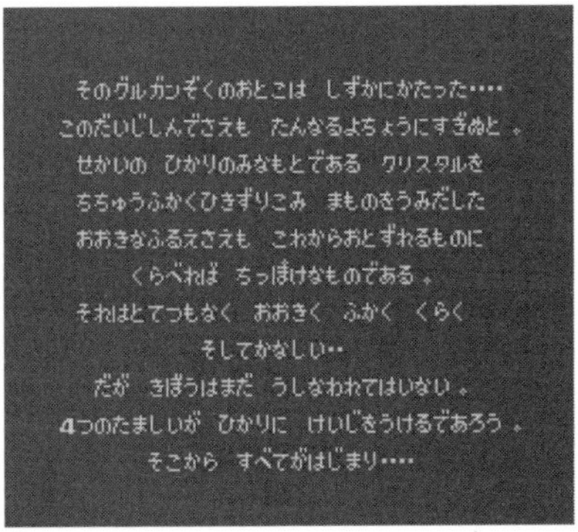

Fig. 10-1.

Fig. 10-2.

Fig. 10-3.

Moving without player control, the four begin to explore the cave and end up forced into a battle with two Goblins (Fig. 10-4). Unlike the scripted first battle of *Final Fantasy II*, this one is easily won. (Here, again, is a battle being used not as a random encounter but in the context of the story.) With this, the player technically takes control of the action, although the layout of the cave is straightforward enough that practically all players will take the very same route to the exit.

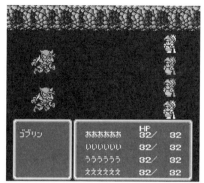

Fig. 10-4.

Inside the next room, the player sees the glittering Crystal talked about in the opening story (Fig. 10-5). But before the youths can reach it, they are attacked yet again (Fig. 10-6). After the fight, the Crystal tells them that they are the chosen four Light Warriors of legend and that it is their job to revive the other three Crystals and save the world. Cut to black and a larger version of the crystal glitters in the darkness (Fig. 10-7); it is fully illuminated after a few seconds, along with the title screen and the "Final Fantasy" theme music (Fig. 10-8). We see a short staff list (Fig. 10-9) and another brief text sequence before returning to the Crystal room, and the game proceeds from there.

Fig. 10-5.

Fig. 10-6.

Fig. 10-7.

Fig. 10-8.

Final Fantasy III contained numerous story-scenes that developed the characters and advanced the plot, more than in the last two games. Although the player characters had reverted back to nameless, featureless shells (although, as illustrated previously, they spoke to each other and to other characters, unlike the mute Light Warriors of the first game), the game was filled with other, named characters who had much to do with the story.

Fig. 10-9.

Many of them play a part in the game's ending, which shows just how much the team had added in terms of non-interactive story sequences.

After the final enemy is defeated, we see some more text set against a *Star Wars*-style background of flying stars (Fig. 10-10). In an earlier game, this might have been the entire ending; but not in *Final Fantasy III*. Next, we watch the four youths leave the castle accompanied by other characters (Fig. 10-11), and they visit the many places and people throughout the world who have aided their adventures. We see them fly from place to place and speak one last time with each of their friends (Fig. 10-12). In this way, closure is brought to the few different story arcs and character relationships. And when the youths return to their hometown—where the game begins—we see a scene depicting the world turning back to normal (represented by brown trees and dark skies turning to green and blue; Figs. 10-13, 10-14).

Fig. 10-10.

Fig. 10-11.

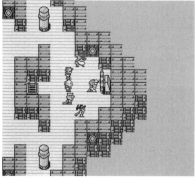

Fig. 10-12.

Fig. 10-13.

Fig. 10-14.

This long succession of scenes alone makes *Final Fantasy III*'s endgame far more movie-like than that of most games preceding it. But it's not nearly done—the cinematics are followed by a lengthy "Cast" (Fig. 10-15, Fig. 10-16) and "Staff" (Fig. 10-17) roll, showing the many characters in the game and then, again, a complete credits list with the full names of everyone involved in the game's production. Finally, we see the "THE END" screen, again on a field of stars (Fig. 10-18). The ending sequence of *Final Fantasy III* was easily the longest and most complex of any video game to that point, and the "Cast" section pointed out that Square wanted its game characters to be compared with movie characters.

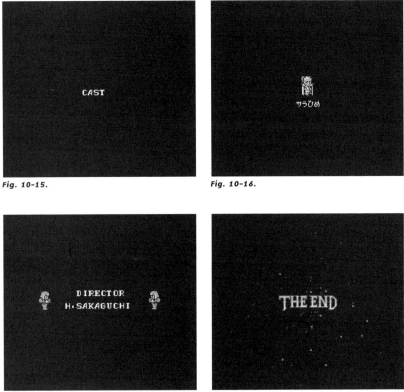

Fig. 10-15.

Fig. 10-16.

Fig. 10-17.

Fig. 10-18.

SUPER SEQUELS

Flush with the success of *Final Fantasy III*, Square immediately began work on *Final Fantasy IV* for the Famicom. They got so far as to mock up a sample screenshot for Japanese game magazines and a list of features, but the game was quickly scrapped as Nintendo's new 16-bit system, the Super Famicom, proved to be quite powerful and potentially a huge retail success much like the Famicom before it.[21] Square wanted to be known for its cutting-edge graphics, so the Super Famicom game that they were developing became *Final Fantasy IV*[*].

* Released as *Final Fantasy II* in America. See Chapter 8.

The improvements over *Final Fantasy III*'s graphics would prove to be small compared to the giant leap made in the cinematics and storyline.

If *Final Fantasy II* was the experiment, the introduction of what Square would later refer to as *ningen dorama* (human drama, or character-based drama) into its RPGs, then *Final Fantasy IV*, was the refined version, created with a new outlook on video game storytelling. Although the stories of the previous three games had been revolutionary, they all had one important thing in common: the player knew exactly how the game was going to end after reading the introductory text. It was a given that the player's group of characters was going to light the Orbs, defeat the evil Empire, and restore the hopes and dreams of the world by reviving the Crystals, mostly because the games' white-on-blue introduction screens set up the conflict in clear terms.

But when we look at *Final Fantasy IV*'s lengthy introductory sequences, we see that although the player is getting more information and character development at the start of the game than ever before, indeed he is only glimpsing a tiny fraction of what is to come; the tip of the proverbial iceberg. The interstitial name-the-characters screens are eliminated from the game's opening[*], and so immediately after the title screen we hear a somber military march fading in during a black screen, and seconds later the picture fades in: a fleet of airships flying above the continent (Fig 11-1). We see the soldiers talking to their captain, Cecil[†], before invading a crystal room like that of the previous game. But the soldiers are not there to talk to the crystal; they are there to take it by force. They kill the guardians of the crystal (Fig 11-2).

* When a new game is started and saved, a 'select game' screen appears after the title screen. But for first-time players, the game launches immediately into the opening cut scene.

† Pronounced SEH-sil, which means he may have been named after professional baseball player Cecil Fielder, who in 1989 was playing for the Hanshin Tigers.

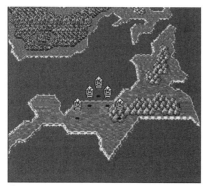

Fig. 11-1.

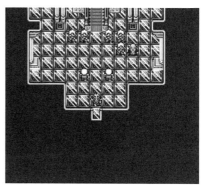

Fig. 11-2.

Back on the airship, the soldiers express some doubt about taking the crystals in the name of the King (Fig 11-3). But Cecil convinces them that what they are doing is right… although, he implies, not even he is sure. They have little time to think about this before they are attacked, and we see Cecil fight in two computer-controlled battles. The ships land in the castle town of Baron, and we see Cecil enter the castle escorted by the King's advisor, Beigan. In the throne room, Cecil hands the crystal over but questions the King's motives. The King lashes out at Cecil and removes him from his command of the Red Wings airship fleet. Cecil's friend Cain, who true to his name will eventually turn on Cecil, goes with him on his new assignment: to destroy the Phantom Monsters of the north (Fig 11-4).

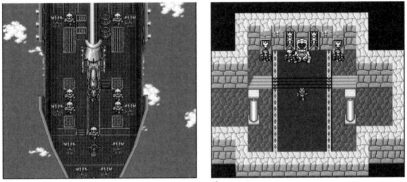

Fig. 11-3.   **Fig. 11-4.**

The player finally gets control of Cecil, but he is still being led through the opening since there are few places for him to go. The careful player can explore all over the castle (but not leave), talking to guards and his former soldiers. Eventually, walking through one corridor, Cecil's girlfriend Rosa finds him and lets him know that she will come up to his room later that evening. After this brief encounter, Cecil runs into Rosa's father Cid, the creator of the airships, who laments that the King wants him to turn his docile flying creations into armored warships. Finally going to bed, Cecil is visited by Rosa, but he turns away from her, lost in his moral struggle (Fig 11-5). The next morning, we see Cain and Cecil leaving the castle to the familiar opening strains of the "Final Fantasy" theme, and against a beautiful backdrop of the castle, the moat, and a blue sky, we see the traditional white text again… and the game begins (Fig 11-6).

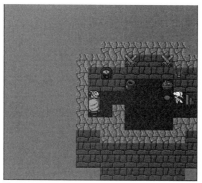

Fig. 11-5.   *Fig. 11-6.*

This opening scene (which can take from five to ten minutes, depending on how thoroughly the player explores the castle and talks to the soldiers) speaks volumes about the changes that *Final Fantasy IV* introduced to the series. The story deals with mature themes and complex characters. In *Final Fantasy II*, the squeaky-clean main characters were attacked by purely evil dark knights; here, our main character *is* a dark knight struggling with his position, paid to kill innocents, trying to reconcile loyalty to his kingdom with his sense of right and wrong. He is clearly involved in a sexual relationship with Rosa. His final mission for the King turns out to be a mass murder: the Phantom Monsters are really just a town of peaceful humans whose magic the corrupt King has deemed dangerous. (Note the heavy political overtones.)

Amazingly, this already complex plot only scratched the surface of the game. The true plot, which would finally involve traveling to the moon to defeat a great evil—is revealed in small chunks throughout the game, bringing far more of a feeling of wonder each time a great plot secret is finally revealed. This was closer than ever to true beginning-middle-end narrative in the true Hollywood cinema sense of the term.

Still, the differences between game and film were obvious. The characters and locations were still made out of small, pixilated drawings and 99% of the game's scenes shared the same camera angle, which wasn't even a physically realistic one; to show as much detail as possible, the characters lay in flat profile on a three-quarters view landscape. The bedroom scene with Cecil and Rosa was intriguing enough for the player to suspend his disbelief... but after a while the player cannot help but laugh at the fact that due to animation limitations, Cecil has worn his full suit of armor to bed. What is important here is that *even though* these extreme limitations were still being imposed, Square pressed on and attempted to make movie-like games even on computer hardware that couldn't handle complex animation.

Final Fantasy V, released in 1992, was again a bit of a step back in terms of "human drama." Whereas *Final Fantasy IV* presented the player with a host of different player-characters that came and went (some turned traitor, some left to pursue other goals, and some died), with *Final Fantasy V* it was back to a standard group of four (although they were not entirely safe from an emotional killing-off). There was very little back-story or moral dilemmas; the characters came together quickly and pressed on until they had defeated the enemy threatening the world. There were plot twists to be sure, but *Final Fantasy V*'s focus was again on the "job change system" of *Final Fantasy I* and *Final Fantasy III* by which the player could assign different classes to the characters from war-

rior to magician and everything in between, with the hopes of building up a powerful group by game's end. This system was so much fun that it was easy to forgive *Final Fantasy V*'s story for being not as thrilling or as multi-layered as *Final Fantasy IV*'s. This was especially so considering that the next game in the series would not only be a new high-water mark but considered by some fans to be the series' creative peak.

For *Final Fantasy VI*, which was to be the last of the series on the Super Famicom, Sakaguchi and team had grand plans. First, they would use a completely new graphics engine, allowing for larger characters and for far more detailed backdrops, many of which were drawn as cohesive paintings rather than assembled from small square "tiles." And the game play would merge the two extremes of the series. It would be a more touching human drama than ever before, but within that framework the player would have the power to customize each character's powers and abilities.

Final Fantasy VI was a story-game *par excellence* in part because it was far more serious and dramatic than all other RPGs. If *Final Fantasy IV* was at least sometimes a story of lighthearted medieval adventure, swords, sorcery and dragons, then *Final Fantasy VI* was a dark, moody, and somber tale of life, death, love, and power. The opening sequence set this chilling tone by being *far* darker and more ominous than that of any *Final Fantasy* game before it. It begins with the *Final Fantasy* logo set in red flames against dark, purple storm clouds while ominous music builds to a frightening crescendo (Fig 12-1). We see three soldiers in giant suits of robotic armor about to ascend a snow-covered mountain (Fig 12-2). They plod up the side of the mountain during the credits sequence, which for the first time is displayed while action is taking place on-screen, even more like a film's opening credits (Fig 12-3).

Fig. 12-1. Note that the following pictures are from the game's original English version, retitled Final Fantasy III for foreign markets. (See Chapter 8.)

Fig. 12-2.

Fig. 12-3.

The game play was much improved over the previous titles, and the graphics were above and beyond any yet seen on the Super Famicom, but *Final Fantasy VI*'s story took center stage. Flashbacks are key and they are shown (and sometimes *played*) in a sepia yellow tone reminiscent of old pictures (Fig 12-4). There was much less distinction between "game play" and "story"; characters will often break into dialogue and action in the course of a battle (Fig 12-5), and the ghosts that ride the Phantom Train to the land of the dead talk to you as often as they fight against you (Fig 12-6).

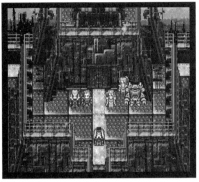

Fig. 12-4.

Fig. 12-5.

The player will have between 12 and 14 characters in his party by the end of the game, and each of them have separate, elaborate story arcs that can be completed individually before the game is over. To get a sense of the grandness of *Final Fantasy VI*'s story, let us briefly examine the 12 major characters and the stories that we lead them through as the game goes on. Note how, as we look at the individual character backgrounds, the grander story arc begins to take shape.[*]

Fig. 12-6.

* For the purposes of consistency, I will use the names from the American translation. Some are different in the Japanese version.

† Named Biggs and Wedge, after Luke Skywalker's rebel flight school companions in *Star Wars*. The names continue to pop up in *Final Fantasy* games to this day in homage to the series.

Terra Branford: At the game's opening, she is under control of the Gestahl Empire. Along with two imperial soldiers[†], she wears giant body armor whose weapons reproduce the effects of Magic. This is a force that has gone unharnessed in this world for a thousand years, ever since the War of the Magi—a grand battle between human beings and a magical race known as Espers. She joins the rebel group The Returners, but is aware of something wrong deep inside her. What Terra does not know yet, and indeed only learns much later, is that she is half-human and half-Esper.

Locke Cole: A thief, although he prefers the term "treasure hunter," born in the town of Kohlingen. As a young man, he brought his girlfriend Rachel into a cave filled with treasure, and she slipped off a rickety bridge and died. He has yet to come to grips with her death and vows to protect his friend…

Celes Chere: A general of the empire alongside Kefka, she was experimented upon in her youth and infused with the power of Magic. She defects from the empire when she realizes its corruption.

Edgar Roni Figaro: He is the 27-year-old king of the Figaro kingdom, a charmer with the ladies, and secretly a member of the rebel group. Either he or his brother could have taken the throne, but it was decided by a coin toss.

Sabin Rene Figaro: Sabin left the kingdom to study under the tutelage of the great martial artist Duncan. As a Returner, he works to learn new martial arts moves and supports the party with his sheer physical strength.

Cyan Garamonde: A loyal, high-ranking soldier in the kingdom of Doma, Cyan is a swordsman extraordinaire. Much like Sabin, he works through the entire game to develop his skills to defeat Kefka and the empire, who attacked his kingdom and murdered his wife and young son in the process. As a high-strung gentleman knight, he clashes the most with…

Gau: A 13-year-old boy abandoned by his psychologically disturbed father, he grew up among animals in the wilds of the Veldt plains. He will attack the party at first, as if he was a monster, but joins them when they offer him dried meat.

Setzer Gabbiani: Setzer is a professional gambler, but more importantly, he owns the Blackjack—the only airship left in the world. His high-flying lifestyle and thirst for adventure and risk-taking causes him to lend his services to the party.

Mog: Among all the Moogles, a race of furry creatures introduced in *Final Fantasy IV*, basically with the intent of selling plush dolls, Mog is the best dancer. He says that the Esper thunder god Ramuh came to him in a dream to tell him to join the party, so he does.

Strago Magus: Strago is a Blue Mage, a type of wizard who can absorb the spells that his enemies cast to learn them himself. He is reluctant to join the party until they rescue his granddaughter…

Relm Arrowny: A 10-year-old art prodigy, Relm seems to have inherited a bit of blue magic from her grandfather—when she sketches monsters, the sketches come to life and attack the monster. The rest of the party can't understand why she seems to have such a bond with Interceptor, the normally violent attack dog that tags along with…

Shadow: A ninja with a mysterious past. It is possible to find out Shadow's connection to Relm, but only if the player doesn't let Shadow die in a crucial scene midway through the game. If the player chooses to abandon him instead, they'll never know his story.

The theme of Final Fantasy VI is **love** in all its forms—romantic love, parental love, sibling love, and platonic love. Sakaguchi asks the player, what is love and where can we find it? One crucial scene crystallizes this theme, while showing how powerful Sakaguchi's directing, Uematsu's music, and Amano's artwork could be when they worked together in harmony. Not only that, it foreshadows the cinematic path that the series had been embarking on and would soon veer completely down.

The so-called "opera house scene" is one of the most remembered in all of *Final Fantasy* fandom. Occurring early on in the game, the scene takes place after the group goes to an opera house as part of their mission and finds the Impresario in crisis—his prima donna, Maria, has disappeared. Coincidentally, group member Celes happens to look exactly like Maria, and she reluctantly agrees to perform onstage so the show can go on and the rebels can complete their mission. When we see the stage, it is a beautifully designed screen—the audience moves about in their seats, the curtain is drawn on the stage area. The action begins.

First we see a scene with the rest of the actors. Maria's true love Draco sings and pines for her, though they are far away, et cetera. Then it is time for Celes' performance. Before this, the player had to read through her lines and memorize them; if the player doesn't select the right song lines for her to sing, the performance is a bust and she has to try again. If the player makes the right choices, the scene flows smoothly. Celes/Maria appears in a 16-bit, pixilated vision of loveliness and sings (via on-screen text accompanied by a not-entirely-unpleasant keyboard sample that sounds somewhat like a human voice following the melody) a very pretty aria.

Final Fantasy VI was as close to a cinematic, movie-like storytelling experience as any game had ever been, and it captivated Japanese audiences. It sold approximately two and a half million copies in Japan alone, making it about the fifteenth best-selling game ever at the time, outstripped only by various *Super Mario* and *Dragon Quest* titles. (After the onslaught of *Pokémon* and two *Final Fantasy* games that saw even greater success, it dropped to number twenty-two in the rankings.)[22] Upon its release in America, *Final Fantasy VI* was expected to sell millions "judging by the [U.S.] population alone," said Sakaguchi. But although it was one of the top-selling games of 1994, the American market had entered a slump that year; moreover, RPGs were still a niche market in the action-oriented West.[23] A 1995

Square/Nintendo collaboration, *Super Mario RPG*, fared very well in Japan and did fine in America with a Nintendo-backed marketing blitz.

Square and Nintendo's bond seemed unbreakable until 1996, when Square revealed (in an announcement that stunned the industry) that it would cease all Nintendo projects and thereafter publish games exclusively on the Sony PlayStation, a CD-ROM based game system. With the massive data storage space of a CD-ROM drive, which Nintendo's new Nintendo 64 hardware lacked, Sakaguchi was able to bring FMV (full-motion video), or fully animated movie sequences, to his games. He explained that the shift was made entirely because the CD-ROM format "allowed for more artistic freedom." It appeared to be the right choice. *Final Fantasy VII*, was the RPG that single-handedly moved RPGs from "niche" to "mainstream" in the US by offering a 3D, computer-animated experience that appealed to America's desire for impressive graphics while retaining the RPG game play; in fact, it sold more copies in the United States than in Japan.

It is important to remember that Square had its choice of CD-ROM based hardware to program for. In 1995, the PlayStation and the Sega Saturn were locked in a dead heat for units sold in Japan, each with about 2.5 million units sold. Before the announcement of *Final Fantasy VII*, it seemed as if the Sega Saturn would be the victor; it had the immensely popular *Virtua Fighter* software. But after the announcement of *Final Fantasy VII*, the PlayStation began a meteoric rise. Within a few years, Sony's sales in Japan had grown to 17.4 million units compared to Sega's 5.7 million units.

Square's move to CD-ROM development was not singular among software publishers. In fact, every other formerly Nintendo-loyal publisher made the shift. The difference was that Square announced that it would *not support* Nintendo's systems, neither the Nintendo 64 nor the portable Game Boy line, whereas other major publishers like Konami, Capcom, and Enix only transferred the *majority* of their efforts to Sony's and Sega's systems while still supporting Nintendo.

To take Enix as a specific example, the company announced that *Dragon Quest VII* would appear on the PlayStation. But it continued to support the Nintendo 64 with the occasional title. One early effort, *Mischief Makers*, was published by Nintendo in the US and, perhaps more importantly, remade its earlier *Dragon Quest* games for Nintendo's portable Game Boy Color system, the first version of the handheld to have a full-color screen. Enix's *Dragon Quest Monsters* titles, patterned after Nintendo's wildly successful *Pokémon* games, were particularly hot sellers.

By Square's own admission, the bridge between Square and Nintendo was not, as many speculated, burned because Nintendo president Hiroshi

Yamauchi felt like a jilted bride. In a 2001 interview with the Nikkei business newspaper, Square president Nao Suzuki took all the blame, not merely for leaving Nintendo but for convincing other publishers to go with them:

> "Our true enemy," he admitted, "was our pride". This was pride that resulted from the heady years of the original PlayStation. When Square originally announced back in 1997 that the *Final Fantasy* series would be PlayStation exclusive from now on, Nintendo president Hiroshi Yamauchi treated the affront lightly, saying that the console selection "couldn't be helped." Suzuki responded by publicly bashing the N64 and convincing Enix to join the PS camp along with them, which, looking back at it now, he realizes wasn't an incredibly smart move. The little grudge match between them that resulted was the main reason Square failed in their bid for a Nintendo license earlier this year.[24]

At this time, Square had been publishing portable versions of its classic games on a system called the Wonderswan, made by the company Bandai. Although Final Fantasy was the hottest-selling title on the system by far, Square knew that a Game Boy Advance license was what they really needed. It was clear from this public admission of culpability that Square wanted to patch things up. Within a year, Square had their Nintendo license. So far, Square has published three Game Boy Advance games: Chocobo Land, Final Fantasy Tactics Advance, and Sword of Mana. Final Fantasy Crystal Chronicles, a title for the Nintendo Gamecube, launched in Japan in 2003 and in the US in February 2004.

"Sakaguchi had always had an eye for cinematics, art, and storytelling," wrote historian Steven Kent, "but working with CD-ROM gave him the opportunity to enhance these features exponentially. *Final Fantasy VII* had epic dramatic cut scenes with symphonic music."[25] Indeed, Uematsu could use CD-quality live recordings of real orchestras. Yoshitaka Amano stayed on as an image illustrator, but the job of character designer went to Tetsuya Nomura, whose art was more suited to 3D renders. Key scenes could be rendered entirely with high-powered computers and presented in movie form.

What this meant was that *Final Fantasy* continued to move away from a "free game" mentality and further down the path of cinematic movie-games—the player spent quite a bit of time *watching* the story play out through movies and more linear game play sequences. But they were beautiful sequences. The move to three-dimensional game play enabled Sakaguchi to show scenes from dramatic camera angles instead of always from the top down. The camera angle could shift mid-scene for maximum dramatic effect. In theory, the sky was the limit.

Of course, it didn't work out quite that way at first. There were still growing pains. The FMV sequences were beautiful, although the actual polygonal characters were still crude, looking boxy and unshaded. And Uematsu couldn't use an entirely symphonic soundtrack since the CD storage capacity was mostly being used for the lengthy, high-quality movie sequences. In fact, all of the music on *Final Fantasy VII*'s soundtrack was still synthesizer-based, although it *sounded* lots better because of the higher-quality samples that the PlayStation sound hardware could produce.

But Square continued to improve on the graphics and music with each installment. *Final Fantasy VIII* (1999) featured a few musical tracks that were performed by live orchestras, as well as a vocal song, "Eyes On Me," sung in shaky English by Chinese pop star Faye Wong. It was released as a single and won Uematsu a coveted Gold Disc award for Best Foreign-Language Song of 1999.

Graphics-wise, the game featured much better FMV and real-time renderings of the game's player-characters. Game play-wise it was more like *Final Fantasy V*; there were only six characters and the focus was on customizing their abilities. The system was so complex and the game so difficult that *Final Fantasy* fans are split on *Final Fantasy VIII*; some think its complexity made it the best in the series, while some disliked it. This split happened in Japan as well, where some deride *Final Fantasy VIII* as their least favorite game in the series. What's more, in his book *Trigger Happy*, Steven Poole noted that there was "palpable outrage" in Japan when the first pictures of *Final Fantasy VIII*, showing the game's Westernized, realistic character designs, surfaced in *Famitsu* magazine.

Development on the next two games in the series started in tandem. One team worked on *Final Fantasy IX* (2000), which more prominently featured Yoshitaka Amano's character designs. The vocal song for the game was called "Melodies of Life" and was performed by Japanese vocal superstar Emiko Shiratori, whose hit album "Cross My Heart" included both Japanese and English versions of the song as well as a vocal version of Uematsu's title theme that he had composed for the original "Final Fantasy." *Final Fantasy IX* was a love letter to *Final Fantasy* fans of the Super Famicom era; it included all kinds of in-joke references and allusions to the classic games as well as more cartoonish, small-proportioned character designs. (Those who enjoyed the more complicated and realistic *Final Fantasy VIII* did not tend to be fans of the "regressive" *Final Fantasy IX*.)

Final Fantasy X, meanwhile, was released on DVD format for Sony's new PlayStation 2 system in 2001. It needed the extra development time because it used the supercomputer power of the system to render the characters and scenes with more jaw dropping detail than ever before. The characters still didn't look quite like their rendered movie counterparts, but they were pretty close. More importantly for the storyline, about 90% of the dialogue in *Final Fantasy X* was performed by a team of over 100 voice actors. Now, the cast sequence at the end of the games was far more meaningful.

Now, *Final Fantasy* titles were selling millions of copies each, not just in Japan but also worldwide. This led to a resurgence of interest in the older games that had gone unnoticed in the US and, to their credit, Square's US branch did eventually deliver, if belatedly, PlayStation versions of the SNES and Famicom games, with additional FMV sequences, bonus options, and in the case of *Final Fantasy I* and *Final Fantasy II*, totally overhauled graphics and music. These were released in three collections of two games each (*Final Fantasy Anthology*, *Final Fantasy Chronicles*, and *Final Fantasy Origins*). As of this writing, only *Final Fantasy III* remains unavailable in any form outside of Japan.

DARK SPIRITS

The *Final Fantasy* games on the Sony PlayStation were, on a worldwide scale, the most visible and most talked-about titles in the series' history. But as the games became more and more popular, Hironobu Sakaguchi was becoming less and less involved with them. He wasn't abandoning his creation, however. Indeed, he was working on the most ambitious *Final Fantasy* project yet; a project that would take the series from film-game to film.

In 1997, around the same time that the long-awaited *Final Fantasy VII* was ready to be released, Sakaguchi announced that he and Square's new Honolulu studio had begun work on a completely computer graphics (CG) rendered *Final Fantasy* movie. Pixar's CG-rendered film *Toy Story* had just been released to critical and box-office success, and it had represented a giant leap in CG-rendered animation, for its technical prowess but also for its ability to move an audience emotionally. Square felt that they could capitalize on their newfound fame as computer graphic wizards and Sakaguchi's gift for directing with a feature film.

In a 2001 interview with the BBC, Sakaguchi recalled that in 1997 "a goal was set to create something within three years that no one had ever seen before. We were looking towards making something that was very realistic but not totally real—the fine line between [anime] and realism."[26] Early images and video teasers showed *Final Fantasy: The Spirits Within* to be just that—it was clearly an animated film and yet its characters and settings were incredibly lifelike.

Still, *anime* was Japanese film and Japanese films did not make nearly as much money as Hollywood productions—not even in Japan. Hollywood movies dominate Japanese theaters; in fact, for fifteen years, the highest-grossing film of all time in Japan was *E.T.* Hayao Miyazaki's *anime* masterpiece *Princess Mononoke* (*Mononoke Hime*) beat this record in 1997, only to lose it a few months later to *Titanic*, which held the record for four years before being beaten in 2001 by *Spirited Away* (*Sen to Chihiro no kamikakushi*), Miyazaki's next film. So the record bounced back and forth between Hollywood's biggest blockbusters and the masterpieces of Japan's foremost genius of animation. The difference is that *E.T.* and *Titanic* were also runaway successes worldwide, while *Princess Mononoke* and *Spirited Away*, even though they were released by Disney in the US and thus had more exposure than practically any other *anime* films, were restricted to a small number of theaters during their US runs.

So it was clear to Sakaguchi that regardless of the fact that his film would walk the creative line between *anime* and Hollywood, *Final Fantasy: The Spirits Within* needed to be pushed as a Hollywood release. Square allied with Columbia Pictures to release the film and hired what could only be called an all-star cast to voice the film's characters. Accomplished Chinese-American actress Ming-Na, the star of *The Joy Luck Club* and the voice of the title character in Disney's animated film *Mulan*,* would play the lead character, scientist Aki Ross. James Woods, Donald Sutherland, and Steve Buscemi, among other well-known actors, would join her, bringing name recognition to the project. (*Final Fantasy*, while certainly well known among video game players worldwide by this time, couldn't be called a household word.)

> * *Final Fantasy* wouldn't be Ming-Na's first experience in video game cinema; she played Chun Li in the critically-panned *Street Fighter*, based on 1992's most popular video game.

In January 2001, just as the film was about to be released, director Sakaguchi and producer Jun Aida were excited about the prospects for their film, going so far as to announce a sequel. "We're working on the concept of a second feature," said Aida at a press conference. "Our hope is to start the production...right after we wrap here, which will be next summer. We will go right into production for the second feature." Sakaguchi added, "I definitely want to bring Aki back as our main digital actress. As with any actress, we'd like to see her in other features...[but] because Aki is a CG character, we can have the advantage of having her at any age. We can even have her come back as a 16-year-old girl."[27]

The project was not without its critics. "From the beginning, I had a feeling that the movie would not succeed," recalled Yasunori Mitsuda, who worked on sound effects for Squaresoft games like *Final Fantasy V* before composing the soundtrack for RPGs like *Chrono Trigger* and *Xenogears*. "Even when I was still working at Square, they were talking about making the movie… I felt it wasn't really a smart move. And if you look at the [fact that Square merged with Enix], you can say that it was not really a smart idea," he said in late 2002, on the eve of the Square Enix merger.[28]

But in 2001, Sakaguchi and Aida were clearly enamored with their creation, and imagined a bright future for Square Pictures, a future of infinite possibilities. But there was one possibility that they were not anticipating: that despite the four years of painstaking work and the $137 million budget that had gone into the project, *Final Fantasy: The Spirits Within* would be a spectacular flop; a critical and box-office failure.

Reviewers shared one universal sentiment: Although the animation was fantastic, the storyline was uninteresting. Video game journalists, familiar with Sakaguchi's idiosyncrasies and the foibles of video game storytelling in general, tended to pin down the problems more precisely. Wrote reviewer Nich Maragos, then of the now-defunct website *The Gaming Intelligence Agency*, "Unfortunately, what *Final Fantasy: TSW* manages to drive home is how character-dependent RPG stories really are, and it emphasizes this point by negative counterexample…where the games are free to devote however much time or space they wish to fleshing out a particular character, *Final Fantasy: TSW* has only 108 minutes to handle seven principal players and still keep the story moving." Most of the supporting characters, wrote Maragos, had "almost nothing in the way of personality"[29]—this, despite being voiced by some of the world's most gifted character actors.

Listening to the audio commentary tracks on the DVD release of *The Spirits Within*, it immediately becomes clear that the film's storyline and world was deeper than could be shown in 108 minutes. But it took four years and $137 million to create those 108 minutes, because of the incredibly minute detail of the animation that made *Toy Story* look hopelessly dated in comparison. Any additional footage would have come at great expense, and "re-shooting" scenes was next to impossible.

Square Pictures would go on to produce one more project, one that would be widely viewed: *The Final Flight of the Osiris*, a short feature that began 2003's DVD release *The Animatrix*, a collection of short works of Japanese animation set in the world of the movie *The Matrix*. The recognition and revenue from this project would not be enough to save them. One report placed the amount of money that Square lost at $80 million. Whatever the damage, Square Pictures was out of business by the end of 2001.[30]

PLAYONLINE

Although Square Pictures was gone, Squaresoft the game creators still thrive, now as part of Square Enix. This puts *Dragon Quest* and *Final Fantasy* under the auspices of one company, although the two main series continue to share their separate identities, development staff, and characters—though *Final Fantasy*'s cute Chocobo character made a guest appearance in a 2004 *Dragon Quest* spin-off that starred the ubiquitous blue Slime as the game's main character.

Dragon Fantasy might be a long way off, however. *Dragon Quest VIII* shows that Horii's latest game adopts a cel-shaded cartoon look, much like *The Legend of Zelda: The Wind Waker* on the GameCube, to best represent Akira Toriyama's 2D artwork. Meanwhile, *Final Fantasy* games continue their push toward ultra-realism. *Final Fantasy X-2*, the series' first ever storyline sequel that showed the continuing adventures of the cast of *Final Fantasy X*, was built around the real-life sex appeal of its digital females. The full-page shot of *The Spirits Within* heroine Aki Ross in a bikini in the pages of *Maxim* magazine was tame compared to the skimpy outfits and sexy poses of *Final Fantasy X-2*'s characters.

The switch from dot-pictures and storyboards done in MacPaint to high-powered computer graphics and full-motion video sequences was a challenge for Squaresoft and for the many other video game publishers who were forced to make the leap and keep up with them. But while many of those other publishers now struggle to find stories, characters, and music that can match the grandeur and scope of the computer graphics available to them, this was simply never a problem for Hironobu Sakaguchi. The great, epic stories and deep, likeable characters were already in place well before the computer graphics could make the game *look* like a movie. All that remained was for the technology to catch up with Sakaguchi's vision. And when it did, the results were tremendous, as *Final Fantasy VII* had more of an effect on Sony's rise to the top of the worldwide home game hardware market than any other single piece of software.

This long-awaited international success of his series left Sakaguchi with the bankroll and the recognition to fulfill his dream of creating a major motion picture, and the CG technology meant that he could do it as an extension of his existing work. So why was the *Final Fantasy* movie a failure? For as much as the *Final Fantasy* team felt that they were making "little movies," they never considered—or never overcame—the fact that filmgoers and video game players have different expectations. That when the crucial element of control is removed, other things have to be there to make up for it. In short,

The Spirits Within was the work of a novice filmmaker with a tremendous budget. But Sakaguchi remained optimistic about the future. In no fewer than three interviews following the movie's failure at the box office, he maintained that Squaresoft has benefited from the movie and that the computer graphics software they have developed over four years would be used in future Squaresoft video games.

Indeed, disappointment with the *Final Fantasy* movie has not prevented *Final Fantasy X*, *Final Fantasy X-2*, and a grand collaborative work with Disney, a cinematic RPG titled *Kingdom Hearts* that featured Disney characters from Goofy to Tinkerbell fighting alongside Tetsuya Nomura's *Final Fantasy* heroes, from selling millions of copies worldwide. An online version, *Final Fantasy XI*, has proven popular, although it will not replace the traditional titles. I wrote about my experience in the world of *Final Fantasy XI* for Wired News, and would like to share it with you before we conclude this discussion.

A FANTASY THAT'S NEVER FINAL*

> "r u a ps2 n00b?"

How to answer? Should I admit that I am indeed a second-class citizen, an untouchable in the city of the bourgeoisie? To the many high-level Warriors and Red Mages running confidently around the virtual world of Vana'diel, players who have been immersed in the massively multiplayer online role-playing game (MMORPG) *Final Fantasy XI* since its late-2003 release for personal computers, the fresh influx of new players this week after the March 23 release of the game for the PlayStation 2 is a pox on their fair city, an irritating mass of unwashed immigrants who beg for free money from the rich and ask annoying newbie questions *all day*.

But PlayStation 2 gamers have a similar sense of we-were-here-first entitlement. *Final Fantasy* has been a predominantly console-oriented series since it first appeared on Nintendo's Famicom in 1987. And indeed, in Japan *Final Fantasy XI* made its debut exclusively on the PS2, the PC version being a mere afterthought in the land where console gaming reigns with an iron fist. As far as the PlayStation 2 crowd is concerned, then, PC gamers are the usurpers and squatters, encroaching on their territory. The world of Moogles, Mythril, and Materia is their turf.

And this situation is, in some way, exactly what *Final Fantasy XI*'s designers set out to create.

Final Fantasy XI's release on the PlayStation 2 marks the fourth and final major step in Square Enix's master plan to create a MMORPG that puts the focus on a worldwide, diverse community. This idea is more radical than it sounds. Yes, the game borrows the very basics of its game play from successful PC MMORPGS, like *Ultima Online* and *Everquest*—kill monsters of gradually increasing difficulty to build up your character's level and amass a horde of virtual treasure. But in *Final Fantasy XI*, you can't do it by murdering the weak; there's no player killing. And you can't do it alone. After the first few hours of leveling-up, expanding your horizons becomes nearly impossible without a party of friends.

So right off the bat, you're encouraged to make friends. The cities of the game are so vast that at first, merely navigating them is virtually impossible without asking directions. And every time I tried this, I was bowled over by the friendliness of perfect strangers. Every person I ever asked for help didn't simply tell me where to go but actually *led the way*, taking time out of whatever they were doing to physically bring me to my destination.

On my second day, a stranger named Tarukun walked up to me out of the blue to give me a Linkpearl, which is like a little magical walkie-talkie connected to a master device called a Linkshell. Any player with a pearl can chat in real time with other players who have pearls of the same set. The group that I was invited to, the TinyTornados, is exclusively for TaruTaru, the diminutive Hobbit-like race of magical creatures to which my player character belongs.

My tiny cousins offered to answer any and all questions I had about the game. There is, I found out, a certain team pride among us few, proud players who chose to be neither musclebound swordsman nor curvy cat-girl. And it was in this circle of new friends that I was asked, right off the bat, if I was one of the new arrivals fresh off the PlayStation 2 boat. I hesitated, but finally figured there was no harm in answering "Yes."

"o. so how do u type?"

A good question, and one that points to the difficulties inherent not only in setting up a persistent online experience that lets players on different platforms and in different countries play in the exact same space, but to merely putting an online RPG on the PlayStation 2 in the first place. Unlike

Microsoft's Xbox, the PlayStation 2 doesn't ship with an internal hard drive, so the $99.99 *Final Fantasy XI* package includes a 40-gigabyte one. Physical installation of the HDD is surprisingly easy; it connects to the 39.99 Network Adapter, then slides into a bay in the back of the console.

That's the easy part. Now you've got between two and three hours of software installation, registration, and character creation standing between you and game play. The *Final Fantasy XI* software comes factory-installed onto the HDD, but after you fiddle with the settings and get the PlayStation 2 to recognize your dialup or broadband Internet connection, you've got to download all the software updates from Sony's servers.

"Boo hoo," mock the PC gamers. Indeed, for that crowd a two-hour setup process is the best-case scenario. And PC gamers see a game that refuses to run as a challenge, whereas console gamers demand refunds. What's more, console gamers want it all for under a few hundred bucks, not the thousand-dollar supercomputers needed to run the PC version of the game, which is a surprisingly taxing piece of software. So this installation process might be daunting to a group used to true plug-and-play, but it's about as smooth as can be expected at this stage.

The thing that PS2 players need to think about that PC players take for granted is, of course, how to type. You could use the on-screen virtual keyboard, picking out letters with your standard PS2 controller. But why, when any USB keyboard will work? Even better is the dual-function controller released by Logitech that puts a full-size keyboard into a PS2 controller. It's a bit awkward at first, but less so than juggling two separate input devices.

If you must use only a standard controller, though, there's an in-game menu of key phrases that you can scroll through as an alternative to hunt-and-pecking. And since Japanese players share the same servers as Americans, there's an auto-translate function for those key words. What the American versions of *Final Fantasy XI* lack is Japanese text input for the growing number of young *Final Fantasy* fans who can speak the language. This effectively removes any possibility of meaningful conversation between the two groups and renders Square Enix's vision of a truly international community nearly pointless.

This is frustrating. But in most other ways *Final Fantasy XI* is a fascinating and fulfilling experience. It's becoming progressively difficult to argue that online game aficionados represent a shut-off group of socially awkward devil worshippers when Square Enix's bold experiment in community-based RPG game play rewards players for being outgoing, considerate, and generous.

CONCLUSION

In the end, the failure of the *Final Fantasy* movie didn't hurt the popularity of the game, but it's not clear yet whether Hironobu Sakaguchi will ever again take the helm of a game design. He is currently involved with his company-saving brainchild in name only. That is, Square Enix retains his exclusive services as an "executive producer," but he no longer takes any meaningful creative role in game development. But it seems Sakaguchi's creative spirit could not be contained for long. Just as we were going to press with this book, it was announced that Sakaguchi would be starting his own independent game development studio, called Mist Walker. Sakaguchi will be teaming up with none other than Yoshitaka Amano to create an original RPG.

But at Square Enix proper, the torch has now been passed once again. *Final Fantasy XII* is in production by a different team at Squaresoft, a group headed by young director Yasumi Matsuno, whose strategy-game spin-off series *Final Fantasy Tactics* reached cult approval but not the kind of sales that mainstream *Final Fantasy* games enjoy. Yoshitaka Amano still creates the logo for each game's package, but little else. Tetsuya Nomura's skin-baring teens now represent *Final Fantasy* more in the eyes of the average gamer than do Amano's ethereal watercolors.

Even Nobuo Uematsu, who, for the first time, shared his composing duties on *Final Fantasy* X with two other composers, was not involved with *Final Fantasy X-2*. It should be noted, however, that of all three men, Uematsu remains the most involved with the *Final Fantasy* franchise on a regular basis—and you can credit that to Japan's infatuation with video game music.

▦ ▦ ▦

CHAPTER 5

GAME MUSIC, MUSIC GAMES

GAME MUSIC

Picture, if you will, the 10th of May 2004. A night at the symphony. The audience arrives at the luxurious Walt Disney Concert Hall in Los Angeles. The house is packed for an anticipated one-night-only performance featuring the Los Angeles Philharmonic and the Los Angeles Master Chorale. The house, a newly constructed 2,265-seat hall, is packed to the gills; tickets had sold out three days after going on sale, months prior to the event. The audience waits with breathless anticipation. Conductor Miguel Harth-Bedoya raises his baton. He brings it down as the chorale sings the opening notes of the first piece of the evening: *Liberi Fatali* from the video game *Final Fantasy VIII*.

A once-in-a-lifetime event, yes, but only if you're not from Japan. In fact, in the year 2003 there were no less than *three* high-profile live performances of game music there. On April 27th and 28th at the Shibuya AX concert hall in Tokyo, *Final Fantasy* composer Nobuo Uematsu's newly-formed rock band, The Black Mages, played a selection of rock-arranged music from the battle scenes of ten Final Fantasy games. Uematsu, who had gotten his start as a musician because he idolized the great piano-rocker Elton John, had never before gotten the chance to perform his own music live in concert.

On July 19th, composer Motoi Sakuraba sat on the stage of the seaside concert hall Zepp Tokyo, surrounded by a dozen synthesizers as he, alongside his friends Toshihiko Nakamura on drums and Atsushi Hasegawa on bass, performed progressive-rock arrangements of Sakuraba's compositions for the renowned RPGs *Star Ocean* and *Valkyrie Profile*. At the party after the concert, Sakuraba met up with his old friend Noriyuki Iwadare, the acclaimed composer of the soundtracks to such RPGs as *Grandia* and *LUNAR*.

And on September 14th, coming off of the success of an orchestral concert featuring classic Nintendo tunes a year prior, Nintendo presented *Mario and Zelda Big Band Live* at the Seinenkan Hall in Tokyo. The performance included Latin, country, and big-band arrangements of tunes from Shigeru Miyamoto's landmark games. For Nintendo fans it was a star-studded event; emcee Benimaru Itoh, a flamboyant *manga* artist and musician who plays a mean *Super Mario* theme on the acoustic guitar, was joined by composer Koji Kondo and Shigeru Miyamoto, who played his one claim to musical fame, the *Donkey Kong* theme, on his own guitar onstage. A vocal theme song from the *Legend of Zelda* series, featuring lyrics written by Miyamoto, was part of the evening's set list.

One important thing that all three of these events have in common is that they each consisted of music that was also released on CD.* Mind you, these CDs were not produced as special-edition prizes for mail-away contests, nor were they included free with magazines. Rather, they were *sold*, at a premium price, in most major Japanese CD stores. "Game music" in Japan is nothing short of a pop-culture phenomenon on its own. Not only are CD releases of game soundtracks hugely popular with fans of the games, but some have even achieved mainstream popularity. And live recordings of game music concerts, as described above, are perennial best sellers.

★ In addition, a DVD video of Sakuraba's concert was released. Recognizing the growing worldwide appeal of Sakuraba's music, the label agreed to make the DVD region-free so that overseas customers could play it on any country's DVD hardware.

Game music got off to an inauspicious start. On April 25, 1984, Namco released *Video Game Music* on cassette and LP on the Alfa Records label for 2000 yen.[1] Containing the original soundtracks from a few Namco arcade games like *Pac-Man*, *Dig Dug*, and *Galaga*, it was the first video game soundtrack ever commercially released. It was, essentially, a novelty record. Namco followed it up later that year with a twelve-inch extended play record that contained the soundtrack to one game, *Super Xevious*. These were the only two video game soundtrack releases in 1984; for one year Namco owned the market.

Only one album was released in 1985: *The Return of Video Game Music*, featuring music from another handful of Namco titles. But the seeds of a phenomenon had been planted with the concurrent Famicom boom. Twenty-seven video game soundtrack albums were released in 1986, about half of which also appeared on Sony's then-new Compact Disc audio format, which cost from two to three times the price of a cassette or LP.

Many of these were also released by Alfa Records and were similar to Namco's albums, but they featured the music of other major video game companies—Hudson, Capcom, Tecmo, Sega, and Konami, among others. One release, called *Famicom Music*, collected the original soundtracks from various Famicom games. Many of these albums were various *arranged* versions of music from *Super Mario Bros.* That is to say, this was not the music as it was heard coming out of the Famicom. Instead, it was played on live instruments or top-dollar electronic synthesizers that far outstripped the Famicom's meager (if relatively powerful for a video game system) sound chip.

In 1987, thirty-nine soundtracks were released. One of them was *Dragon Quest In Concert*, a live recording of Koichi Sugiyama's music from the first two *Dragon Quest* titles, performed by the Tokyo Strings Ensemble in Tokyo's Suntory Hall on August 20th of that year. It was arguably with this concert and subsequent CD release that game music became something more than a novelty item—it became legitimate music. Sugiyama was a popular composer, but there was still something inherently childish, or nerdish, or at least comical about listening to a CD full of Famicom-generated tones. But a concert by a string orchestra, well, that was downright *classy*.

In any case, it was after 1987 that things began to snowball. Sixty-two titles in 1988. Eighty-seven in 1989. One hundred thirty-five in 1990. The numbers grew little by little until 1998 saw over and *four hundred sixty-three* video game soundtracks released, all in the span of one year. Things quieted down a bit after this period of unbridled enthusiasm; "only" two hundred fifty game music CDs were released in all of 2001.

So what *were* all these CDs? For the most part, they fell into the same categories as the handful of titles that were released in 1987: original soundtracks (or OSTs) that reproduced the entire musical score exactly as it was heard on the video game system, and *arranged* albums that featured music composed for a game but performed on either high-powered synthesizers that sounded much better than the game system's hardware or other live instrumentation. Arranged albums fell into any and all genres, from orchestral to hip-hop dance to piano solo to New Age to rock guitar and everything in between.

Many of these CDs are basically tie-in products; much like soundtrack CDs are released along with Hollywood films here in the US, video games in Japan will typically get their own soundtrack CD regardless of whether the music is of

> **Sakuraba's new CDs sell to Sakuraba fans even if they have no intention of playing the latest *Star Ocean* game.**

Dragon Quest quality. But for some select series and composers, the music takes on a life of its own, separate from the games, and the soundtracks practically sell themselves. Sakuraba's new CDs sell to Sakuraba fans even if they have no

intention of playing the latest *Star Ocean* game. Many CDs aren't even tied in to a specific game release at all, but are compilations featuring tracks from previous games in a series or, in some rare cases, selected tracks from a wide variety of games.

So why did this phenomenon spring up only in Japan? A trip to nearly any music store there will solve one piece of the puzzle. Find the 'game music' section in the CD racks—there is always one, whether you are in a multi-floored Tower Records, a tiny mom-and-pop-shop selling used discs, or even the CD section of a department store. This applies to most every genre of music. Japan is a music lover's paradise; music stores have huge, sprawling selections to serve the startlingly eclectic musical tastes of the nation's highly homogenous populace.

Once you've found the Game Music section, note that in almost every case it is next to, or sometimes mixed in with, a similarly large selection labeled 'anime music.' Soundtracks to *anime* are just as popular in Japan as game music soundtracks, and they're more closely related to game music than they are to movie soundtrack CDs. This is because both are *original scores*, which is exactly what movie soundtracks are *not*. Although all Hollywood films feature original music, this doesn't always make it onto the CD rack in Wal-Mart. Instead, a 'movie soundtrack' often contains a handpicked selection of current popular music that may or may not actually be played during the movie whose logo and stars adorn the CD cover. So in Japan, there was already a market and a fan base of original instrumental compositions. That's one piece of the puzzle.

Take home your new game music, break the shrink wrap, take care not to damage the protective *obi*, or spine card, which wraps around the side of every CD sold in Japan—if the CD ever goes out of print, as many do each year in Japan's whirlwind of popular culture, having the *obi* et cetera in pristine, complete condition will send the CD's collectible value soaring. Then put the CD into your player as you peruse the extensive liner notes, messages from the composer, and various bonus inserts that inevitably come packaged with nearly every CD in Japan. Listen to the first track or so, and you'll start to realize another reason for game music fandom: this stuff is just plain *great*, on a higher plane of quality than most of what passes for in-game music outside of Japan.

Why? How? Is it because of their perfectionist attitudes? Perhaps. Is it because the video game industry in Japan is seen as an entirely legitimate career for a young musician of the *shikaku sedai* "visual generation," much like the talented young artists of the generation who eschewed oil painting and sculpture for careers in *manga*? That's probably part of it, too. In any case, the difference is so profound that former head of the Sega Music Group, Spencer Nilson, when interviewed by JC Herz for her book *Joystick Nation*, seemed convinced that there was something *intrinsic in the Japanese* that explained their ability to create incredible music with the Sega Genesis sound hardware, something Nilson's American teams simply weren't able to do:

"The Japanese are *amazing* at what they can do with the chip. It's night and day sometimes… They use a whole different type of code. It's *perfection*… It's much more entrenched in their way of doing things and in their culture."[2]

Nilson points out that the Japanese composers at Sega, rather than compose sweeping music and try to compress it down into 16-bit sounds, compose music in programming language, creating tracks that, first and foremost, sound good on the computer hardware.

It is difficult to resist comparing this from-the-bottom-up method of music composition, where the machine's capabilities are taken firmly into consideration during the creative process, to Miyamoto's method of designing his inventive, animated, colorful characters during the early Famicom and Super Famicom days. Rather than draw characters in sketchbooks, then try to shrink them down to a small block of pixels, Miyamoto would always draw the dot-picture first, and then make the instruction-manual and packaging graphics from that. So in these early decades, Japanese creative work on video games seems to have *begun* with the ones and zeroes, not *ended* with them. This may have made all the difference.

As this genre, this phenomenon, grew in sheer numbers and broadened in variety, Nobuo Uematsu's *Final Fantasy* music grew along with it. Now, over a decade and a half since his first CD release, from the early days of squeezing out innovative melodies on primitive computer hardware to composing majestic John Williams-esque scores that carry the dramatic action of recent *Final Fantasy* titles, Nobuo Uematsu has managed an incredibly extensive discography. To get a sense of the scope and variety of his work as well as the many, varied types of game music soundtracks released by the hundreds every year in Japan, it is highly useful to look at each of Uematsu's *Final Fantasy* albums in turn.

All Sounds of Final Fantasy I·II (12/21/1988): An OST collecting all the tracks from the first two *Final Fantasy* games, plus two synthesizer-arranged medleys that began and ended the disc. This was released a week after *Final Fantasy II*, so it was clearly a tie-in album to that game. The front cover was identical to that of the Famicom *FFII* cartridge, and a foldout poster inside featured Yoshitaka Amano's artwork from the game, including a world map and bestiary.

Symphonic Suite Final Fantasy (7/25/1989): Following closely in the footsteps of *Dragon Quest*, a *Final Fantasy* orchestral concert was arranged the following year. The concert contained seven "scenes," medleys of tunes from the first two games, arranged by Katsuhisa Hattori, who conducted the Tokyo Symphony Orchestra at Yuport Hall on May 20, 1989. Again, a foldout poster in lieu of a booklet contained liner notes, photos of the event, and Amano's illustrations.

Legend of The Eternal Wind (5/25/1990): An arranged album of *Final Fantasy III* music, *Yuukyuu no Kaze Densetsu* is quite a significant, yet odd, soundtrack release for a few reasons. First, it was released in lieu of an OST, not alongside one. Second, preceding each track was a narrative, spoken in English, that told the story of *Final Fantasy III* in increments. This made it an early example of a *drama CD*—audio dramas, in the old *Little Orphan Annie* radio style, that mixed narrative with music. Finally, this album features Uematsu's first attempts at writing vocal songs, two tracks that did not appear in the game itself, sung by female vocalist Ohtaka Shizuru. Vocal themes would figure prominently into the *Final Fantasy* catalog and make appearances in the actual games as soon as technology allowed. What's more, this CD was the first *FF* arranged album to truly encompass Uematsu's entire range, segueing neatly from up-tempo rock "battle music" to calming ballads to orchestral majesty.

Final Fantasy IV (6/14/1991): The OST release of the music from *Final Fantasy IV* is, sadly, a rather disappointing one. It's not that the music wasn't good; quite the opposite, as *FFIV*'s soundtrack, using the souped-up Sony-designed sound chip on the Super Famicom, was some of Uematsu's best work to date both creatively and technically. The problem was that, to fit the lengthy soundtrack onto one CD, each piece of music was "looped" only once rather than twice as was typically done. Game music had to be written to loop back on itself; most OSTs played the music twice through and then faded out just as the third repetition began. Because the music was not looped twice on the *Final Fantasy IV* release, the tracks were only a minute or so each.

Final Fantasy III (7/15/91): *Final Fantasy III*'s OST was released a month *after FFIV*'s. The reason seems to be that Square was in the process of forming its own CD label, Square Brand, at this time, and *FFIII* was temporarily lost in the shuffle. By the time they were ready to release *FFIII*, *FFIV* took priority because it was the hot new game. But that didn't stop *FFIII*'s OST from being released on its own, which is further illustration that CD releases had already gone beyond being mere marketing tie-in products.

Final Fantasy IV Celtic Moon (10/28/1991): The first arranged album to be released on the Square Brand label, *Celtic Moon* was Uematsu's most ambitious effort to date and perhaps the best arranged album that he has ever produced. Recorded in Dublin, Ireland in the last two weeks of August 1991, *Celtic Moon* had the feel of an Irish pub session with seven accomplished traditional musicians, a few of whom were on the cusp of stardom. Accordion player Sharon Shannon released her solo album in Ireland just as *Celtic Moon* was being recorded; it was a huge surprise hit that sold over fifty thousand copies. Later, arranger and fiddle player Maire Breatnach, flautist

Cormac Breatnach, and tin whistle/uilleann pipes player Ronan Browne would be heard the world over on the soundtrack to the Irish dance and music Broadway spectacular *Riverdance*. Browne, a founding member of the breakthrough fusion ensemble *Afro Celt Sound System*, would later release, in Japan only, two albums of various game music arranged for uilleann pipes, called *Melody of Legend*.

Uematsu's music seems to have lent itself almost effortlessly to Irish traditional arrangement. Indeed, early game music and Irish traditional have a lot in common: simple, repeating, easy-to-learn melodies arranged to get the maximum sound out of a small set of instruments.

***Final Fantasy IV Piano Collections* (4/21/1992):** Except for one bonus track at the album's finish, this album is entirely made up of piano solo arrangements. The original pressing included a full-size book of piano sheet music for all fourteen pieces, but they weren't for beginners. They were quite complex and consequently highly enjoyable to listen to, but difficult to play.

***Final Fantasy V* (12/7/1992):** *Final Fantasy V*'s OST release fixed the main problem of *FFIV*'s, expanding the length of each track. This required that the soundtrack be a double-disc release, with the accompanying price increase. Of course, the higher price of ¥3300 wasn't that much more expensive than what consumers were paying for single-disc releases at that time (most were around ¥2800 and some were ¥3000), so it didn't seem to matter.

***Final Fantasy V Dear Friends* (3/25/1993):** For *Final Fantasy V*'s arranged version, Uematsu again traveled to Europe, this time to Helsinki, Finland. Recorded one week in early January, *Dear Friends* prominently featured the close harmonies of female vocal group Angelin Tytöt, singing songs set to *FFV*'s music in Saami, the ancient language of Scandinavia's native Laplanders. Some tracks are straightforward arrangements of the Super Famicom music, others are highly experimental, giving the album a New Age feel.

***Final Fantasy V Piano Collections* (6/21/1993):** The second Piano Collections also featured a book of sheet music, this time set to songs from *Final Fantasy V*. The fan favorite battle music "Big Bridge (Battle With Gilgamesh)" featured as an unlikely selection on this disc. The original Square Brand pressings of these CD/book sets went out of print early and still fetch high prices on online auction sites.

***Final Fantasy VI* (3/25/1994):** The final Super Famicom installment of the series (and the last *Final Fantasy* game to appear on a Nintendo console for nearly a decade) was, at 24 megabits in size, half again as large as *Final Fantasy V*. The game was much longer and was split into two distinct halves that were emotionally quite disparate. Thus it needed more music. *Final*

Fantasy VI's original soundtrack was three discs long, almost unheard of for a Super Famicom game. It remains to this day one of Uematsu's most impressive works.

Final Fantasy VI Grand Finale (5/25/1994): Another arranged album, and another trip to Europe for Uematsu and company. This time, to do justice to the fan favorite "opera sequence" (see Chapter 4), the entire album was recorded in Italy by the string Ensemble Archi Della Scala and the Orchestra Synfonica Di Milano. For the album's final track, soprano Svetla Krasteva brought the "Aria De Mezzo Carattere" to life. The recording would later accompany the realistic FMV sequences that were added onto the PlayStation remake of *Final Fantasy VI*.*

> ★ Although performed by an orchestra, this is not generally listed among 'orchestral' albums, because that designation usually refers to a recording of a live concert performance.

Final Fantasy VI Piano Collections (6/25/1994): The third and, for many years, final Piano Collections arrangement. In the summer of 2001, NTT Publishing (Square's second music label) re-released the three Piano Collections albums, without the books of sheet music, which were eventually released separately and can be found in most every sheet-music store in Japan.

Pray (6/25/1994): Released on the same day as *Final Fantasy Piano Collections*, *Pray* was the first disc in a new series: *Final Fantasy Vocal Collections*. Twelve of Uematsu's most famous songs were given lyrics and performed by Risa Ohki, an Osaka College of Music-trained singer, keyboardist and composer who had been a member of three rock bands since her recording debut in 1986 and whose songs had appeared in various Japanese television commercials. All this, including the names of the products for which her songs had shilled, appeared in a brief, straightforward biography in the album's liner notes.

Phantasmagoria (10/26/1994): Uematsu's first and only album of non-game music, *Phantasmagoria* featured Uematsu on keyboards and synthesizers blended with a host of other musicians playing various traditional acoustic instruments. Some tracks featured poetry read over them, some written by Uematsu himself. The end result was a pleasant, innovative album that might be classified as World music, although the music couldn't be identified as belonging to any specific part of the world. The final track was a vocal version of the *Final Fantasy* main theme song, which had been recorded previously and used for the *Final Fantasy VI* television commercial.

F.F. Mix (11/26/1994): Continuing to expand the genres and styles of music that the *Final Fantasy* arranged discs encompassed, Uematsu enlisted a group of artists to remix some *FF* tunes into thumping dance beats. Tracks like "Main Theme of Final Fantasy IV (phat stylee remix)" and "The Prelude

Crystal Mix" made up about a third of this budget-priced release. The rest of the disc featured arranged versions and unreleased tracks that had previously been available only on hard-to-find single releases, like *Final Fantasy IV Minimum Album* and *Final Fantasy V Mambo De Chocobo*.

Final Fantasy 1987-1994 (11/26/1994): Released on the same day as *F.F. Mix*, *Final Fantasy 1987-1994* was a collection of tracks from the previous arranged albums. But it wasn't merely a greatest-hits disc. Four of the tracks were remixes and another two were entirely new. As a bonus for the diehard *Final Fantasy* music fans, the first pressing included a small hardcover book, filled with essays penned by Uematsu about music composition, enclosed with the disc in a handsome sleeve.

Love Will Grow (11/25/1995): The follow-up to *Pray*, the second Vocal Collections disc included Ikuko Noguchi alongside Risa Ohki. Another interesting aspect of the Vocal Collections albums is that Ohki could sing beautifully in not only Japanese and English but also Portuguese and French, meaning that the music on the albums, much like Uematsu's instrumental compositions, was not tied down to any specific real-world culture or location. It had, much like Uematsu's compositions, a *mukokuseki* (non-country-specific) appeal.

Final Fantasy VII (2/10/1997): The first *Final Fantasy* release for the Sony PlayStation CD-ROM-based video game system, *Final Fantasy VII* was a huge PlayStation game at three discs. Its OST release soon after took up even more space, a full four discs. Although the CD game format afforded Uematsu the chance to use real audio formats for his soundtracks, he didn't. To save disc space and thus increase the number of tracks he was able to fit into the game, he continued to use conventional programming techniques, although the music sounded much better thanks to the PlayStation's superior sound chip.

Final Fantasy VII Reunion Tracks (10/22/1997): Perhaps four discs full of music may have been too much to handle? *Reunion Tracks* was for the most part a pared-down version of the *FFVII* soundtrack, featuring a much more accessible lineup at a more affordable price. The final three tracks were orchestrated versions, making *Reunion Tracks* attractive to fans that had purchased the full OST release.

Final Fantasy VIII (3/1/1999): This OST is notable for a number of firsts. It was the first *Final Fantasy* soundtrack to include a handful of pieces recorded with live instrumentation in the game itself. One of these songs was the series' first vocal theme to appear within the game: "Eyes on Me," sung in English by Hong Kong pop superstar Faye Wong. For composing "Eyes on

Me," Uematsu would win his first-ever Gold Disc award in Japan for Best Foreign-Language Song.

Final Fantasy VIII Fithos Lusec Wecos Vinosec (11/20/1999): FFVIII's arranged album featured a few songs that were identical to the original soundtrack, because they'd already been arranged for orchestra. For this album, a handful of songs that had originally appeared in rougher, synthesized form in the game were given the full-orchestrated treatment. Like *Reunion Tracks*, it was much easier to listen to one disc of the best tracks, rather than four discs containing *every* track.

Final Fantasy VIII Piano Collections (1/21/2000): Early the next year, the Piano Collections series made a comeback after a six-year absence. This seemed to be related to Uematsu's growing partnership with new Square musician Shiro Hamaguchi. Whereas different people arranged each of the other *Final Fantasy* albums, Hamaguchi had done *Reunion Tracks*, *FLWV*, and now this arrangement.

Final Fantasy IX (8/30/2000): Another four-disc release. To record *Final Fantasy IX*'s vocal theme, Uematsu and Hamaguchi worked with Japanese vocalist Emiko Shiratori. Like Faye Wong, Shiratori already had an established fan base but her solo work was more in tune with the style of previous *FF* vocal albums. The song, titled "Melodies of Life," was originally released as a single on Shiratori's, label King Records. It was used to promote the upcoming game and OST release as well as Shiratori's upcoming solo album, *Cross My Heart*. That album was released two months later and contained, in addition to "Melodies of Life," another Uematsu-penned song as a new vocal version of the *Final Fantasy* main theme.

Final Fantasy IX Plus (12/6/2000): As a matter of fact, Final Fantasy IX's total OST wouldn't fit on four discs. There were many brief minute- or thirty-second-long tracks that didn't loop during the game play but instead accompanied the game's many FMV sequences. Many of these were left off the original release but were collected here on a budget-priced separate album. Bonus tracks, including arrangements of older FF songs that appeared in FFIX, as well as songs that never made the final cut, were also included.

Final Fantasy IX Piano Collections (1/24/2001): Performed by Amsterdam-born Louis Leerink and arranged by Hamaguchi, the fifth in the Piano Collections series seemed to indicate that the tradition was starting up yet again. The arrangements on this disc, above all others, are stunning in their complexity; at times it is difficult to believe that one is listening to a piano solo.

Potion: Relaxin' With Final Fantasy (2/21/2001, 12/19/2001): *Final Fantasy* music, like most RPG music, needed to span several styles and genres. For example, rock music was appropriate for battling, while light, relaxing melodies worked for exploring cities and towns. *Potion*, along with a second volume released later that year, was a greatest-hits collection of beautiful, slow, heartstring-tugging tunes from all the prior *Final Fantasy* albums. Both featured one newly arranged bonus track; the first was from fellow Square Sounds composer Yoko Shimomura, whose OSTs to *Super Mario RPG* and *Legend of Mana* were earning her a rabid fan base.

Final Fantasy X (8/1/2001): The OST to *Final Fantasy* X had even more firsts. It was Uematsu's debut on the PlayStation 2, and it was the first *Final Fantasy* soundtrack in which two other composers, Junya Nakano and Masashi Hamauzu, would share composing duties. Okinawan vocalist Rikki performed *FFX*'s theme song, "Suteki Da Ne" ("Isn't It Wonderful"), in keeping with the Okinawan style of the game's setting and character designs.

Final Fantasy X Piano Collections (2/20/2002): If not for the *Final Fantasy* live orchestral concert that took place in Tokyo on the same day, the release of *Final Fantasy X Piano Collections* would have been the biggest *Final Fantasy* music-related event to take place on the twentieth of February, 2002.

20020220 Music From Final Fantasy (5/9/2002): A recording of the second *Final Fantasy* orchestrated concert, the first since 1989, 20020220 was a double-disc set that featured the voice actors for *Final Fantasy X*'s main characters as emcees to introduce each landmark piece of music with light humor and background. The one-off show was such a fantastic success that a Japanese tour and US concert were planned for 2004. The mirror-image title of the CD comes from writing the date of the show in Japanese year/day/month order.

Final Fantasy XI (6/5/2002): An online game like *Final Fantasy XI* doesn't need all sorts of orchestrated movements to bring dramatic flair to storyline cinemas because, well, there are practically none. Like the early *Final Fantasy* game, the music is far more area-based; the same song loops repeatedly, simply depending on your location in the game.

Final Fantasy I·II Original Soundtrack (10/23/2002): When Square released upgraded versions of the first two *Final Fantasy* games on the PlayStation in late 2002, they needed upgraded soundtracks. Uematsu and The Black Mages band mate (see below) Tsuyoshi Sekito delivered far more than that. Their end product amounted to a double-disc collection of every tune from the first two games redone in a variety of styles and with amazing instrumentation.

The Black Mages (2/19/2003): The release of this album will go down in game music history as being one of the defining events of Uematsu's career. Although fan favorite *Final Fantasy* music had always included the hard-rocking battle arrangements, few were ever given the fully realized treatment. *The Black Mages*, the self-titled debut album of a *Final Fantasy* rock band featuring Uematsu on keyboards, Sekito on guitars, and four more Square musicians, was the prelude to the concert described at the beginning of this chapter.

Final Fantasy VII Piano Collections (12/3/2003): As Piano Collections discs became more and more popular and the time between *Final Fantasy* releases grew longer and longer, Square knew they had to release *Final Fantasy VII Piano Collections* very late in the game, so to speak. However, releasing an album entirely devoted to songs from a very old game speaks volumes about how some game music had grown far away from being mere merchandising tie-in.

Final Fantasy Song Book Mahoroba (3/10/2004): The most recent *Final Fantasy* album from Uematsu (as of this writing) is another vocal collection, though not the third in the Vocal Collections series. The songs on this album, sung (and written in some cases) by Manami Kiyota, are all in Japanese. Overall, they are softer and lighter versions of the tunes, interspersed with a few instrumental arrangements.

Even this extensive list is nowhere near exhaustive, as it leaves out:

CD singles: Examples include *Final Fantasy IV Minimum Album* and *Final Fantasy VI Special Tracks*.

Albums that feature *Final Fantasy* music but not tied to a *Final Fantasy*-titled game: Examples include the soundtrack to the *Final Fantasy* spin-off kart racing game *Chocobo Racing* and the *Game Music In Concert* series, live recordings of concerts featuring Super Famicom game music arranged for orchestra.

Other albums with compositions by Uematsu that feature no *Final Fantasy* music: Examples include the original soundtracks for *Chrono Trigger* and *Hanjuku Hero In 3-D*.

Final Fantasy albums with no original Uematsu compositions: Examples include *Final Fantasy X-2 Original Soundtrack* and *Final Fantasy Tactics Advance Radio Edition*.

If all these were included, still only scratching the surface of the massive market for game music CDs, the list would more than double in length.[*]

* Readers who seek a complete *Final Fantasy* discography, complete with CD cover scans, item numbers, and various miscellany should read the excellent website Daryl's Library (www.ffmusic.info).

What does all this mean? Reading through the list above, you can sense the evolution of video game music CDs as a cultural phenomenon and as a product. We've seen releases progress from single-disc original soundtracks with the occasional knocked-out, synth-arranged bonus track to four-disc gargantuan releases with arranged albums that run the gamut from rock to Celtic to opera. There are other popular video game music series to which any of these examples could apply, but Uematsu has been the jack-of-all-trades. If there is a trend in video game music, he has dabbled in it, been a leader in it, or begun it altogether.

It was only a matter of time, then, before video game music fandom started to make its way across the Pacific. Of course, the music had always been available in the US because the *games* were. And many an aficionado has stories of trying to transfer his favorite music to cassette tape while the game was playing. Square, for its part, realized that it might do well selling US versions of its soundtrack CDs. They released three: the single-disc OST to *Secret of Mana*, another for a US-only Square RPG called *Secret of Evermore*, and *Kefka's Domain*, the full three-CD OST for *Final Fantasy VI*, which had been released in the US as *Final Fantasy III*.

Things were then pretty quiet for a while. Square's US branch went out of business only to be re-established in Los Angeles[*] when Square shifted its alliance to Sony, whose American offices were in nearby Foster City. In 1999 they released *FFVIII Music Collection*, the full four-disc OST. Like the earlier discs, it was available only through direct mail order with the company, a practice that was cost saving if impractical and unlikely to produce more than a handful of purchases. So it was with the intent of getting *Final Fantasy* music into American record stores that Square partnered with Tokyopop, another LA-based company that produced *manga* magazines, *anime* videos, and the like. While Tokyopop's CD distribution tended to reach most reliably into game and *anime* specialty stores, their CDs could also be found in mainstream record stores.

[*] Square's original US branch was in the same Redmond, Washington business park as Nintendo.

Over the next few years, Tokyopop released six *Final Fantasy* game music CDs among a handful of other releases[†]. For the releases of *FFIX* and *FFX*, Tokyopop produced single-disc best-collection OSTs. The *FFIX* collection included an American-exclusive bonus track. For the release of *Final Fantasy Chronicles*, a PlayStation title that included ports of the Super Famicom games *FFIV* and *Chrono Trigger*, each game's OST plus a bonus track was released separately.

And in late 2001, the first two full albums of arranged *Final Fantasy* music were released in the US, called *N Generation* and *S Generation*—'N' and 'S' standing for the manufacturers of the systems on which the featured games were released. The track list to *N Generation* was identical to *Final Fantasy 1987-1994* (see above), and Uematsu selected the listing for *S Generation*.* Sales were ultimately not enough to continue; *N* and *S Generation* were particularly tricky to sell in America because they weren't tied to any specific game release.

† Mostly merchandising tie-in CDs with little to no musical value, like the OST to Sega's *Sonic Adventure 2* or Namco's *Tekken Tag Tournament* fighting game.

★ Your humble author penned the liner notes to these two discs.

That, however, is not the true story of game music fandom in America. What actually happened had nothing to do with Square's partnership with Tokyopop and had everything to do with the Internet. It started as just a few files that enthusiastic fans had transcribed into MIDI format. As access speeds and technologies grew faster, the lucky few American fans that had access to Japanese music stores ripped the songs from their CDs and uploaded them in MPG, MP2, and finally MP3 format.

The type of Americans *otaku* that were likely to be fans of game music were also likely to be computer savvy. So game music started to spread like wildfire as the Internet did the same. "Game music MP3s" became the preferred and prevalent format, not only for its ease of use and accessibility but because it was the only way to get the music in the first place. This started a grassroots fan base, but it also drastically reduced the potential audience that would be willing to go out and *buy* CDs if they were ever released in America. And maybe it was true that, as the argument went, piracy of pop singles from the radio bounced off of giant record companies like a pebble off a tank…

…But it certainly wasn't true for a small company looking to get a genre off the ground. And this went doubly when the 'company' in question was a group of fans looking to produce their own arranged CDs. That was the aim of Project Majestic Mix, which started in 1997 as the brainstorm of musician and Uematsu fan Stephen Kennedy. At the time, Kennedy was attending the College of the Ozarks at Pt. Lookout, Missouri, majoring in sound engineering and video production. It took Kennedy nearly two years of constant research and phone calls to Japan to finally get contact information for Nobuo Uematsu, who at the time was based in Honolulu while writing the music for *FFVIII*. Uematsu directed Kennedy to Square Sounds, who owned the rights to all of his work.

Many, many years and eight thousand man hours later, *Project Majestic Mix: A Tribute To Nobuo Uematsu* was finally released, a truly unique take on Uematsu's music from a host of musically inclined fans. "For a long time," wrote Kennedy in the group's mission statement, "the adolescent 'blips' and 'bleeps' of our time have shrouded many composers' true talents... Our aspirations for this project were to take old songs fellow gamers have grown to love, and arrange them in ways we've only pondered hearing them; ways that would not only be entertaining to us, but even to those who knew nothing of the games."

★ The emergence of eBay also helped to get Uematsu's *Final Fantasy* CDs distributed to fans around the world willing to pay the exorbitant prices that such auctions reached. Sadly, most of the game and *anime* music CDs on eBay ended up being Taiwanese knockoffs of the original Japanese products.

The Project Majestic Mix phenomenon was doubly amazing, because it was an entirely volunteer project *and* the massive costs of royalty fees and production were underwritten by over $40,000 of donations from about 1300 fans. Kennedy and company first solicited check and money order donations through their website (www.majesticmix.com). But the donation process became significantly easier when PayPal, the online credit card-based payment service, grew in popularity and ease of use alongside the online auction site eBay.★

Now, with money in the bank and solid working relationships from which to license music, Project Majestic Mix lives on. A second album, the cleverly titled *SquareDance*, took the concept of Uematsu's *F.F. Mix* several steps further; it was a double-disc extravaganza of classic Square tunes remixed in a thumping club style. Further plans for Project Majestic Mix include a trance album featuring music from video games including *Final Fantasy* and *Secret of Mana*, of course, but also *ICO* (see Chapter 10), *Metroid*, and Microsoft's *Halo*.

And then there's OneUp Studios (www.oneupstudios.com), a group of musicians who appear on each Project Majestic Mix release and play at various video game fan conventions under the name The OneUp Mushrooms. They've released their own CDs. The first was a tribute album that celebrated the work of another Square composer named Yasunori Mitsuda.

MAKING A DRAGON CRY: YASUNORI MITSUDA[3]

I interviewed Yasunori Mitsuda in November 2002 at a restaurant close to Mitsuda's Procyon Studio. A former Square staff composer turned freelance, his soundtracks for such games as Chrono Trigger, Xenogears, Chrono Cross, *and* Tsugunai *have made him world renowned. Some consider his work to be even better than Nobuo Uematsu's. For me, Mitsuda's music is always the highlight of whatever game it appears in—his songs make an otherwise boring game memorable and a great game a classic.*

Whether the style is orchestral, Irish traditional, or otherworldly, it's possible to enjoy Mitsuda's music without ever having played the game for which it's composed. I found myself humming his songs in my head as we walked into the restaurant, a Denny's-styled chain called Jonathan's, picked because of the free drink refills. It was as noisy as an American family restaurant, and Mitsuda's voice is soft and shy. I strained to hear him over the din.

"I was a *very* active child," Mitsuda begins. "I loved exercise and sports— baseball, basketball, kendo, judo, and track and field. My older sister had a piano, and although I wanted to play too, I really hated practicing. So you couldn't call me a musician in those days, just an athlete." All through school, however, Mitsuda developed an appreciation for music. "When I got to high school," he says, "I started to get interested in films as well. So I decided that I would make music for films, and went to a junior college for music to study composition."

Mitsuda is reluctant to publicize his alma mater. "Because there aren't really any good teachers there anymore," he says. So if people knew I went to this school, they might want to go there…and I'd actually rather they didn't." Still, Mitsuda remembers his teachers fondly. "They were mostly professional musicians, and I would follow them around and assist them. That gave me more experience in a lot of different fields, not just music theory."

While he was still learning composition, Mitsuda took some part-time work that would prove to be the beginning of his career. "I worked for Enix as a sound manipulator. I worked on *Elnard* (called *The 7th Saga* in the US) for the Super Famicom, and did sound effects for some PC games on the PC-8801. I don't remember the names of them, though."

On graduating, Mitsuda applied for an open position as a composer for Squaresoft, even though he had never played any of their games, not even *Final Fantasy*. He remembers initial dissatisfaction with the position. "The thing is, even though it said Composer on my business card, I was only doing sound effects and programming. I worked on *Hanjuku Hero*, *Romancing SaGa 2*, and *Seiken Densetsu 2*. Oh, and I did some stuff for *Final Fantasy V* too— you know the dragon's cry at the beginning? That was me."

How exactly does one make a dragon's cry? "Well, you take a waveform of the notes, then you add noise, and mix them together until it sounds like a

dragon's cry [laughs]. I was playing with it, and [Nobuo] Uematsu just came running up, and said, 'What's that sound? We've got to use that sound!' But anyway, I didn't like being stuck as a sound programmer. And one day I finally snapped, and I went to [Hironobu] Sakaguchi, and I told him that if he didn't let me compose songs, I'd quit. And so he said, okay, you're going to do *Chrono Trigger*."

And just like that, Mitsuda was given composing duties for what would become one of the most memorable RPG experiences of all time. *Chrono Trigger* was a collaboration of epic proportions. *Dragon Quest*'s scenario writer Yuji Horii and character designer Akira Toriyama would partner with the *Final Fantasy* designers to create an original RPG. With some of the best graphics on the Super Famicom and a time-travel story far more offbeat and crazy than anything *Final Fantasy* could, by design, ever be, *Chrono Trigger* needed a unique and appealing soundtrack to match.

"I wanted to create music that wouldn't fit into any established genre… music of an imaginary world. The game's director, Masato Kato, was my close friend, and so I'd always talk with him about the setting and the scene before going into writing." Mitsuda's perfectionist nature was beginning to show, and this would actually land him in the hospital before he could finish the music. "Originally, I was working on it all by myself. And I worked so hard that I got stomach ulcers, and I was sent to the hospital. And after that, Uematsu-san came in to help out."

After *Chrono Trigger*, Mitsuda partnered with Nobuo Uematsu to score *Front Mission: Gun Hazard*, then *Radical Dreamers*, a graphical text adventure released on Nintendo's ill-fated Satellaview add-on for the Super Famicom that let Japanese satellite customers download small games via satellite reception. Although *Radical Dreamers* was technically the follow-up to *Chrono Trigger*, the two games shared very little in common save for Mitsuda's exceptional music. After that, he acted as music director on *Tobal No. 1*, a martial arts fighting game that was Square's first PlayStation release. His next project would be his first true solo work, an RPG called *Xenogears*.

Opinion is harshly divided over *Xenogears*. Its fans consider it nothing less than an epic work of literature. Its detractors find the game play frustrating, the story overwrought, and the religious overtones trite. But most everyone agrees that Mitsuda's soundtrack is exceptional. The Celtic influences that had barely trickled into *Chrono Trigger* and *Radical Dreamers* were turned on full-force for *Xenogears*. "I had read the design document, and I wanted to put those religious themes into the music. But I didn't just want to make simple religious music; I wanted music that felt religious, but from a different angle."

"Also, I had a feeling that a Celtic boom was about to hit Japan. And it did, right after *Xenogears* came *Titanic* and Riverdance. And a lot of Irish musicians started to come to Japan. So it was just as I predicted," he adds with a satisfied smile. Riverdance, the Irish music and dance spectacular that hit it big on Broadway, featured such master-class Celtic performers as Maire Breatnach on the fiddle and Davy Spillane on the uilleann pipes. To record the live tracks for *Xenogears* and its arranged version, titled *Creid* (a Gaelic word meaning "believe"), Mitsuda traveled to Ireland to work with Breatnach, Spillane, and other accomplished musicians, including Joanne Hogg, the vocalist for the renowned Celtic/Christian band Iona.

Mitsuda left these talented artists room to improvise. "I had written about eighty percent of the arrangements," he recalls. "The rest I left open, for the artists to just fill in. A lot of the ideas for the arranged version don't come until you get in the studio anyway. The guitar solo in the opening theme, 'Small Two Of Pieces,' was improvised in the studio. Also, Davy Spillane's solos, like on the title track of *Creid*."

Regardless of their feelings on the game as a whole, *Xenogears* had Squaresoft fans asking who composed that brilliant music. *Final Fantasy* composer Nobuo Uematsu had long been revered as game music's master, but it was becoming clear that Mitsuda was, if nothing else, heir apparent to the throne. *Xenogears* was enough of a personal success for Mitsuda that he readied for his next great leap. "I felt that I had done all that I wanted to do with Square—in other words, I was satisfied with what I had accomplished there. It was the first time I ever got to be completely free with my work, but on a company level, I was beginning to lose that freedom. And I didn't want to. I also wanted to be able to take on side projects."

So Mitsuda quit Squaresoft in 1998 and began working on a freelance basis, establishing Procyon Studio and scoring games like Nintendo's *Mario Party*, Hudson's *Bomberman* for the N64, and an RPG called *Tsugunai* on the

PlayStation 2. But his two most high-profile works as a freelancer are *Chrono Cross* for Squaresoft and *Xenosaga* for Namco. *Chrono Cross* retained his now-trademark Celtic style, but *Xenosaga* was mostly orchestral, although it featured many of the same performers from *Xenogears*.

"The world of *Xenosaga* is different, isn't it? It called for a different atmosphere. With *Chrono Cross* I tried to reduce the instrumentation, to strip it down to a bare minimum, like how some songs are just the guitar. But with *Xenosaga*, I went in with the opposite goal; I wanted to see how much I could add! Lots of horns, lots of strings...lots of everything."

It is beyond a doubt the most technically ambitious soundtrack project on the PlayStation 2. "Of the forty-five tracks, only three used the built-in sound hardware of the PS2. The rest were true CD-quality audio files. Twenty of them were mike-recorded with live instruments, and the others were recorded by me with synthesizers," Mitsuda recalls.

> **I wanted to see how much I could add! Lots of horns, lots of strings...lots of everything.**

Mitsuda's success at creating memorable soundtracks may come from the fact that he looks at game music composition from a different angle than his peers do. "When you look at the end product, it might seem like all I did was put the music to the game. But the way I figure it, I not only make music that works in the game—I make music that I would want to listen to by itself."

Interestingly, Mitsuda doesn't think that other game music composers feel the way he does. "Whenever I talk to my colleagues, all of them say that I should compose music without ever thinking about putting out a CD. They see this as a side project. But, of course, what I want you to know is that the first priority is that the music has to match the scene of the game. The second priority is that it has to be a piece of music that I can listen to by itself."

Mitsuda demurs at the suggestion of a *Chrono Cross* arranged album, saying that he is "pretty satisfied with the soundtrack as it is." So what are his dreams? "I want to reunite all the members of Millennial Fair—the group from *Creid*—and have a live concert of that music. I also think I'd like to try writing the soundtrack to a musical play. Right now I'm on vacation. But I'm thinking about making a solo album, something close to *Creid*. I want to get a lot of musicians together and make something new.

"I just entered my thirties, and they say that musicians hit their prime in their thirties," he says. "So, the good stuff should be from now on."

MUSIC GAMES

I keep telling our musicians, why don't you stop making music for other peoples' games and try to design a music game instead?

— Shigeru Miyamoto

Music, in cinematic entertainment like film, animation, or video game, is not there merely because it is pleasant to listen to. The soundtrack is just as vital to the storytelling as the imagery. Writes Maureen Furniss in *Art In Motion: Animation Aesthetics*, "It is common for beginners to be enamored with the visual components of animation and give very little attention to the soundtrack. However, most people will find that the secret to success for many award-winning films is the care with which aural elements…have been handled."[4]

And indeed in video games, whether or not it is the sole 'secret to success,' we find a certain level of care taken in the aural elements of even the earliest successful ones, from the pleasing tones of *Pac-Man* to the in-game melodies of *Donkey Kong* that change to enhance the escalation of the action, the heightening of the tension. A bad game can be partially redeemed by a great OST, but few great games have bad soundtracks.

Music, then, is a powerful thing in the hands of a game designer who knows how to use it. But what if the player had *control* over that music? For as long as video game computer systems have been able to produce musical melodies, game designers have pondered that question. Early games that put the player in control of music were rarely games at all; instead, they promised to use the allure of video games to transform unsuspecting children into musicians. One high-profile product called *Miracle Piano Teaching System*, sold for the NES, included a half-size piano-style keyboard that plugged into the NES' controller port, as well as a NES cartridge containing dozens of lessons from beginner to expert. The *Miracle* was highly praised by educators but at nearly five hundred dollars for the entire package, few NES owners bought it.

A more common type of music video game let the user play at composing music. A well-known example would be the music composing tool in *Mario Paint*, a creative Super Nintendo game that let players draw artwork, animate it, and set it to music. Using an included PC-style mouse controller, players could drag musical notes into position on a staff, set the tempo, then play back their composition (in the editor, Mario ran across the top of the staff and jumped on each note as it played).

This was all very interesting, but merely prelude. On December 6, 1996, another "bizarre cartoon game from Japan" ended up inventing an explosively popular new genre out of whole cloth. That game was an early Sony PlayStation title called *Parappa The Rapper*. The game featured the adventures of a talking, cartoon, paper-thin dog decked out in funky clothes that learned to rap from six similarly odd *sensei*, such as a karate-chopping onion. *Parappa* blended its singular visual style with catchy music, off-the-wall lyrics, and a unique game play concept: the *sensei* would rap one line, then the player, as Parappa, would match them by pressing the correct controller

buttons with the right tempo. A smash success in Japan, it could be argued that *Parappa* was the pivot point on which the PlayStation turned from expensive geek toy to mainstream home appliance. Parappa became the Mario of the PlayStation in Japan; in the US it was critically acclaimed and popular, if not as earth-shakingly so.

Parappa was the first console game developed by a Sony designer named Masaya Matsuura. At thirty-five years old in 1996, Matsuura already had a career that would be the envy of any young musician. Born in Osaka, Matsuura was educated at the prestigious Ritsumeikan University, where he became fascinated with electronic music and teamed up with vocalist Mami "Chaka" Yasunori, a fellow Osakan, to form a band called PSY'S (pronounced "size"). They were signed to Sony's record label in 1985, when

Matsuura was twenty-four. PSY'S became widely known for being one of the first bands to garner pop music recognition for cutting edge computer-generated sounds. Matsuura and Chaka released over a dozen albums that generated a host of hit singles.

In 1993, looking for new challenges, Matsuura became the first Japanese musician to release his own CD-ROM multimedia title, a music-based effort for the Macintosh called *The Seven Colors*, which won the Multimedia Grand Prix for music software that year. In 1996, just after releasing his second CD-ROM for the Macintosh, a music-making title called *Tunin' Glue**, Matsuura disbanded PSY'S in order to work full time on his latest project.

★ *Tunin' Glue* was also released for the Pippin Atmark, a hybrid computer/game console released in Japan by Bandai.

As luck would have it, a friend who had worked at Sony Music but was now with the newly-formed Sony Computer Entertainment emailed Matsuura one day to say, "Hey, why not make something for our new platform?"

"I liked that [approach]," recalls Matsuura. "It was very casual, and I was a little surprised." Matsuura knew that console games needed great, eye-catching graphics no matter what the game play, so he asked a New York City-based artist named Rodney Greenblat to design the characters and scenery. Matsuura and Greenblat met at the MacWorld computer expo in Tokyo years before; Greenblat had also done a Macintosh CD-ROM multimedia game that he was showing off at the same time Matsuura was displaying his. "Also," says Matsuura, "I knew that Sony had a contract with him already. So it was convenient."

The game play was designed to be as accessible as possible, which, says Matsuura, is why rap was chosen in the first place. "For the player to recognize and feel the fun in interacting with music, it requires game play that is easy to understand. Of course, playing an instrument like a guitar is very interesting, but that's for someone who already has an interest in music, which many game players don't. But everybody has a native understanding of *language*.

"Rap is very unique in this regard, since it is musical expression but one that features words. And their usage is very different from the normal way that we say things. The rhyming, the *sound* of the words, is very important. But not everyone understands this." Even in the Japanese version of the game, Matsuura used English, the mother tongue of rap. But it was a very peculiar kind of English, to say the least. "People tell me you can learn English by playing *Parappa*. And of course that's true, but—um—I don't know if you should."

So the *sensei* would rap, then Parappa, the player, would rap back by pressing buttons with the right timing. But it wasn't simply *Simon* with rap music; the experience was dynamic, it changed along with the player. The background music would become out-of-tune and droopy if the player couldn't rap well, the characters on screen would start to nod off instead of dancing, and if the player was "Rappin' AWFUL" as indicated onscreen, the scenery itself would begin to fall apart. It was this sort of direct relationship between the player and what was happening onscreen that helped to make the player feel as if he was actually *making music*, not just playing a call-and-repeat game.

Matsuura could have stopped there and been content with having created a stellar new genre of game. But he wanted to craft a cinematic experience around it. "One of the things that frustrated me when I was a musician was that I had to play on television shows. I love to compose music for myself and for everyone else, but I felt very strange on TV, because the visuals that accompany my music shouldn't be video of me and my face. So I wanted to make characters and a story that would fit well with my music."

Parappa was unique among video game stories in that it was a love story; there was no bad guy to kill, no world to save—just a dog trying to win the love of a sunflower. It was ultimately a game of cooperation and learning, not competition. And Matsuura didn't think it would set the world on fire. Matsuura calls himself "more of a niche person." He imagined *Parappa* might do thirty or forty thousand copies. It ended up selling one and a half million copies in its first eighteen months.

Parappa having set the standard, numerous other publishers began to work on games in the music genre. Hoping to stay ahead of the curve, Matsuura and crew started two new projects, which were released within a few months of each other in 1999. *Um Jammer Lammy* was a sister game to *Parappa* that blended the original's game play with a rock guitar sound. The *sensei* called

out rock songs and Lammy, a guitar-playing punk-rock-chick lamb, answered back with guitar solos. To celebrate the game's US release later that year, a concert featuring the game's musicians was held in New York City, at the Roxy theater. That same year, he released three more *Parappa* and *Um Jammer Lammy* soundtracks on the Sony Music label.

Matsuura's third game, *Vib-Ribbon*, featured similar rhythmic press-but-tons-to-the-music game play but was nearly devoid of graphics. The screen showed only a black-and-white sketch of a rabbit that walked along a curving, looping line. Different loops and patterns in the line, placed rhythmically along with the music, had to be 'jumped' by Vibri the rabbit using different controller buttons. Although *Vib-Ribbon* included many musical tracks, it was unique in that the player could insert any audio CD and *Vib-Ribbon* would analyze the music and then set the game play to its rhythm. Two PlayStation 2 fol-low-up games, *Mojib-Ribbon* and *Vib-Ripple*, created original musical games out of a player's downloaded emails and digital camera pictures, respectively.

ビブリボン／Vib-ribbon   ©1999 Sony Computer Entertainment Inc.

Matsuura's constant experimentation has thus led him to create many original, groundbreaking games in a very young genre. But there is one type of game that sprung up in the aftermath of *Parappa* that Matsuura has, for some reason, yet to try. They are games that use specialty controllers in the shape of the instrument that the game emulates: a DJ's turntable, an electric guitar, a pair of maracas. Major companies—Sega, Namco, Nintendo—have published these games. But the games that started it all were the Beatmania, or *Bemani*, series by Konami.

Beatmania was essentially a video-game simulation of a club DJ turntable. The controller featured five piano-style keys and a rubber turntable that spun around. The onscreen graphics were sparse: just six vertical bars, one for each button on the controller. Smaller horizontal bars fell rapidly from the top of the screen. When they reached the end of their vertical column, the player pressed the corresponding button. With perfect timing, the player performed a dance track. Numerous popular dance mixes in genres from drum-and-bass to house to trance were licensed for the game, as well as many songs com-posed by Konami's in-house musicians.

It was the perfect game to revive Japan's flagging arcade industry, because the game design's intrinsic qualities made it well suited to coin-op entertain-ment. First, it was possible to create significant upgrades to the game machines easily, by swapping out the CD that contained the songs and inserting a brand new one. Thus, as soon as players' interest began to wane, arcade operators could buy a disc of all new songs, swap out the marquee glass at the top of the cabinet, and promise an entirely new experience.

Second, *Beatmania*'s concept was easy to grasp in seconds but nearly impossible to master. "Press a button as soon as the little bar reaches the bottom of the screen—how hard could that be? Here's my hundred yen. Oh, it's *very* hard. But there's no reason it should be. I must not be concentrating. I know I can do this. I'll try again." Simple but difficult, *Beatmania* was *Space Invaders* set to music.

Third, *Beatmania* was a spectator sport. *Space Invaders* masters looked like zombies at their machines, but the on-screen action wasn't much fun to watch or listen to. But in the hands of a master, *Beatmania* was a musical performance. To watch a player's nimble fingers dart across the keys as an incredibly complicated, perfectly timed music mix pumped out of the giant speakers that adorned the top of the machine was entertainment in and of itself.

Later games in the *Bemani* collection were even more performance-oriented, featuring all sorts of instruments. The game play was the same, but the songs and controllers were different—*Guitar Freaks*, *Drummania*, *Keyboard Mania*. These were popular, but one spin-off in particular skyrocketed to popularity, no longer a mere video game but a cultural phenomenon. Rather than playing an instrument, this game was focused around a giant metal platform with four arrow-shaped pads. The player stood on the platform and stomped on the pads to the beat of a thumping dance song, illustrated by the vertically scrolling lines of arrows on the screen.

The game was, of course, *Dance Dance Revolution*, a video game, a dance performance, and a solid workout all in one. Originally released to Japanese arcades in 1998, *DDR*'s concept of controlling a video game with one's feet was not entirely new. The Nintendo licensee Bandai had released a foot-control pad called the *Family Trainer* for the Famicom, which Nintendo had licensed for the US and called the *Power Pad*. But *Dance Dance Revolution*'s musical nature and energetic game play made it about a thousand times more fun than any of the Power Pad software.

> **Dance Dance Revolution: a video game, a dance performance, and a solid workout all in one.**

DDR was also a spectacular sight to behold, an oasis of lights, music, and action in the middle of a dark arcade. Set inside a giant cabinet with massive speakers, flashing marquee lights, and two giant metal dance controllers, it took up a massive amount of floor space but it was worth its weight in gold; the sight of a *DDR* player, arms flailing, feet stomping, was enough to attract many more potential players to the machine. It worked much better than the traditional 'attract mode' animations that played on arcade game screens, although *DDR*'s screens had those too, displayed during those rare occasions when nobody was playing the machines.

DDR started out difficult, as players struggled to learn how to best use the controller. In one sense they were re-learning how to play video games, at two hundred yen every three minutes. Things got a lot less expensive for *DDR* fans when Konami released the first home version of *DDR* on the PlayStation in Japan on April 10, 1999, along with a soft plastic footpad for home use that resembled the Power Pad controller. This meant that for a relatively low cost, players could play over and over with no interruption.

This led to the emergence of expert-level players. And so with each upgrade to the machine, Konami had to include not only a full set of new songs but also much harder arrow patterns in order to keep players coming back. Players kept coming back, and the video arcade had again found its savior as *Street Fighter* and its progeny, which had caused their own spike in arcade popularity, began to fade away, *Bemani* was there to take its place.

As *DDR* grew in popularity machines were introduced into California arcades, which typically featured the latest Japanese games, as early as 1999. There, not only video game geeks but also crowds of streetwise, fashionable high school and college students took to the game.

With the release of *Dance Dance Revolution Third Mix* in early 2000, *DDR* started to appear in arcades all over the United States, coast to coast. Fan communities started to spring up. One, a website called DDR Freak, ended up being the official-unofficial source of *DDR* information, listing locations around the US where machines could be found, where to buy the import games and pads for the PlayStation, and how to play the game. RedOctane.com sold imitation versions of Konami's *DDR* home pads, and soon invented its own pads. Even at over one hundred dollars each, fans lined up to buy them.

The home version promised to bring *DDR* to a wider audience of players than the hardcore import-gamers. Later versions of the game for the PlayStation 2 and Xbox systems incorporated fans' wishes and expanded the song lineups.

What the US release of *Dance Dance Revolution* did best was spur mainstream media coverage of the phenomenon. By the end of 2001, the Wall Street Journal, CNN, Reuters, ABC News, USA Today, and the New York Times had run stories on *Dance Dance Revolution*'s popularity. Many of these articles pointed out the fact that video gamers were beginning to lose weight by playing *DDR*, in sharp contrast to the stories that had blamed the NES for obesity in American youth. DDR Freak was mentioned in most of these stories; the editors of the website were even featured on the ABC talk show "The Other Half." Host Danny Bonaduce, formerly of "The Partridge Family," came away from the segment so enamored with *DDR* that he bought his own arcade machine.

If later editions of *DDR* and other *Bemani* games had one flaw, it was the steep difficulty curve, which only got steeper as time went on. As new, updated editions of the games were released they were tailored more and more toward intermediate to expert players who needed harder and more complex challenges. This followed a pattern similar to the once-mainstream martial arts fighting game genre, led by Capcom's *Street Fighter II* series, from a decade before; the games started out with wide appeal but as the various iterations got more and more complex, they seemed to skew toward the existing hardcore, expert-level fan base.

Realizing that *Bemani*'s evolution created a hole to fill in the market, other publishers came in with new ideas. Sega's *Samba De Amigo* became a cult classic, blending pop *musica Latina* favorites like "La Bamba" and "Livin' La Vida Loca" with maraca controllers that the player had to shake. Onscreen visuals borrowed the colorful style and dynamic reaction of *Parappa*—the main character was a perpetually grinning, wildly gyrating monkey.

Namco's *Taiko no Tatsujin*, or *Drum Master*, was perhaps the most ethnically Japanese music game yet released.[*] The game's title and in-game text were all in Japanese, the controller was a life-size wood and imitation leather *taiko* traditional Japanese drum, the song list was made up of Japanese traditional melodies, television themes, and *anime* music, and the graphic style of the cabinet and onscreen action looked like a traditional Japanese *matsuri* festival in progress.

[*] As seen in the film *Lost In Translation*.

Taiko appealed to older Japanese and younger kids with a song list and graphic style that they could appreciate without being club-hopping teenagers. Furthermore, the game play was simple to learn *and* simple to master, so it was instantly rewarding. Moreover, whereas *Guitar Freaks*' controller, for example, was merely a plastic toy-like replica of a guitar, *Taiko*'s controllers were like real *taiko* drums, which produce such a massive booming sound that they are fun and exhilarating to play. *Taiko no Tatsujin* captured like no other rhythm game before it a sense of sheer joy that comes with actually making music.

And then in late 2003 came *Donkey Konga*, a collaboration between Nintendo and Namco that mixed the game play of *Taiko* with Nintendo's *Donkey Kong* characters and a new controller designed specifically for home play—a set of bongos that was quieter and easier to play than the cheaply made plastic *taiko* that shipped with the home versions of the original game. What's more, *Donkey Konga* had that *mukokuseki* appearance; both American and Japanese players could 'read' Miyamoto's characters as being part of their own culture, so it had more worldwide sales potential. It was also great fun.

And yet ultimately, although home versions of the arcade instrument-controllers and *Dance Dance Revolution* floor pads get more accurate with every iteration, the music games that work best at home are still the ones designed from the ground up to use the home system's standard controller. One shining example of those post-*Parappa* games, and its designer, is profiled below.

MICROSCOPIC GAME DESIGN: KEIICHI YANO AND *GITAROO-MAN*

Gitaroo-Man for the PlayStation 2 is an example of a "sleeper," an unlikely title that comes out of nowhere, with practically no marketing hype, and ends up attaining cult-hit status through word of mouth. The publisher, Koei, was and is still mostly known for historical military simulations, not crazy, colorful music games. But as the music game boom took off in Japan, led by *Parappa The Rapper*, every company wanted a piece of the pie. So Koei snapped up *Gitaroo-Man* while it was in development at a tiny developer on the outskirts of Tokyo called INIS.

Gitaroo-Man creators Keiichi Yano, his wife Masako Harada, and Arka Roy.

Much like *Parappa*, *Gitaroo-Man*'s story sequences featured a bizarrely adorned cast of wacky characters. But unlike *Parappa*'s focus on rap, its musical soundtrack was just as wild and varied; each level featured something new, from J-pop to smooth jazz to acoustic guitar. In any case, the American media found *Gitaroo-Man*, much like *Parappa*, to be one of those "bizarre cartoon games from Japan," and prized it for its foreign wackiness. So you can imagine my surprise when I was introduced to *Gitaroo-Man*'s designer, Keiichi Yano, at the Tokyo Game Show in 2002 and found out that he had spent most of his life living in Los Angeles.

"I was born in Tokyo," says Yano, the vice-president and director of development at INIS. His wife Masako is the company's president and CEO. "But at the age of two, we moved to the States. First we were in Hawaii for about two and a half years, and then we moved to LA. At home I spoke Japanese. I didn't know this until recently but apparently my mom scolded me when I tried to speak English—but obviously, you go to school and you're speaking English with your friends." At school age, Yano discovered music, starting on the piano and saxophone at nine years old, and playing in the jazz and marching bands all throughout high school.

And of course, like every other child of the 1980s, Yano had an Atari 2600 system and a library of game cartridges; *Pitfall* and *Combat* were his favorites. For Yano, games and computer programming were a side interest, but something he had grown up with. His father was literally a rocket scientist; he worked at NEC writing programs for rockets in Assembler language. "I never really *learned* programming from him, but I grew up fascinated by it and thought, like everybody else, that it would be really cool if I could make, you know, like a *game*. So I had him buy me an NEC PC-88 computer, which used to be the standard game PC in Japan, and I started learning BASIC programming on that."

Still, Yano's main interest was his music. He went to USC and, after a brief but unsuccessful flirtation with mechanical engineering ("I wanted to design cars"), Yano took a scholarship in Jazz Studies. After graduation he moved to Japan, with every intention of going home within a year. However, a part-time job doing BASIC and Director programming for a Tokyo multimedia company turned into a five-year stint.

Yano left the multimedia company in 1997, teaming up with his wife and her brother, a professional musician, to form INIS. "The intent was to do consumer video games—of course, neither I nor Masako nor anybody on the team was in the games industry. So we started with nothing, and it took us a while. We had to snowball little by little, build up the resources to create a great game. And it took about three years. Up until then, we had done a lot of contract work, prototype games for Yamaha. Those were the early days of INIS, lots of little things here and there. I didn't start using [the programming language] C until *Gitaroo-Man*, so that was my first venture into any real programming at all.

"Since we all came from musical backgrounds, we always had the idea of doing some type of entertainment software that was musically inclined. Then *Parappa The Rapper* came out, and we said, oh, that's interesting—somebody's thinking the same thing. So we wanted to take the music genre to the next level. We wanted to keep the rhythmic element that kept *Parappa* so accessible, but we wanted to add a melody, which was an element that no other music game had attempted. And around this time, we'd been working with Koei on a CD-ROM title that was based on Moritaka Isato, who is a famous idol singer over here. And they wanted to get into doing in-house game development, and we said, yeah, we've got this game, so they checked it out and said okay."

Securing a publisher for their original game was only the start of the battle for INIS. "There were some hurdles. One was that the prototypes weren't really product-quality game designs yet. The game system ended up coming to me in a dream. My game systems usually

My game systems usually come to me in dreams, and it's right before I fall asleep, so I debate whether or not to wake up and write it down.

come to me in dreams, and it's right before I fall asleep, so I debate whether or not to wake up and write it down. This time, I wrote it down, and we had a working version of it by 2000. And basically everybody just loved it and thought it was really cool."

The game system was much harder to master than *Parappa*'s simple button presses. During the "attack" phase of the game play, the player hits the Circle button in a tight rhythm while moving the analog control stick to follow a curving, looping line. The curves of the line and the subsequent spinning, tilting motions of the controller are a visual and tactile representation of the melody. The "defense" phases are pure rhythm; as icons representing the four face buttons of the PlayStation controller zoom toward the screen's center, the player must press the corresponding buttons with perfect timing to dodge the enemy's "guitar attacks."

But wait—attacking? Defending? What's all that about? It all relates back to Yano's Jazz Studies major, of course. "When you're playing jazz, and you're taking solos from each other, it's this kind of battle-oriented thing. You're saying, "hey, look, my phrases are better than yours," while the other guy's saying, "well, screw you—*my* phrase is cooler." And so, coming from Jazz Studies, I had the notion that music was a battle-oriented thing." So, Yano thought, why not visualize jazz "battles" in the style of classic shooting games like *Combat* and *Space Invaders*? "Why not have laser beams come out of guitars?"

But *whose* guitars, exactly, and what would the beams look like? Advance glossy photo spreads in video game enthusiast magazines are what get titles noticed, so if *Gitaroo-Man* was going to sell it would need eye-catching graphics. "We didn't have anybody internally that we thought we could be fairly confident with, so we investigated some character design people. We wanted to go with a pop look, with somebody that was kind of *now*. So from our pool of five candidates, we decided on 326." 326 is the pen name of Mitsuru Nakamura—the numbers 3-2-6 can be read in Japanese as *mi-tsu-ru*.

326 had already built an established fan base in Japan among young adults who loved his wild, graffiti-like style. Like many artists in Japan he had published large-dimension illustration books full of his art; he'd also done bill-boards, posters, and television commercials. Television commercials are a pop-culture phenomenon of their own in Japan. Well-designed commercials that featured new pop music songs could shoot the single to the top of the charts[*] or, in this case, put an artist in the public eye.

★ This happened in 2001 with Nintendo's GameCube launch title *Pikmin*—the song from the game's commercial was wildly successful as a single.

Selecting 326 as the game's illustrator and character designer also ended up solidifying the game's final musical lineup. "The office that 326 belongs to is actually a music office with some fairly high-profile musicians," says Yano. "And so we thought, well, hey, if we could use their musicians at the same time, great! One group that they had that was popular on the indie circuit was called COIL, and we ended up working together on the tunes. They did the writing on about a third of the guitar songs, and we did the arrangement.

"But prior to all that, we'd went with Koei's team to a hotel room, and brought about a hundred CDs with us. We listened to songs all day, trying to figure out what kinds of songs would be cool. We wanted to include stuff from all different genres. And at the same time, we were constructing the story, so we were trying to match up where the songs would fit.

"Like, this is where the hero's gonna fall in love…" reminisces Yano, clearly thinking about one of the game's key story scenes. Late in the game, after a series of tough battles, the game's hero U-1[†] finds himself alone on a beach with the girl of his dreams. In every previous chapter, the cowardly, shy youngster U-1 transforms into Gitaroo-Man to battle enemies; in this one, the newly confident youngster begins to come out of his shell as he plays a soft acoustic song to his love interest. If the player is adept at the song, the girl nudges her way over to U-1 and rests her head on his shoulder; if the player has trouble, she leaves.

† U-1 is sort of a bilingual pun. U-1 is pronounced "you won" in English, but it's shorthand for the Japanese first name Yuuichi. Keiichi Yano, as you might imagine, signs his name K-1.

It's a touching and memorable scene. Like the rest of the game, it's also incredibly difficult. "That's one of the best and worst comments that we get," says Yano. Ultimately—and this is to INIS' credit—whether a player finds *Gitaroo-Man* to be difficult or easy seems to depend on whether said player is musically adept in real life. "A lot of our musicians would blow through it, but our playtesters would say, 'You *can't* make this any harder!'"

Another potential divide that makers of music games have to work through is how to sell the same quirky title to both American and Japanese audiences. As one might imagine, this didn't turn out to be as much of a problem for the Tokyo-born, LA-raised Yano. "There was a big Japanese community there, even a Little Tokyo. I still think I'm a very LA kind of guy, but my roots are in Japanese culture. I'd rent anime—there were places that rented Japanese videos—and I'd come to Japan at least once a year. So I never felt any kind of a culture shock. It was something that was in my blood."

"Compared to the average Japanese person," interjects INIS director Arka Roy, "he has more of a grip on their culture because he really educates himself on this kind of thing, on what's cool." Roy, as well, is certainly qualified to talk about the peculiarities of Japanese popular culture. By way of describing himself, Roy points out all the parallels between his background and Yano's: born in India, moved to Canada with his family when he was two, moved to Japan a few years after graduation. Roy's original intent was to stay in Japan for about a year as an English conversation teacher (the bubble economy had not yet burst, so being fluent in English was like "having a license to print money"), but he soon found himself working with an old college friend, a fellow math major, at a multimedia company called 9003.

In 1993, 9003 released a piece of CD-ROM personal computer software called *AquaZone*, a virtual fish tank simulator that was the first of the "pet simulation" games that would later take over Japan and the world for a brief time. In fact, the developers of the hit Tamagotchi digital pet toy acknowledged *AquaZone* as an influence. "I was in that company for seven years, and then a game designer, a famous one named Yoot Saito, started a company and asked me to join him as vice president."

The company was called Vivarium, and its first game was a groundbreaking release for the Sega Dreamcast called *Seaman*. *Seaman* looked like a fish simulator, but the difference is that this fish *talked* to you, and you had to talk back using a microphone that attached to the Dreamcast controller. Using sophisticated voice-recognition software, *Seaman* would hold 'conversations' with you—a virtual pet whose communication advanced far beyond the simple beeps of the Tamagotchi key chains.

"One thing I've noticed," says Roy, "not just for games but for everything is that Japanese companies are not really *done* with a product until it's really,

really good. They'll just keep working at it—weekends, all-nighters—to get every last detail completely perfect. And even back when I was growing up in North America it just seemed like Japanese products had a certain smartness about them in design, and maybe in function in some cases. It's a lot of work, this real pickiness, but the results are very good ones.

Yano elaborates. "It's game design on a microscopic level. While American designers focus on the macro level, on the big idea, Japanese game designers focus on the little parts that make the game fun. As Miyamoto puts it, it's all about the polish, how the game controls on the micro level. And that all comes from that fact that Japan is an island country. We're very good at microscopic things, and we really notice microscopic details.

"For example, let's say you're sitting in a Japanese train car. You're very close to the next guy, especially in the mornings during rush hour. If he smells, you notice it. If he has flecks of dust on his shoulder, you see them. You notice all these small details because you're always so close physically, and that leads to the Japanese culture's orientation toward details. I would say one of the less obvious points is that people in Japan are also very fashion-oriented, so the look of Japanese games is always going to be very high-fashion. And I think that's what makes Japanese games unique and fun, and sets them apart from other games."

"I have the feeling that I'm in a very good position, that I understand both cultures very well, so I can leverage that to have a game design that can appeal to both." Does that mean a future INIS game might use more American artists? "I've always wanted to do that, and the next game might be it. I'd want to take a whole bunch of people—pop artists, garage bands… What's great about a music game is that you can take a lot of artists and a lot of styles, produce it into this one thing that kind of coheres, and it's not so strange because the game design keeps that coherence."

■ ▢ ▨

Regardless of the impression that the interviews in this chapter might give, game music is not only important to epic RPGs or quirky rhythm-action games. Every game can benefit from extra polish on the soundtrack. Would playing *Super Mario Bros.* be nearly as pleasurable if the music wasn't so pleasing and infectious? Would extended sessions of *Tetris* on the Game Boy be as addictive if Tchaikovsky didn't accompany them? Interesting music benefits any game design, but a stirring, carefully designed soundtrack is crucial to creating a cinematic game experience, even when the cinematic game in question is a shooting game, the modern-day equivalent of *Space Invaders*.

CHAPTER 6

A TALE OF TWO *GAIJIN*

Although Miyamoto downplays the importance of story in his games, it is difficult not to notice that every time he has turned his attention to a new genre, besides refining the game play, he adds a story with appealing characters. Sometimes he adds them to a game genre that historically never carried a narrative. One example of this is *Star Fox*, a 1993 spaceship shooter game—the genre born of *Space Invaders*—for the Super Nintendo system that featured realistic 3-D graphics powered by a coprocessor that was included on the *Star Fox* cartridge. *

* This is one advantage that the cartridge format has over CD and DVD-ROM: the game hardware can be "upgraded" with processor or memory chips on the cartridge's circuit board.

Star Fox was ahead of its time in two different ways: technologically, it brought 3-D gaming to a mainstream audience and wowed SNES owners with graphics they never thought possible on the hardware. But perhaps more importantly, it was one of the first tentative steps toward an East/West game design partnership, being that the product of Nintendo's Kyoto game design merged with the technical expertise of a small group of young programmers from London. Two of them, Dylan Cuthbert and Giles Goddard, have since permanently relocated to Kyoto and established their own companies there. They are now officially part of the Japanese games industry even though they will always be *gaijin*—foreigners, outsiders.

Close together in age and birthplace, Goddard and Cuthbert were in large part products of their time. In the early eighties, personal computers were becoming so cheap and so powerful that few families could resist the allure. In the US, video game companies like Atari and Coleco attempted to expand into PCs in those early days. In Britain it was companies like Sinclair and Amiga.

"My mum gave me a Sinclair Spectrum for Christmas when I was about ten, and I got into programming BASIC on that," recalls Goddard. "Because I didn't know how to program, I would get these magazines that had programs inside for you to type in by hand. And they wouldn't work. And I'd try to fix them and realize that they were broken anyway and would *never* work. So I tried to learn how to fix them myself, and that's how I learned BASIC."

When Goddard was around fifteen, he saved up to buy a more powerful Amiga computer. He stayed away from making games, preferring to concentrate on experimental programs and 3-D demos. One day he ran wires out of the joystick port over to tinfoil switches that he had jury-rigged onto his bedroom door. When the door opened, the switch tripped and an alert popped up on the computer screen. Another early experiment on the Amiga was a music program that used the system's built in drum samples.

Dylan Cuthbert's early experience with programming also dealt with electronic percussion. "When I was about ten, around 1982, a friend of mine asked me to write a software interface for a drum machine that connected to his computer. He lent it to me for a few months while I worked on it. I wasn't actually able to do it, so instead I wrote games—a mini-version of *Pac-Man*, and a really crap version of *Space Invaders*."

ARGONAUT

By their mid-teens, both Goddard and Cuthbert knew that they wanted to work with computers for a living. But the public educational system in the UK wasn't giving them the skills they knew they would need. "The college [high school] courses nowadays are much better, but this was the late '80s. Computer studies meant learning how to punch holes in paper tape," recalls Cuthbert. "I wasn't learning anything. And so I started looking for work. And Jez San, the boss of Argonaut Software, called me and said that if I wanted a job there I'd have to start the next Monday. And I dropped out of school. I was a year away from university, but I never went back, never looked back."

Six months earlier, Giles Goddard had left school and joined Argonaut. "I was sixteen and had never done any real programming before. But I wanted to work for a company that was doing 3-D games on the Amiga. And the only company doing that was Argonaut Software. I sent them demos of stuff I'd done, and they asked me to come up to London."

At Argonaut, Goddard and Cuthbert were hardly outcasts for having dropped out of school. In fact, nearly everyone at Argonaut had quit school to work there.[*] The company was made up of about half a dozen programmers, all working out of founder Jez San's house in North London. Argonaut had scored a minor hit with the PC space adventure game *Starglider*, and were working on the sequel. Goddard's first job was to port *Starglider II* to the up-and-coming Apple Macintosh, while Cuthbert worked on the sound programming for the Amiga and Spectrum versions.

After that, Cuthbert began playing around with a new game console called the *Konix Multi-System*, which had been developed by a British company of the same name. The system looked like a "toilet seat" and had a steering wheel controller on its face. The chips inside the system were manufactured by Flair Technology, which was a division of Spectrum makers

[*] "There was one guy," recalls Goddard, "that actually had a proper education. His name was Danny Emmett and he was a really good 3-D developer. He'd draw up these big sheets of graph paper and would draw, using a pencil, a 3-D model on three axes. And then he'd sit there, without writing anything down, and type in all the coordinates on the number pad with one hand." Giles demonstrates, tapping five fingers at breakneck speed on the table. "And he'd just press Enter and this 3-D shape would appear on screen, flawless. I've never seen *anything* like it since."

Sinclair. Konix showed Argonaut's Multi-System game at the European Computer Trade Show, but the company went under soon after. The game was never finished and Argonaut had to explore other consoles if they were going to break into the home video game scene.

The Nintendo Entertainment System was available in England at that time through an exclusive license with Bandai, a Japanese toy conglomerate that had an established UK subsidiary. But it was not nearly as popular as it was in the US and Japan. "Atari had the console market in England," recalls Goddard. "Of course, the console market in England was really nonexistent anyway. It was only a few lucky kids who had the Atari VCS." This is not to say that the British were not playing video games. They were, but it was on programmable computers like the Spectrum and Amiga.

Still, Argonaut experimented with everything they could get their hands on, and that included the NES. "We were all working on the NES, trying to get 3-D working on it. And one of our programmers actually got it to work." The 3-D engine that Argonaut had developed for the NES could only display simple wireframe graphics and ran painfully slow, but it worked. "We showed that you could actually make a 3-D game on a NES. And then there was this new kid on the block called the Game Boy. And Jez grabbed that and said, 'Let's do 3-D on the Game Boy then.'"

And then there was this new kid on the block called the Game Boy. And Jez grabbed that and said, 'Let's do 3-D on the Game Boy then.'

Cuthbert was the sole programmer on the game, which they called *Eclipse*. Argonaut licensed the game to the publisher Mindscape. Meanwhile, without telling his employees, Jez San took their 3-D demos with him to America for the Consumer Electronics Show, which at that time was the game industry's preeminent trade show. "I didn't even know he was showing my game around," says Cuthbert. "Why would he—we were already signed with a publisher! But he showed our 3-D games to Nintendo of America, and they said we had to show it to Japan because no one over there had ever managed to do 3-D on either machine. They didn't think it could be done.

"So Jez got back from the CES and said, 'Next week we're going to Japan, so pack your suitcase.'" At 19 years old, Dylan Cuthbert was on his way to Kyoto for a dramatic meeting with Nintendo's top brass. Miyamoto and team were so amazed by the Game Boy game that they bought all the rights from Mindscape and had Cuthbert and team join R&D1 in Kyoto, the team headed up by the inventor of the Game Boy, Gunpei Yokoi. Their assigned director was *Metroid* creator Yoshio Sakamoto.

The young men from Argonaut went back and forth between London and Kyoto constantly, staying in the best hotels and flying business class. "Nintendo was very rich back then, and we had great fun. I went over seven or eight times for the Game Boy game alone. Big leather chairs on the plane. Made it worth the knackering jetlag," remembers Cuthbert.

Nintendo president Hiroshi Yamauchi renamed the game X. "Yamauchi would just wake up in the middle of the night with a new name for a game. And he'd call the director right then and say, 'this is what you're calling your game.' It was a better name, of course. *Eclipse* or *Lunar Chase*, which is what we were calling it at that time, didn't mean much to the Japanese. X was more striking."

X was something new for the Japanese audience. Concept-wise, as a 3-D mission-based space adventure game in the vein of *Starglider*, it was something they'd never seen before. And perhaps more importantly, technology-wise it was far more advanced than anything else on the system. "It had an intro screen that was full 3-D, after the title screen but before the game began. You saw these little mini-movies where the commander, who was a polygonal head, told you about the next mission. Back then, no one was doing that." X was released to moderate success. Recently, the Japanese weekly game magazine *Famitsu* voted it as one of the four most influential Game Boy games ever created.

THE MARIO CHIP

But it was another concept, born out of that same Kyoto meeting in the summer of 1990, that would prove even more influential and change Argonaut's and Nintendo's fortunes forever. "After we showed them our 3-D engines, they showed us a prototype of the Super Famicom," says Cuthbert. Miyamoto showed the Argonaut programmers half-finished versions of the three games that his teams were feverishly working to finish for the Japanese launch of the Super Famicom that November: *Super Mario World*, a futuristic racing game called *F-Zero*, and an airplane stunts game called *Pilotwings* that featured events like hang gliding and skydiving.

All three games used a hardware feature of the SNES called Mode 7, which was a built-in routine that allowed the system to scale and rotate a flat, two-dimensional bitmapped background. In *Super Mario World* this was used to zoom Bowser in and out of the screen during the final fight. In *F-Zero* it allowed the racetrack to be an entirely contiguous design that spun in real-time underneath the racers, giving the illusion that a "camera" was following behind the player's car. And in *Pilotwings*' skydiving sections, the ground below zoomed in fast as the player dropped toward the target.

The Super Famicom's competitors, NEC's PC Engine and Sega's Mega Drive, did not have sprite rotation or scaling, and so the difference was already stunning. Sega's games looked like more colorful versions of Famicom games, but Nintendo's offerings looked entirely new. But Miyamoto wanted more. Mode 7 only allowed for one background at a time to be manipulated, and the player's airplane or race car had to remain in one place. "They showed us *Pilotwings*," says Cuthbert, "and they wanted the plane to rotate around in real-time 3-D. They asked us if there was any way we could do that in three months."

This was an impossible task even for the talented Argonaut programmers. "And we said no, not in three months we can't. But if we make a special chip for you, you could do it in future games. And so right in the middle of this meeting, Jez calls up his friends at Flair Technology, who had done the 3-D graphics chips for Konix, and said that Nintendo wanted to know if we can design a chip for them that can do 3-D on a game cartridge. And he says, well, yeah, we can do it if there's enough money. And, of course, there was," Cuthbert laughs.

Giles Goddard: "The chip was a DSP [digital signal processor] chip, and we had to use it because of the problem of fill rate. The SNES could display lots of colors and had a much higher resolution compared to the NES, but it didn't have the power to fill in all of the pixels and make closed, solid polygons rather than wireframe graphics. So we really needed some kind of extra hardware if it was going to look good."

A year before *Star Fox* released, Nintendo released its go-kart racing game *Super Mario Kart*, which had a DSP chip that enabled the system to scale many different sprites as well as the background, meaning that the characters could get smaller and larger according to how far they were from the "camera" position—that is, where the map beneath them was placed. "But 3-D is very different from sprite scaling," says Goddard, "because you have to actually draw each pixel rather than just have a set piece of artwork that you can just scale and move around. So the chip needed a completely different design." The chip, which they called the Mario Chip, ended up being a RISC CPU—a reduced instruction set computing, central processing unit—that could easily power a small-scale computer on its own. "It was fairly programmable; you could do whatever you wanted with it. You could draw sprites with it if you wanted to." But the Super FX Chip, as it was eventually named, was used exclusively for 3-D graphics.

STAR FOX

"Originally, Argonaut had started to design a *Starglider* game, as they always do," laughs Cuthbert. "And it was really bad. It was fully 3-D with some sprite-based graphics, but it wasn't fun. And we went over for a month to work with Nintendo on it." Miyamoto took one look at the game and sucked wind in through his teeth. For the Japanese, this was the wordless signal that something was very, *very* wrong.

"This game," Cuthbert admits, "had no actual designer. It had been pulled together by a bunch of programmers who were just making cool 3-D graphics with no game planning to back it up. And Nintendo didn't like it." Even so, it was entirely necessary for

> **Miyamoto took one look at the game and sucked wind in through his teeth. For the Japanese, this was the wordless signal that something was very, *very* wrong.**

the Argonaut programmers to be deeply involved in the process, because they were the ones with the technical expertise. "The basic engine was programmed beforehand, in the UK," explains Goddard, "and the game was designed in Kyoto. We had to come over there to do

it. They wouldn't have been able to make a game with the chip as fast as we could. And the Mario Chip had such a short lifespan that there wasn't really much time to experiment and find out how to use it. You had to just do it.

"We knew it wouldn't be the be-all, end-all of DSP chips. Game hardware was advancing very fast at that time—the PlayStation came out less than two years after *Star Fox*. And so obviously the Mario Chip wasn't going to compete anywhere near the PlayStation. So we only had literally a two-year window where you could realistically expect to be able to sell Mario Chip games."

But even with development time ticking away, Miyamoto was still unimpressed with Argonaut's design and wanted to start back at the beginning. He asked one of the developers on his internal team to create a simple game on the chip. The game simply had a triangle that represented the spaceship. Instead of flying in all directions in true 3-D, the ship flew in a straight line through a tunnel. Miyamoto insisted that the game be based on this straight-line game play because it was instantly comprehensible. They had a workable game design—now, the real work began.

"They told us that this time, they would need us here permanently," recalls Cuthbert. "So in February 1992, we got all of our bags and they put us up in a hotel downtown for a year. And we began full-on development. We pretty much worked our butts off, from nine-thirty in the morning to eleven at night."

"None of us really had defined roles," says Goddard. It was just three of us programming the game, and whatever needed to be done, we just randomly picked who was going to do it. It was a unique way of developing because there was no single person working on any specific area. Every part of the game got everyone's best effort—there were no parts that suffered because of other parts."

To get around the Japanese programmers' lack of expertise with the Argonaut-designed chip, the English programmers wrote a scripting system that would allow the designers to plug in their designs with a minimum of changes to the program code. It was a slick design that they were unfamiliar with, but it worked like a charm. Meanwhile, Dylan and Giles put their heads together to program the massive boss machines that were at the end of every stage, which were too complicated to be plugged in through catch-all script programming.

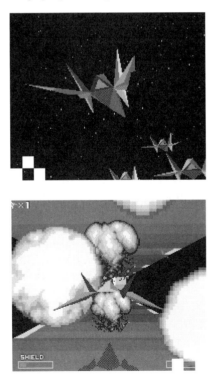

By October, the engine was polished to perfection, but the game still had no storyline or characters. It was at this point that Miyamoto brought out his trusty sketchbook and drew a team of anthropomorphic pilots to man the fleet of ships: the brash lieutenant Falco Lombardi, the awkward Slippy Toad, the aging but loyal Peppy Hare, and the courageous young team leader, Fox McCloud. The characters were not merely window dressing; they talked to each other during each stage, making *Star Fox* the first "shooter" game that incorporated a running, developing storyline right in the thick of the action. The next two months were hell as Cuthbert and Goddard scrambled to incorporate 2D pictures of the cast and digitized voices into the design.

Their effort paid off. In just sixty days, *Star Fox* went from being a glorified 3-D technical demo to a story game that was pure Nintendo. "I can't think of any other action games at the time that did that," says Goddard. Dylan Cuthbert was particularly proud of the game's cinematic sequences, especially the final ending demonstration. "It's really worth beating the game to see. We put a lot of effort into it. We introduce all of the boss machines, and then we have this Superman-style credits sequence with an amazing orchestral score, which is the best thing about the ending. A Nintendo composer named Hirosawa did the music. He had real skills at orchestral-style composition. He made it sound just like *Star Wars*."

Star Fox released in Japan in January 1993, and then in April in the US. It was accompanied by a massive marketing blitz featuring in-store *Star Fox* competitions and gigantic write-ups in *Nintendo Power* magazine. It set a record for over-weekend sales, shifting close to one million units in its first weekend in the US. It did equally well in Europe when it launched later that year—so well, in fact, that it brought in enough money for Nintendo to officially establish its own UK branch.

In many ways, Argonaut's chip was the star. American children, in 1993, knew the name Argonaut. It was a massive leap for the small company, but not so much for the individual designers. "I got a bonus of about five thousand pounds," says Cuthbert. "And when you're twenty years old, that's amazing. But really, it wasn't a lot for a game that sold a few million copies."

THE FINAL DAYS OF SUPER FX

Nintendo and Argonaut's contract obligated the developer to create three games for the Super FX chip. So after *Star Fox* wrapped in December, the team of Goddard and Cuthbert was split up. Now, with more programming experience under his belt, Giles headed up the development of a racing game called *Wild Trax FX* while Cuthbert, who had led the *Star Fox* team, went to work on the sequel.

Goddard being asked to work on a racing game was not accidental. In London he had nearly single-handedly crafted a game called *Days of Thunder*, based on the NASCAR racing movie starring Tom Cruise. When the team was called away to Kyoto to work for Nintendo, Goddard was in the middle of programming a stunt car racer for the Amiga ST personal computer. And when they received the first Super FX development hardware, Goddard got "halfway through" a similar game before starting full time on *Star Fox*. And when that ended, he went back to his old code, teaming with Colin Reed—another Argonaut programmer who had moved to Kyoto to work on Super FX games—to flesh out the racing game.

Flair Technology was designing the Super FX chip on a tight schedule, and the version that ended up being used in *Star Fox* was a half-speed version of the original design. While Nintendo worked on the first Super FX game, Flair continued to perfect the chip. *Wild Trax* was the first game to use the upgraded Super FX2 chip, which was double the speed of the original. But it still had nowhere near the 3-D power required for realistic driving simulation. "*Wild Trax* started off with highly realistic car physics—proper torques and acceleration, friction…everything that car simulations do nowadays. And it looked really good, running at twenty frames per second.

"But then we had to turn that demo into an actual game, and every time we added little bits to the design, it started eating into the frame rate until we were down to 10 FPS. And at only ten frames per second, you can't see the effect of the car physics at all; you miss all the little nuances. You can get away with it in *Star Fox* because nobody actually knows what a space fighter ship moves like. But people know how a car handles."

In that respect, then, Cuthbert had the easier job because he was again working in the world of fantasy, and the designers of *Star Fox 2* could let their imaginations run wild with the double-speed chip. This meant that certain areas of the game played in true 3-D. That is, the map was a wide-open area on which the ships could change direction rather than a straight line with limited wiggle room. It was on these maps that the player could engage in strategic, team-based dogfights that pitted Fox and his friends against the Star Wolf team, a sort of looking-glass group of four evil animals that dogged the Fox team throughout their adventure.

In other ways, too, *Star Fox 2* was a more strategic game. Rather than simply being led on a few branching paths as in the first game, the player had his choice of missions to select on a map screen. He could see what planets the Star Wolf team was advancing on, and could try to clear those planets before his archrivals. If he waited too long, he would have to fight the Wolf Team before he could progress to the level itself.

Cuthbert and team finished *Star Fox 2* in early 1995. But by the time they were done, Nintendo was gearing up to release their fully 3-D next generation game hardware, the Nintendo 64. And they made the decision that all Super FX 3-D projects would not be released—the rationale being that they wanted to show players a clear distinction between the two-dimensional games of old and the forthcoming three-dimensional revolution. Unfortunately, after *Star Fox 2* was removed from the release schedule, the Nintendo 64's release was delayed to summer 1996.[*]

★ Some, but not all, of the strategic game play of *Star Fox 2* was used in the Nintendo 64 game *Star Fox 64* in 1997. The Star Wolf team was finally brought to life in that game.

The completion of the project, however, fulfilled the terms of Argonaut's original contract with Nintendo. Argonaut only worked on one more title before fully parting ways with Nintendo, a robot-battle game called *Vortex* that was published by a small third-party publisher called Electro Brain. A Super FX fighting game in the style of *Street Fighter*, un-imaginatively called *FX Fighter*, was previewed in *Electronic Gaming Monthly* magazine but quickly shelved; "it was awful," explains Cuthbert.[†]

† Errata: *FX Fighter* was eventually released for the IBM PC, years later. It was *phenomenally* awful.

Nintendo, meanwhile, experimented with other uses of the Super FX chip. "They made a really good version of *Pilotwings*," says Cuthbert, which was never released or even announced publicly. In fact, the only other game for which Nintendo used the chip was Shigeru Miyamoto's final SNES project,

Super Mario World 2: Yoshi's Island. Besides the doubled speed, the Super FX2 chip had the ability to display its screen data as sprites instead of simple filled polygons. This meant that an image could be scaled and rotated in real-time 3-D, but the player would see a seemingly hand-drawn graphic instead of a featureless block of color. Miyamoto used this to make Mario's newest adventure seem like a child's pop-up storybook come to life. When the Nintendo 64 was released shortly after, though, Miyamoto no longer needed a chip to do that.

THE PARTING OF THE WAYS

And what of the Argonaut programmers who'd come all the way to Kyoto? After *Star Fox 2* was canned, Cuthbert looked at the brand new Sony Play-Station and decided he wanted to work on this impressive-looking CD-based system. And so he headed to another new continent, joining Sony Computer Entertainment America in their Foster City, California offices to program a "sort of 3-D action hero platformer game" called *Blasto.*

Soon after finishing the project, Cuthbert decided that he truly belonged in Japan, not America. "I enjoyed California for the short time I was there, but I couldn't stand it any longer. You have to drive everywhere; you couldn't just walk somewhere for a drink. It wasn't the kind of relaxed, unplanned atmosphere of Japan. So I called up my friends at Sony Japan and said, 'well, give us a job, then.'"

By the time Cuthbert started work at Sony's Japan studios, the next-generation PlayStation 2 console was already in development. Cuthbert's programming expertise and ability to adapt to new and experimental hardware environments made him an ideal candidate to work on technical demonstrations for the PS2—graphical displays that would show off the machine's advanced capabilities. The demo that Cuthbert designed was, if nothing else, memorable: a 3-D model of a bathtub that contained vivid, lifelike water, toy submarines, and a giant rubber duck. It was shown off at the 1999 Electronic Entertainment Expo, and for a while, the duck was what most people thought of when "PlayStation 2" was mentioned.[*]

* Later, Squaresoft and Sony showed off a technical demo that used exceptionally high-quality versions of *Final Fantasy* characters, and the duck was rendered obsolete.

Cuthbert stayed with Sony long enough to program one game: *Piposaru 2001,* a follow-up to a PlayStation game called *Saru Getchu* (*Ape Escape* in the US). *Ape Escape* was one of the first games designed specifically around the two analog joysticks on the redesigned PlayStation controller. Players used one joystick to move the main character and the other to use weapons and various other implements to round up a troop of escaped monkeys. The cute monkey characters caught on in Japan, selling lots of stuffed monkeys and even some promotional toys at McDonald's. With the true PS2 sequel far off, Sony made the decision to turn Cuthbert's project into an *Ape Escape*-branded title.

"...It wasn't an *Ape Escape* game originally; in fact, the game design didn't have any apes at all. It was a game based on interaction between the player and groups of objects... [Making] all the characters into apes meant all the levels looked the same. Before that, we had all sorts of different levels—hordes of elephants, things like that."

Giles Goddard, meanwhile, never left Japan—he quit Argonaut to work full time at Nintendo's Kyoto offices. "As *Stunt Race FX* was coming to a close, they were working on developing the Nintendo 64 hardware with Silicon Graphics. So I went over to the SGI headquarters to give them advice on how game developers would want to use their hardware." Goddard returned to Kyoto with the specifications for the N64, and set to work making some technical demos using a Silicon Graphics supercomputer called the Onyx, which emulated the N64 hardware. "It was a dream job," recalls Goddard. "I had a supercomputer right next to my desk and I could do whatever I wanted with it. And so I spent about a year just doing demos, and stuff like that."

Silicon Graphics provided every Nintendo programmer with an Indy workstation, a lesser-powered (but still top-of-the-line) PC. Included in the package that SGI provided was a video camera that could be used with motion-capture software. "I cut some ping-pong balls in half and attached them to my face so the camera could read the movements of my head. And I'd just walk around all day with ping-pong balls on my face, sitting in front of the video camera. As I moved my face around, it would pick up the movements of the ping-pong balls. And there was a 3-D face on the screen, with bones underneath it. And so you'd lock the ping-pong balls to specific bones. As the balls moved, the bones moved. As the bones moved, the face would move along with it. That was early motion capture. What I find quite amusing is that they still use exactly the same technique today—they just have more expensive ping-pong balls."

Goddard's experiments captured the attention of his fellow developers. "My desk was right next to the Mario team, and they were looking for an interesting title screen or an interactive front end for *Super Mario 64*." Miyamoto was walking by Goddard's desk one day, saw his ping-pong ball demonstration, and asked him to do this but with a giant Mario face onscreen. Everyone agreed that it "looked really good," and the team programmed various animations and programmed a grasping hand that the player could use to stretch and deform Mario's face. Playing with Mario's face was a compelling activity in a game full of compelling activities. Players could spend hours fiddling with Mario's face as if it was a giant ball of virtual modeling clay. It was not a *game*, but it was *play*—in other words, it was pure Nintendo.

Goddard and Reed's next project, his first full N64 game, was *not* pure Nintendo. In fact, the other members of EAD (Nintendo's Kyoto development studio) were "dead against" *1080° Snowboarding*. "Miyamoto loves skiing, so he suggested we make a ski game. But we sat down and realized that skiing isn't fun in a video game because you can't do tricks or anything. So he agreed to do a snowboarding game, which is what I love.

"We had two options: either make a cutesy, character-based, typical Nintendo game, or do something different with a realistic, older teen-oriented look. *Stunt Race FX* was a cutesy racer and I was sick of that. The thing about those kinds of games is it's a free-for-all when it comes to effects and physics, because it's a fantasy world. We wanted a world where you couldn't do anything that you couldn't do in real life, something that was as realistic as possible but still fun.

"The rest of EAD were against it. They didn't think it would sell in Japan if it didn't have cute Mario characters. So we kept it in secrecy inside EAD until it was looking really good, and then we showed it off and they were really quite impressed with it. And it ended up doing well in Japan, as well as an N64 game could do at that time. It was more of a hit in America, though."

Although Miyamoto was officially the producer of *1080°*, he was "very much hands-off" according to Goddard. "He had a few ideas—he suggested that players could use the Z-trigger on the N64 controller to bend the snowboarder's knees, to soften the blow of impact. That turned out to be an important aspect of the game, because you could then do more dangerous tricks and it would all still obey the laws of physics."

Goddard has unflattering words for the wave of "extreme sports" titles that followed in the wake of *1080°*'s unexpected success. "The sort of in-your-face style of snowboarding game where you're just running as fast as you can throughout the entire game is not EAD style at all, and that's not the kind of game I like either. It's very easy to get cheap and make a game that's entertaining for the first five minutes, with lots of things coming at you. And this is great for E3 demonstrations. But after the first five minutes, you're bored because there's no underlying game play."

Goddard left Nintendo soon after finishing *1080° Snowboarding*. It was an amicable split; he retained close ties with the friends he'd made at the company, but he wanted to tackle new challenges in the country he'd made his home. He worked with a Tokyo-based company called Video System on one PlayStation 2 title, but it wasn't long before Nintendo contacted him again. A Nintendo-contracted developer called Param was converting a Nintendo 64 Disk Drive game called *Kyoujin no Doshin* (*Doshin the Giant*) to the GameCube, and their one and only programmer had quit. In desperation, they called Nintendo to ask if they could spare any top-level programmers who could take up the task and single-handedly finish the conversion. Nintendo put them in touch with Goddard, and he went right to work. He tossed out everything the other programmer had done and began reprogramming

the game from scratch. The new version of *Doshin* attracted a much wider audience on the more popular GameCube, and an English version of the game was even released in the UK, although not in the US.

A Star Fox team reunion party, 1996. L-R: Hiro Yamada (Nintendo), Angus Guschwan (then of Sony), Giles Goddard, Yoichi Yamada (Nintendo), Jonathan Beard (then of Sony), Shigeru Miyamoto with a pair of chopsticks in his ear, Dylan Cuthbert.

STARTUPS

While at Sony in Tokyo, Dylan Cuthbert was already hatching a plan to move back to the Japanese city closest to his heart. On September 4, 2001, Cuthbert and fellow Ape Escape designer Ken Shimoga started their own company, Q-Games, in a tiny office just northwest of central Kyoto. The philosophy of the company was entirely different from Argonaut's technology-first-games-second approach: "Fun games—with good technology if it's *necessary*," says Cuthbert. "We want the good technology, but we *really* want the game to be quality. We want the player to be happy, not for us, the designers, to be amused by pulling off programming tricks.

Dylan Cuthbert and Ken Shimoga

"At Argonaut, the idea was that we were going to get some really cool 3-D technology going and only later come up with game ideas to go around it. It was a very Western design mentality, and I realize now that you need to temper that with the Nintendo mindset of using the technical tricks for a *reason*. You can't just do things for your own gratification."

Q-Games, now a thirteen-person organization, is in the business of "next generation games," games for the hardware systems that will follow the PlayStation 2 and GameCube. So why is there PlayStation 2 development hardware underneath everyone's desk? "We might do something for the current generation," Cuthbert muses.

Giles Goddard's company, meanwhile, is programming exclusively for the GameCube for the time being. Vitei, a name chosen by Goddard because "it was one of the only five-letter website addresses left," boasts more GameCube development kits than actual employees. The entire company consists of Goddard and Akintunde Omitowoju, a Nigeria-born programmer who worked on Nintendo's *Metroid Prime* at Retro Studios in Austin, Texas before joining Goddard in Kyoto. Their first project is still under wraps, although Goddard promises that it will be visually different from anything else on the system.

FINAL THOUGHTS ACROSS THREE COUNTRIES

Having worked in the UK, US, and Japanese games businesses, what would Cuthbert say are the major differences? "England was far more civilized," he begins, "The American side is much more about corporate politics and trying to get one's position to be upgraded from assistant director to director, from programmer to senior programmer. It's all working out how to get senior in front of your name within the structure of the company. And I really didn't like that. In England, the culture is far more technology-based, people really into cool technology."

Giles Goddard felt that the technological divide is what set up the major difference between England and Japan. "As a *gaijin* working at NCL in Kyoto, the work aspect of it was very good because I was working at Nintendo with all these brilliant game designers. And you don't even realize that they're brilliant game designers until you go out into the world and hear people talking about them, these people you work with day to day.

"And there's no ego problems with NCL at all. But they're all really high-level. All the data you get back from artists is really good quality. Programming isn't really the strong point of EAD; it's the designers and artists who are really good. So it was great to work with them. We brought a lot of programming expertise that would not have been there otherwise. The Japanese programmers always work by the book, they don't think for themselves. And that's really bad when you're programming games.

"When we programmed the Amiga, there was no information at all. So you basically had to find out for yourself how to program it, which was no mean feat as there were not really any manuals around. We brought that whole way of self-taught, freestyle programming to Japan. There was no hobbyist programming in Japan at that time; there still isn't. We brought this experience that they had never really seen before."

Goddard closes our conversation with a story that illustrates how even illustrated artwork is treated in a strictly by-the-book manner in Japanese schools. "When I was working with Video System, I had to look at resumes from schools all over Japan. And we had a bunch of portfolios from one particular school, which had sent all their students' stuff over in one book.

"And all the pictures were the same. Literally. There was one section that was cubes, and everybody had drawn a cube. In the next section everyone had drawn an apple. And that was the way they were presenting their students, showing how well they could draw what they were told to. And that epitomizes the Japanese way of doing things, where individualism is not even considered. In the West, every single picture would be different, wouldn't it?"

■ ■ ■

CHAPTER 7

ADVENTURES IN AKIHABARA: THE JAPANESE GAME MARKETPLACE

The name "Akihabara" loosely translates to "field of autumn leaves." When this section of Tokyo was first christened, it was home to many lower-class samurai whose cheap wooden houses often burnt down *en masse* whenever a domestic fire got out of control. After a particularly bad blaze in 1869 that pretty much destroyed the area, not to mention a good part of the rest of Tokyo, the imperial government decided to leave it as a wide-open field to "act as a firewall to protect the Imperial Palace. Eventually trees took over this wasteland and it became famous for the vast quantities of dead leaves that littered the ground in autumn."[1]

You won't find any leaves in today's Akihabara—it's difficult enough to find a place to sit down. Akihabara is the electronics capital of Tokyo, of Japan, and of the world. The cognoscenti abbreviate it to "Akiba" or just "Aki." A wide boulevard called Chuo-doori (literally, *central street*) runs parallel to the train station, and for a mile down the road all you can see are tall buildings literally covered in bright fluorescent signs, buildings packed with stores offering all sorts of electronics and home electrics: air conditioners, refrigerators, televisions, DVD players, minidisc recorders, anything you can think of. Over two hundred and fifty electronics stores are packed into this tiny section of Tokyo.

During spring and summer, Chuo-doori is filled with people. Masses upon masses of shoppers, tourists, and Japanese going about their daily lives pack the sidewalks and spill out onto the streets. They maneuver deftly, balancing huge shopping bags as they weave in and out, past fellow shoppers, past streetside vendors selling everything from *takoyaki* (fried octopus balls) to cheap costume jewelry to pirated copies of Microsoft Windows. It is like Disneyland, but twice as crowded and twice as exciting. Akihabara's customers range from expert computer hackers, who prowl the side streets looking for used parts and rare hardware, to professional musicians looking for new equipment, to confused tourists looking for duty-free deals. On any given day, you can easily spot an Aki first-timer, hands heavy with bags, wallet light with emptiness, eyes darting about in hopes of glimpsing a Citibank sign.

Ducking down a side street to hide from the excitement, you enter a tiny covered shopping area to find rows and rows of ancient stalls manned by ancient Japanese men selling electronics from a bygone area: vacuum tubes, transistors. Once, Akihabara was filled with tiny stores like this. Now they are disappearing one by one, replaced with another high-rise filled with high-definition TV sets and miniature cell phones. And, of course, for the last three decades the stores of Akihabara have been filled with every video game you could ever possibly imagine.

Parents in the United States doing their Christmas shopping tend to be overwhelmed at the sheer number of different video game titles in the Toys 'R Us games aisle. The average Akihabara store has about ten times that amount. Not only are there many more games available, but the average shelf life of any of those games is also far longer than it is in the US. Prices tend to be lower in Akihabara because of the stiff competition. In even a largish city like Kanazawa, where I lived for a year, there were only a few such home electronics stores. But in Akihabara's dense forest of *denki-ya-san*, every store must struggle to get noticed with attractive prices.

The tall, flashy stores with neon lights are the ones your eyes will be immediately drawn to, but if you want to find the true adventures of Akihabara you should ignore them. The appeal of giant, neon-encrusted stores like Sofmap and LAOX is that they tend to have giant displays of video game characters and playable demonstration units. Until its closing in 2004, a giant store called AsoBit City was home to a life-sized Mario statue and a mammoth Xbox play area, encased in translucent green walls, that featured the very latest games set on free play, with comfortable chairs and headphones to try them out.

These large chains are also guaranteed far more copies of the latest game or hardware release on its first day of availability. Furthermore, they generally open for business earlier than other Akihabara stores. It is in front of these stores, then, that we witness the legendary long lines of gamers waiting for hours at a time for new products on their first day of release.

Head down to any major electronics store in Tokyo the morning of a new game's release date and you're sure to see a line of customers stretched out from the front door. There might even be store employees holding signs and announcing into megaphones that such-and-such game will be on sale that day, even announcing the price and the opening time of the store.

An employee of Bic Camera in Shibuya, Tokyo holds up a sign advertising that the very first copies of Final Fantasy X-2 will go on sale at their store before anywhere else in Japan—on sale no less (above, left). A line of otaku forms, waiting patiently for the store to open (above, right).

Inside the store, Square Enix executives give a presentation on a makeshift stage, briefly interviewing the first otaku to get his copy of the latest Final Fantasy game, along with extra first-day-of-release goodies.

Masato Takeno described such an event in his 1988 short story "The Yamada Diary." "As I passed the big-name discount camera store in front of the station, I saw that a line of seventy or eighty people had formed, waiting for the store to open. This was a weekday, yet junior high school kids, even grade-schoolers were lining up at the storefront computer game counter."*

Takeno's story is a science-fiction tale of a game that imitates the life of its player (or perhaps vice-versa), but his description of the lineup outside the store is purely realistic in many ways. Seventy or eighty people might be on the low side for a big-city store, but those in line do typically represent a wide range of ages, from elementary school kids skipping class to businessmen skipping work. As mentioned in Chapter 4, it was written into law that *Dragon Quest* games must be released on a weekend, even though most games are released on Thursdays. The big-name titles, of course, are usually released during school vacations.

★ Anthologized in *Monkey Brain Sushi: New Tastes In Japanese Fiction* (Kodansha, 1991). Translation by Alfred Birnbaum.

Furthermore, many people join these lines on impulse, just like this story's protagonist. Yes, many of them are game *otaku* who have anticipated the release date for some time and who have already pre-ordered the title to assure they get a copy on release day. But many of them are simply casual game players who might enjoy the excitement and companionship of waiting in line for hours in the early morning.

This practice was born not so much out of crazy *otaku* behavior but out of necessity. Demand for Famicom cartridges, especially *Dragon Quest* games, vastly exceeded supply, and sales were strictly first come, first served.

This was also the situation in the US when Nintendomania ruled, of course. The difference was that in Japan, video games had a set release date—one day, announced in the weekly *Famitsu* magazine or on signs in the game shops, on which the game would be available across the country in every store.

Meanwhile, in the US, there were no set release dates. The closest that *Nintendo Power* ever got to reporting on release windows was down to the *month*, and even then they weren't always accurate. Customers had to keep calling stores to see if the games were in, and then rush down before they sold out. They were often too late. Eventually, US game companies did begin to publicize actual release dates for new games. It started out as clever ad campaigns for a few major releases—the release date for *Mortal Kombat II* was "Mortal Monday"; *Sonic The Hedgehog 2* came out on "Sonic 2sday."

Nowadays, most games in the US have official release dates, but there still aren't any lines in front of stores here because most US video game retailers have "preorder" programs, where the customer can put down money on a game to guarantee a copy at launch. Japan is coming around to this practice but lining up is still prevalent.

Still, lines snaking out of storefronts to pick up a hot new product are not unheard of around the world, to which a young boy named Harry Potter might attest.

CLASSIC MUSEUM STORES
FOR COLLECTORS IN AKIHABARA

As visually interesting as the giant stores can be, there is a certain breed of game *otaku* that rarely sets foot in them and *never* spends money there, yet perhaps drops more cash in Akihabara on any given day than even dedicated gamers might spend in a month. These particular *otaku* are the kindred spirits of the American collectors with a rat's nest of 1970s-vintage wires behind their televisions and stacks of Atari 2600 games lined up on their bookshelves. They collect classic video games, eschewing the new and flashy for retro nostalgia. Some collect the earliest primitive game consoles from the pre-Nintendo era, some are nuts about the Famicom, still others snatch up 'neo-classic' systems like the NEC PC Engine or Neo-Geo.

And they know how to work the system, where to get their out-of-print gaming fixes at reasonable enough prices. But the many, many *gaijin* gamers who invade Japan each year—whether on school exchange programs, post-collegiate English teaching stints, for business, or just on vacation—don't. So if you plan to visit Japan in the near future or just want a little inside information on what to look for in Akihabara, this next section is just for you: a gamer's guide to Akihabara's exciting collectors' shops.

The first category of stores is what I cynically dub the 'museum-stores.' Their prices are almost outrageously high, but they stock nearly every rare and out-of-print game that you have ever heard of, and then some. You don't need to spend any money to enjoy yourself in stores like Media Land or Trader—just shove your comically oversized *gaijin* body down the claustrophobically narrow aisles that so typify these stores, and gawk at the shelves full of pieces on display, relics from another time. Note how neat and organized the games are, separated by console of course, but also alphabetically. Note that each item for sale bears a tiny paper tag that explains the condition of the item and what, if anything, is missing. Note how high the prices are.

This is not to say that Media Land or Trader aren't worth your patronage. Media Land's first floor is a great place to find heavy discounts on brand new games and heavier discounts on slightly older ones that proved less popular than initially imagined. And Trader's prices tend to be quite reasonable at times, even on their massive collection of early video game hardware. And you can't beat the selection. But you shouldn't buy a thing there unless you've poked around some other stores, one of which is so popular that it operates over half a dozen stores in Akihabara alone.

Those in the know realize that I'm talking about Liberty, a chain of used CD/DVD/game stores that pay lower prices for bought-back merchandise but pass that savings on to the shopper. Liberty is the best place in Akihabara and maybe even Tokyo to shop for video game music CDs. Any one of their panoply of outlets in Aki and elsewhere in Tokyo contains a massive selection of new, used, and out-of-print CDs for fair, if not bargain, prices, all based on the condition and completeness of the disc. Liberty outlets also contain a great selection of used video games at much lower prices than the museum-stores. The condition of the games isn't usually as good, and the super-rare items don't often show up there. But that's a good thing, as Liberty teaches first-timers and even old pros about what is and is not truly a rare find.

Another fantastic Aki shop that the informed frequent is called Friends (*Furenzu*), and it is nearly impossible to find. It requires a bit of walking down Chuo-doori, away from the glitz and glamour of the electric city, and even once you reach it, it's tough to spot because the only landmark is a tiny red LCD sign that scrolls the store's name in *katakana* characters. The best thing to look for is the giant red awning of an Italian restaurant called *Segafredo**; Friends' shop is located a floor above and to the left of the restaurant's entrance. Friends carries most everything from a wide range of Famicom Disk System software and classic Famicom-era memorabilia to a small wall of cheaply priced Sega Saturn games. And a cluttered glass case underneath the cash register is home to a variety of one-of-a-kind items.

> * Not related to the video game company Sega, as far as I can tell.

And then there are the off-the-wall places. One, called Chaos Shop, is located up a narrow staircase adjacent to its big brother store, Messe Sanoh. The main Messe Sanoh shop consists of two floors. The first is like Media Land's ground level: newly-released and slightly older titles at bargain prices. The second is filled with video game tie-in merchandise, game music CDs†, and other such memorabilia. But Chaos Shop is the one that American expatriates spend time in when they're feeling a little homesick, as it is Akihabara's imported-games store, featuring shelves full of games, toys, and books produced for the American games market. Chaos Shop is the only place in Aki that Japanese gamers can get their hands on Western exclusives like *Grand Theft Auto Vice City*, at about twice the price it sells for in the US. It's still worth a visit even for Yankees, however, as there's a ton of strange stuff there from all over the world.

> † For the most part, Messe Sanoh's game-music CD section features nearly every music CD ever printed by Nihon Falcom, the developers of the popular RPG series *Ys* (pronounced 'ease'). Next to the CDs are a wide variety of *Ys* games for personal computers.

Now that you know *where* to shop in Akihabara, here's some advice on *how* to shop:

Condition is king—a little damage might mean a big price reduction. There is, largely, a fixation on (some might say an obsession with) cleanliness and condition of the games. Fortunately, stores are all too happy to accommodate (see the following section, "The Debate Over Used Games"). This is actually an advantage for *gaijin* game collectors on a trip to Japan. In large part, they are not competing for the same items as the Japanese who prowl these stores. As long as the game is complete with its original instruction manual and cardboard box, does it matter if the box has a few scuffs? It's better than the condition in which you find most classic American games, if you can find them at all, and it's roughly equivalent to what you've seen on eBay, at about half the price—sold!

Don't buy it right away; it's not going to disappear. On your first trip to Akihabara it's easy to be totally flabbergasted—there they are, every Japanese video game you've ever lusted after, sitting right beside each other on the shelves. Hasn't anybody noticed them there? Why, those are *rare games!* Those would go for *twice* that price online! Better buy them all up right now! That's what you think, anyway. The reality is that, with very few exceptions, you'll probably find a better price on each one of those games after an hour or two of shopping around. And imagine how well you'll do if you avoid buying things on the first *day*, coming back later to grab everything at the rock-bottom price. Sure, you might miss one or two great deals and have to pay a little more here and there, but in the long run you'll save lots of cash.

Or, don't buy anything in Akihabara, ever. "*What?*" you ask, incredulous. But it's true, to an extent, that practically everything that you can acquire in Aki is to be had for a lower price somewhere else. Yes, Akihabara is an adventure that any Japan-bound video game fiend should experience. Yes, it is incredibly convenient; every rare video game ever made is packed into a two-block radius. And yes, buying brand new games, and games that have been out for a few weeks, is cheapest in Aki because of the cutthroat competition between major stores. But nearly everything in Akihabara is cheaper elsewhere, if you've got the time to hunt it down.

OUTSIDE OF AKIHABARA

Even if your trip to Japan won't take you outside of the Tokyo city limits, there are plenty of bargains to be had outside of Akihabara. West of Shinjuku station are branches of the same chain stores that populate Akihabara, like Liberty and Trader. The prices are around the same as the Akihabara branches, but the selection is better because there are fewer tourists picking through the shelves. These particular stores are located very close to the famous Shinjuku Sportsland arcade, which boasts a basement level that looks like a museum of martial-arts fighting games, from the earliest iterations of *Street Fighter* to the latest versions. Occasion-ally, arcade games that are months away from nationwide release are beta-tested at Sports-land, so there is no telling what you might find. The other side of Shinjuku station meanwhile boasts a Virgin Megastore, Tower Records, and a giant Kinokuniya bookstore with a massive selection of Western books and magazines for the homesick expatriate.

Another great place to buy used games and shop around for all sorts of vintage game-related merchandise is Manda-rake (pronounced mon-da-ra-kay), a famous chain that sells all sorts of used *manga*, *anime*, and anything else related to the *otaku* lifestyle. Mandarake outlets are the Mecca of *anime* fans; anything and everything can be found within these massive superstores, usually at a reasonable price. A few years ago, 'anything and every-thing' expanded to include classic video games. Now, most Mandarake outlets have a wide variety of rare and unusual video games of all kinds, stored and sold with the same high standard of care as the stores' array of collectible *manga*.

> **Occasionally, arcade games that are months away from nation-wide release are beta-tested at Sportsland, so there is no telling what you might find.**

The original Mandarake was established in 1987 in Nakano Broadway, a multilevel shopping mall of *otaku* specialty stores. Now, Mandarake fills large spaces on three floors of that mall, with a very good video game shop on the fourth floor. To get to Nakano Broadway, leave from the North exit of JR Nakano station, then walk straight up through the Sun Mall shopping cen-ter. There are two more Mandarake outlets in Tokyo: one in Shibuya, and one in Akihabara. Even more are scattered across Japan: two in Osaka, one in Nagoya, and one in Fukuoka that boasts many visitors from Korea—the flight from Seoul to Fukuoka is only ninety minutes.[2]

Other major cities in Japan each have their own "Akihabara," a section of the city or a particular street known for electronics and games. In Kyoto, it is the section of Teramachi Street just south of Shijo-doori (4th Street). Furthest south is Wanpaku Kosou, instantly recognizable by the English lettering "Licensed By Nintendo." The bottom floor of Wanpaku features games for recent hardware, and the upper floor, accessible via a tiny metal staircase, contains a decent selection of classic games and hardware that tend to be priced a bit high. Better deals can be found at Ninomiya, an electronics chain store with a bright red-and-white sign. The second floor boasts some of the city's best deals on new and used games, with fair prices but a slightly less impressive array of classic hardware.

There are few video game specialty stores on the covered section of Teramachi up north, although various *anime* stores abound, and the collectible record stores between Teramachi and Kawaramachi have video game sections that are worth a look. Also, if you happen to find yourself in Kyoto, remember that a short walk south of Teramachi-Shijo is Kiyamachi-Rokujo, the site of the original Nintendo building.

Before taking the train from Kyoto to Osaka, stop in the stores by the stations. If you're taking the Keihan line, you'll find a Book-Off used bookstore in the Sanjo Keihan station with a decent selection of used games but a much broader selection of used books, including lots of cheap, slightly worn game strategy guides. Or, if you're taking the JR line to Osaka, stop by the branch of the Softmap computer store, accessible via underground walkway from Kyoto Station. Its video game section is difficult to find but highly recommended.

Even stores in Den Den Town sometimes hold special promotions. In this case, it's a chance to play the Square Enix RPG Star Ocean 3 weeks before its release date.

After an hour-long train ride to set your bags down and rest your hands, you'll be in Osaka. Osaka's "electric city" is called Den Den Town, and some consider it even better than Akihabara for price, selection, and convenience. The 'must-visit' video game shops of Osaka are stretched out over about a mile of densely packed shopping street, with Den Den Town at one end and the giant Namba shopping/nightlife district at the other.

The best way to traverse this gauntlet in one day might be to take the Sakai-suji brown train line to Ebisu-cho station, and take a right past the turnstiles to exit out onto Sakai-suji Street. You should already be face-to-face with video game shops like Super Potato and Retro TV Game Revival. All who visit Retro TV Game Revival come away thinking that it might be the best vintage gaming store in the world. From the earliest 'dedicated' Nintendo home systems to a huge array of games for rare systems like the Sega SG-1000 and PC Engine, all at fair prices, Retro TV Game Revival seems to have it all. Super Potato is Retro's sister store, with a few classic games and systems but mostly great deals on newer items. Another used game store, Plus+, is across the street and features even better prices but a smaller selection.

Continuing up the street you'll first come across the Den Den Town branch of Sofmap, then Big Tiger, another sister store to Super Potato. On the left side of the street you'll see the Namba branch of Mandarake. Stay on the left side of the road and keep peeking down the cross streets, because eventually you'll come upon the Namba branch of Sofmap. Every Sofmap is worth a visit. Although the new games on sale on the shops' bottom floors are often identical*, the used game floors are always different.

Coming out of Sofmap, bear to the left and walk a little further up the road to Namba proper. Namba is a maze of covered shopping streets, like Kyoto's Teramachi but far more labyrinthine. Giant electronics stores, used bookstores, and tiny toy stores punctuate the region's massive video arcades, pachinko parlors, and karaoke halls—poke your head in and see if there are any Famicom games in the glass case under the cash register.

* Sofmap will often discover crates of new, unsold games in their warehouse, and then sell them dirt-cheap in their major branches—brand new, shrink-wrapped games that are over a decade old in some cases, for the Sega CD or even the Famicom.

If you find yourself in Nagoya, head to the Osu section of town to find a covered shopping street dotted with electronics and games stores. In Kanazawa, head outside the trendy Korinbo downtown area and up near Shigeru Miyamoto's alma mater to find Book-Off stores and a chain of used-game stores called Takarajima (Treasure Island), easily spotted for the cartoon pirate that adorns each shop.

Indeed, no matter where you are in Japan, the country is a video game lover's paradise. But a few years ago, a string of lawsuits threatened the very existence of used-game stores.

THE DEBATE OVER USED GAMES

How much control does Nintendo have over a piece of software once it leaves the store? Does the buyer have the right to copy the disc and sell the copy to his friends? Not in the US or Japan, nor practically anywhere else in the world save for a few small nations where intellectual property rights are quite literally a foreign concept. If the buyer owns a video rental store, can he purchase video games at retail, then set them out for rental? In the US, yes. In Japan, no. If the buyer grows tired of the game, can he sell it? In the US, yes. In Japan, yes—for now.

The battle over used game sales in Japan is quite similar to the debates over video game rentals in the US in the late eighties, chronicled in David Sheff's *Game Over*. Nintendo's side of the argument was that video game rentals would decrease sales of their games. Movie videocassettes only became available for rental after the film had racked up dollars at the box office. Moreover, video rental stores paid the studios premium prices for new tapes before they were made available to the public. But video game rentals would be available day-and-date with the game's release. There was no protection for Nintendo.

Blockbuster Video's side of the argument was simple: no matter what the consequences for Nintendo, Blockbuster had the right to do whatever they wanted with the games they purchased. The courts sided with Blockbuster, and that was the end of the discussion.[*] To Nintendo's credit, after losing the court battle they began to work more closely with Blockbuster to hash out a mutually beneficial solution. These days, hit GameCube titles like *Animal Crossing* appear in Blockbuster Video before they hit store shelves—at a hefty price per unit, one must assume.

[*] Nintendo did sue, and win, for another charge. Blockbuster included photocopied instruction manuals with the games it rented out, and kept the originals. This was done so that, if a renter lost or destroyed the instruction manual, Blockbuster could simply make another. Even so, this was clear copyright infringement.

[†] To all who have ever complained about the so-called "high price" of Japanese animation videos in the US: during the VHS era of Japan, new anime series sold for the equivalent of $100 for a thirty-minute tape. Even today, new animation DVDs cost between $50 and $100.

The situation is markedly different in Japan. Videocassettes, which typically retail between $50 and $100[†], are marked either "For Sale" or "For Rental Only." Video rental establishments *must* purchase rental version videos at a much higher price, of course. This criteria does *not* apply, amazingly, to music CDs, which are rented out at nearly every video store in Japan and are *quite* easy to copy. This has led to the rise of controversial new copy-protected CDs that do not work properly on a personal computer.

And what of games? Video game rentals are in fact *unheard of* here, even though video games, compared to audio CDs, are nearly impossible to duplicate. The law equates games with movies, and no company so far has produced "For Rental Only" copies of video games. Recently, some companies have begun to supply rental stores with demo discs of their new games, which contain sample levels or promotional movies. These can usually be rented for free—of course, the same demo discs are generally *given away* in the United States.

What about used games? In the US, there was never any debate over used game sales. This is surprising given Nintendo's litigious streak in those early days. Perhaps if they'd won their suit against Blockbuster they'd have moved on to used game sales, but this never transpired. At this point, used game sales are so common in the US that no person or company would be able to question their legality.

Stores that sell used video games are actually *more* common in Japan. But the road to legality has been long and bumpy, ending only in an April 2002 Supreme Court ruling! This followed two conflicting decisions in the district and, later, the high courts of Tokyo and Osaka. Tokyo-based Enix was the plaintiff of one suit, Osaka-based Capcom the other. At question was whether games fell into the category of "cinematographic works." That is, if the distribution of video game software fell under the same legal restrictions as the distribution of films. Here's how the cases broke down—note the topsy-turvy, seemingly arbitrary nature of the Japanese legal system at work:[3]

May 27, 1999: The Tokyo District Court rules that video games are *not* cinematographic works and therefore the sale of used games is permissible under copyright law. Enix appeals.

October 7, 1999: The Osaka District Court rules that video games *are* cinematographic works and therefore the sale of used games is *not* permissible under copyright law. The defendant appeals.

March 27, 2001: The Tokyo High Court rules that video games *are* cinematographic works, and therefore the sale of used games is *not* permissible under copyright law.

March 29, 2001: The Osaka High Court rules that video games *are* cinematographic works, and therefore the sale of used games *is* permissible under copyright law.

At this point, used game retailers had no idea what to do. Sofmap Store 13 in Tokyo, once the largest and most-visited stores in the chain, first stopped selling Enix games and then shut its doors completely. Most other stores continued to sell used games pending the decision of the Supreme Court. Finally, on April 25, 2002, it ruled that "in the case of the transfer of ownership of copies of cinematographic work that are used in conjunction with household TV game machines…the right to transfer to the public the ownership of copies of the works concerned shall be exhausted by the legitimate first sale…and copyright shall not have an efficacy on the conducts of re-transfer to the public of the copies concerned."[4]

In short, the court evoked "exhaustion theory" or the "first sale doctrine," which in layman's terms state that once the copyright holders sell the copy of their work, where that copy ends up is determined by the person who bought it. That's what your $50 buys you—a guarantee that you can sell what you just bought. The rights of distribution, it is specifically stated, extend to transfer of ownership, *not* rental.

Questions of legality aside, the fact is that today, used video games are sold widely in both the US and Japan. And the difference in how used game sales are run in both countries is like night and day.

It is a simple fact that used game retailers in the US and Japan treat their products differently. This stems from how the game *players* treat their games after they buy them. Japanese gamers tend to keep their games in pristine condition. This is more easily done these days, now that most games come in sturdy plastic DVD cases with storage slots for memory cards and instruction manuals. But this was no small task when most games shipped in cardboard boxes with flimsy paper or plastic inserts. Indeed, simple use tends to wear out the boxes and it's difficult to find perfect copies of even mega-popular Famicom games like *Super Mario Bros.* in like-new condition.

★ An aside to hardcore game fanatics: Like all generalizations, this may not apply to you personally. In fact, since you're reading this book it probably doesn't. It certainly doesn't apply to this author, who is much more Japanese about his game collection.

But it is *far* easier to find them than it is to find perfect, boxed copies of the US version. Because, where boxes are lost in Japan to the ravages of time *in spite* of having been well taken care of, it is common practice in the US to let game boxes and manuals kick around the living room until they fall apart—if, in fact, they are kept for more than a day or two and not immediately thrown in the trash.*

What's more, it is my observation that Japanese gamers sell back used games earlier and more frequently than their American counterparts. When a brand-new game is released in the US, you usually have to wait a week or more before one or two copies find their way back to stores. In Japan, the waiting time is more like a *day*, and there is always an ample supply. With a waiting time like that, the chances that a game will be abused in the interim are minimal.

Moreover, since Japanese gamers tend to be fastidious about having things in mint condition, it is only natural that condition would play a large part in used-game sales. And indeed, it makes a big difference. Before buying back a game, the clerk will of course check to make sure the game still works, but will also check for the presence of everything originally included with the new copy: instruction booklet, box, posters, etc. The CD will be fully examined, and even a tiny scratch brings down the buy-back price. A game that might fetch ¥1000 when complete, if brought back with only an instruction booklet and a one-centimeter surface scratch might only bring ¥50 or less—even if the game works perfectly!

Such a game would probably be marked "JUNK" and sold for ¥100 out of a cardboard box on the floor. Games in better condition would be placed into a plastic bag specially sized to fit the product. The price would be marked on a sticker affixed to the plastic (*never* the box itself!), or written on a slip of paper. That slip of paper would detail any imperfections noticed on inspection: a small tear on the box, a missing poster. The price would be marked down accordingly. This does *not* only apply to the collectible museum-stores of Akihabara. It applies even to tiny used game stores in rural Japan. Video games, new and old, are treated like collectible comic books across the country.

Why? One reason is that for quite a while, the average video game store in Japan was independently run. The huge, city-block-filling camera and electronics stores of Japan's major cities sold Famicom games, of course, but these were few. Most games were bought from independent retailers. In most cases these were *literal* mom-and-pop establishments. This meant that each store was free to set its own, case-by-case rules about buying back used video games.

In the US, however, large discount chains sold most video games: Sears, Toys 'R Us, K-Mart. These large chains would never set up any type of used game sections, no more than they would have started dealing in used toys or furniture. It was common to find used games at garage sales, but this was hardly a reliable source. For a long time, the only way to buy or sell your used games with any semblance of reliability was to patronize the mail-order companies that advertised in the back of video game magazines. You'd send in your old games and a list of games you wanted to buy. If you were lucky, you'd get them within a few weeks with no substitutions.

The US finally had a nationwide used game bricks-and-mortar retailer when Funco, the most successful of the mail-order trade-in houses, opened Funcoland chain stores in strip malls across the country. The main trade was NES games, but games and boxes were never kept together—boxes went up on the wall as a display, and games were kept behind the counter. The games were not priced with stickers or tags. Instead, a circular that looked like a racing form was available at the store every month that kept track of price fluctuations. Funcoland paid less for games with no boxes or instructions but charged the same price for a game in any condition.

Eventually Electronics Boutique, a computer-software mall chain, began to sell used software. So did Software Etc., a division of the computer retailer Babbage's. To compete with Funcoland in the nation's strip malls, Babbage's launched a line of stores called GameStop, which specialized in used games. Funcoland failed to keep up with the competition and Babbage's bought them out, eventually renaming all their gaming specialty stores to GameStop. GameStop and Electronics Boutique currently comprise the major gaming specialty retailers in the US.

How do they treat rare games today? Eventually, to clear more shelf space for new titles, many stores started to rip up and throw away the boxes for cartridge games. Some still keep the boxes for the few games they receive, but they don't alter the price if no box is present. And to the great chagrin of collectors, the box is usually pasted with stickers—price on the front, a new UPC code on the back, and maybe even clear stickers that seal the box shut. All of these can ruin the box if not removed with great care.

This would *never, ever* happen in Japan. They would balk at the practice of ripping up boxes and selling the unboxed copy at full price, or selling a scratched, bare CD for anything over a few dollars. The absurdity of the entire situation escalates when the game in question is actually a rare collectible. Japanese game store clerks are generally well aware of the rarity of most games, and while this means it is not likely that you will find a true bargain in a used games section, it also means you can sell your rare games at a decent price at most stores.

Japanese stores will buy back any classic video game system, even ancient pre-Famicom systems. In fact, since these items are rare in Japan, stores are only too happy to purchase them for resale at a premium price. But neither Electronics Boutique nor GameStop has ever purchased anything older than the NES, and the number of stores that carry even those products are dwindling. As of February 22, 2004, GameStop stopped buying back NES, SNES, N64, and Sega Dreamcast games, accessories, and hardware.

What this means is that classic game collectors have turned in droves to buying and selling games online, mostly on the online auction site eBay, turning over cash to strangers because they can find no other way to purchase collectible games in good condition. The chains have taken themselves out of the running by destroying merchandise—when they buy it at all. The few surviving independent retailers tend to treat rarities with respect, but only a handful of these stores actually exist in the US.

VIDEO GAME TIE-IN MERCHANDISING

Used games, new games. Is that where all Japanese gamers' entertainment dollars go at retail? Hardly. Japan's love for video games and game characters means that, just like the *anime* and *manga* cultures, all sorts of licensed goods featuring video game characters can be found in many different types of retail establishments all over the country.

By far the largest tie-in product to video games is, as discussed in Chapter 5, game music soundtrack CDs. In general, you won't find video game music CDs in the same places that you find video games. There are a few exceptions; Liberty stores in Akihabara and elsewhere, in addition to used video games, feature a wide selection of new, used, and rare soundtrack CDs. Retro TV Game Revival in Osaka's Den Den Town has an enviable selection of fairly priced used and rare soundtracks, including a shelf or two of scratched CDs that play perfectly but may have a few cosmetic defects. And the branch of the electronics chain Ninomiya, near the national park in Nara prefecture, has floors devoted to both games and music.

But in general, you'll have to go elsewhere to get your *Final Fantasy* soundtrack fix. You don't have to look far and wide for specialty stores, however. In general, most every music store in Japan has a game music section, sometimes, but not often, mixed in with *anime* soundtracks. In general, the smaller the store, the smaller the game music selection. Larger arrays of game music can be found at giant music stores like Tower Records and Virgin Megastore, both of which maintain large branches in the Shinjuku section of Tokyo and in other major metropolitan areas.

But if you've got time to spare, every tiny record store is worth checking—they might have just the album you're looking for. If you're on a tight schedule, however, check out *anime otaku* specialty chains like Animate and Gamers. Both have branches in Akihabara and elsewhere, and besides their panoply of licensed goods featuring characters from *anime*, and *manga*, and games, these stores have extensive selections of game and *anime* soundtracks, usually stocking any CD that is still in print. The one drawback is that they don't sell used CDs. However, the king of used *manga* chain stores, Mandarake, does. Most Mandarake outlets have a good selection of them, in fact. (The Akihabara branch, however, doesn't; the store is entirely devoted to sales of pornographic personal computer software.)

Animate, Gamers, and Mandarake are also excellent for tracking down the many licensed goods—from stuffed toys to business card holders and everything in between—that feature the likenesses of video game characters. If you visited the Kyoto branch of Animate in the summer of 2003, you would have seen plush Chocobo birds from the *Final Fantasy* series, the cartoon drum characters from *Taiko no Tatsujin* printed on T-shirts, plastic file folders emblazoned with scenes from Konami's RPG series *Genso Suikoden*, and a replica of the very Bomb Ring from the introductory scenes of *Final Fantasy IV*, crafted from sterling silver.

Before half the store tragically burned down in early 2004, the Akihabara mainstay Yamagiwa Soft, in addition to hosting several floors of music CDs, DVDs, and games, featured a large section of exclusive merchandise. This included plush dolls of the Kobun characters from the *Mega Man Legends* action game series, perfect replica police uniforms from the *Resident Evil* series that cost hundreds of dollars, and pewter figurines featuring the most memorable characters from the *Final Fantasy* series, just to name a few.

These products are, however, generally produced in limited quantities and only available at such specialty stores. Far more ubiquitous are the toys sold in vending machines, sometimes called *gacha-gacha omocha*, *gachapon*, or *gashapon*. The name comes from the sound the machines make: the *gasha-gasha* of the crank mechanism, and the *pon* of the plastic capsule falling down the chute. The concept is identical to the rows of machines that vend gumballs and cheap plastic toys, but the quality of the toys in *gashapon* machines is much, much higher than their Western counterparts. A bank of *gashapon* machines might feature mostly figurines and other toys of *anime* characters, but a few games—Capcom's fighting games like *Street Fighter*, Nintendo's *Mario* games, and the like—tend to inspire sets of *gashapon* as well. The higher quality comes with a price. A spin on most machines usually costs ¥200 or about $2.

Another type of toy-vending machine is the skill crane game in which the player manipulates a mechanical claw above a pit full of toys and other prizes and tries to snatch one of them up. They're called *UFO Catchers* in Japan probably because the action of the game resembles nothing so much as an alien spaceship abduction, especially given the wild flashing lights and noise that accompany these games. Typical American arcades have one or two such machines; a large Japanese video arcade might have an entire *floor* devoted to them. Many have only a few prizes inside, and like the small but expensive toys in the *gashapon* machines, they will be of high quality and value, identical to toys sold in stores but often exclusive to those machines, which makes them irresistible to collectors.

What's more, the prizes in the machines might be separated by type. One game might be full of identical Hello Kitty dolls, another full of Winnie-The-Pooh. Large, plastic figurines of (usually female) characters from Capcom's *Street Fighter* fighting game series are one popular type of UFO Catcher prize. They usually come in cardboard boxes with plastic windows so the player can see what figurine he is aiming for. The boxes have holes punched in them so that the machine's claw can grasp the sides, or the player can try to grab the handle at the top of the box. Such statuettes can usually be fitted together into one large diorama, meaning that the player usually tries for a complete set.

In fact, most of these *gashapon* or UFO Catcher toys are organized into clearly defined sets; a paper insert inside the capsule or box usually shows all of the toys in the series. For example, the *Mario Party gashapon* set included figurines of Mario, Luigi, Yoshi,

> **Large, plastic figurines of (usually female) characters from Capcom's *Street Fighter* fighting game series are one popular type of UFO Catcher prize.**

Peach, Donkey Kong, and Wario. But collectors want everything. Thus, quite a few retail stores have sprung up in places like Akihabara and Den Den Town that sell nothing but these toys. They usually come at a sizeable markup, but it's usually cheaper than

leaving it to random chance. What's more, given that the sets of toys in the *gashapon* machines and UFO Catchers are swapped out for new ones so rapidly, these stores are the only place to find toys that are over a month or two old.

So, there's plenty of video game licensed merchandise to be found *outside* of grocery stores. What about *inside*? Besides the typical food items marketed to children upon which you might expect to see a video game character's face emblazoned—*Super Mario* candy, *Sonic The Hedgehog* soda pop—you can find video game and *anime* characters on microwaveable bags of curry sauce (*Pokémon, Kirby*) and packets of seasoning for fried rice (*Hello Kitty*). Curry rice in particular is a favorite food in Japan. Japanese curry is closer to British curry, a thick, mild brown sauce served over rice, with toppings that range from pork cutlets to shredded cheese. It is in particular a favorite 'fun food' for Japanese children, who prefer individual boxed portions with their favorite television character on the front, just as American children would gladly eat canned Spaghetti-O's over homemade pasta.

Curry rice tastes better when it's endorsed by Pikachu (top) or Kirby (above).

As briefly touched on above, there is much crossover between *anime*, *manga*, and video game properties. In both Japan and America it has historically been a one-way street: characters, stories, and worlds are established in *anime*, *manga*, comic books, and Hollywood movies, and video game versions of those stories are produced after the fact.

But there are exceptions. One early one was the *Super Mario Bros.* animated movie in 1986, *Super Mario Bros. and the Great Plan to Save Princess Peach*. Nowadays, *anime* and *manga* based on video games are commonplace. *Dragon Quest manga* was wildly popular in the weekly magazine *Shonen Jump*; this gave way to an animated series. A direct-to-video animated miniseries based on *Final Fantasy V* was released in 1993, and there have been *anime* and *manga* series based on Namco's *Tales of Eternia* and Sony's *Arc The Lad* RPG series. Trying to stay ahead of the curve, Square Enix announced at a 2004 press conference their intent to create 'polymorphic' content that could not be identified as belonging primarily to the video game, *manga*, or *anime* spheres. Rather, it would be used in each medium simultaneously.

Besides *manga* based on video games, which are cheaper to produce than *anime* and thus more likely to be experimented with, the publishing industry also makes big money on video game strategy guides and art books. Strategy guides are most popular for the complex RPG genre, but they are released for practically every other video game that requires any thought whatsoever. Such guides are a major tie-in item that actually sparks sales of the games themselves. Potential buyers can flip through the guides sitting on store shelves and use them to determine whether or not to buy a game, depending on how interesting the puzzles and action look.

While strategy guides are always released in paperback (though in full, glossy color), 'art books' are usually handsome hardcover volumes with elaborate slipcovers. These books, usually released for RPG games illustrated by a famous *manga* artist, collect all of the artwork used in the game, as well as original character sketches by the artist. The market for these books is limited but voracious. Fans of the artist demand to have all of his or her works in collection. In 2001 Yoshitaka Amano released "The Sky," a $300 box set collecting all of his artwork for *Final Fantasy* games *I* through *X*. Used copies still fetch that price today.

At times the video game itself is sold packaged with one tie-in product or another. Sometimes this is a bonus for placing a deposit with an advance order for the game before it releases. In 2003, Nintendo's RPG *Giftpia* came with a keychain that held specially-designed *hanafuda* cards. Some copies of Square Enix's Game Boy Advance RPG *Shinyaku Seiken Densetsu* (Sword of Mana) shipped in a special box that contained plastic figurines of characters from the game. These sorts of preorder bonuses are incentives for the consumer to buy the games brand new rather than used.

Only a few years ago, the Japanese game market would have stood in sharp contrast to the American one. But recently—especially as young Americans in their twenties begin to embrace with retro-nostalgic fever the imagery and iconography from Nintendo's earliest games—many licensed video game toys, clothing, and other products have claimed shelf space at specialty retailers and trendy stores like Hot Topic. And if you look hard enough, you can find at least one or two examples of every Japanese tie-in product category that have been released in America, from *Final Fantasy* art books to *Super Mario Kart* battery-powered go-kart racer toys.

Indeed, the market in America is changing and expanding, but whether an American game store will ever resemble a Japanese one is doubtful. Still, the process of localizing and marketing Japanese video games in America has changed dramatically over the past few decades, and it is worth examining to see yet another facet of the Japanese video game industry.

▨ ▨ ▨

CHAPTER 8

LOST IN TRANSRATION: THIS GAME ARE SICK

The notion that the Japanese confuse the letters R and L when writing in English always struck me as an exaggerated stereotype. Then I started shopping in Japan's music stores. After discovering such artists as Freetwood Mac, Meat Roaf, and Eric Crapton, I began to feel a little less bad about referring to awkward English versions of Japanese video games as "transrations."

But the word "translation" doesn't even begin to describe the complexity of the process by which Japanese video games come to the United States. To be sure, the translation of the text from Japanese to English is a difficult and laborious process, but it represents only

> **The notion that the Japanese confuse the letters R and L when writing in English always struck me as an exaggerated stereotype.**

one of many changes that may, and sometimes *must*, be made before the game can be released in America. For purposes of this discussion, let's look at four major types of changes: *symbolic* changes, *graphical* changes, *game play* changes, and *language* changes.

Symbols are a powerful language all their own, and in early video games where graphics were abstract and text space was at a premium, the use of symbols to communicate large ideas could be invaluable. But different cultures read different symbols in different ways. In his book *Anime Explosion,* Patrick Drazen noted "some images [that] Western viewers automatically invest with a great deal of power are taken by Japanese viewers with little more than a mental shrug."[1] In great part he is referring to Christian crosses, which appear from time to time in *anime,* even children's shows like *Sailor Moon,* but also in video games.

Although Japan has a "small minority of devout and practicing Christians," Drazen explained, "in general the Japanese have only been interested in the tangential trappings and trimmings of Christianity."[2] This stands in stark contrast to America, where video game companies have to be worried that a cross (or worse, Satanic imagery like a pentagram) might be construed as blasphemous.

This was of course a serious concern in the days when "Nintendo games" were targeted directly at children, but even today publishers are worried. Bill Swartz of Mastiff, a US-based firm that localizes Japanese video games, said as much in a 2004 interview: "There are well organized forces that work hard to punish software makers and sellers for what they consider religious transgressions. As a very small and brand new publisher without deep pockets we need to pick and choose our battles."[3]

Thus, the practice of censoring religious symbolism in video game localizations continues today. For example, a few crosses were taken out of the US release of Mastiff's PlayStation 2 game *La Pucelle Tactics*, an anime-styled strategy RPG with some religious story overtones. These days, however, such editing tends to be taken seriously and done with near-surgical precision, taking care not to go overboard or affect the overall experience. In most cases, that is—not all companies are as respectful of the original work as Mastiff is.

Race can often be used as a symbolic message as well. The Japanese, living in a racially homogenous society, have fewer qualms about racial stereotyping than Americans do. When I lived in Kanazawa, we had a local bank near our school that was the only place I could withdraw money. This simple act was complicated by the fact that above the ATM machines in the bank's lobby was a giant poster telling the ATM users to beware of pickpockets and thieves. The poster consisted of two *manga*-style scenes showing little old Japanese ladies being ripped off by four *gaijin*, drawn with curly hair and big noses. One was even pointing at the ATM machine to distract the little old lady, saying *watashi wakarimasen*, which means, roughly, "Me not understand." The sentence was written in *katakana* script and from left to right, two other conventions used in *manga* to show that a foreigner is speaking.

So it shouldn't be surprising that David Sheff pointed out that in the Nintendo game *Gumshoe*, the enemy characters were all warlike American Indians, changed to "generic bad guys" for the American version. Or that the only black character in *Casino Kid* was a thief; his skin tone was altered for the US game.[4] Or that the character of Jim in *Square's Tom Sawyer*, an RPG based on the Mark Twain books, was drawn with giant lips; the game was not released in the US.

Other graphical changes are also made even when there is no symbolism or offensive content. Sometimes the graphics are changed simply to be more appealing to American players. In certain NES games, the *anime*-styled characters would be redrawn in a style more like the American comic books of the time, with more realistically proportioned and detailed features. More recently, the main character of Tecmo's survival horror title *Fatal Frame* was changed from a young-looking adolescent to a curvier high school student.

Some major graphical alterations happen when the game in question is based on an *anime* series, and the game publisher would rather that Americans didn't know that. So the famous *manga* character, a strange duck-like ghost, in Bandai's Famicom game *Obake no Q-Taro* was changed to a curly-haired angel for the game's US release as *Chubby Cherub*. The hero of *Gegege no Kitaro*, a Famicom game based on an *anime* about a strange little boy who hunts ghosts, was changed to a ninja and the game was released in the US as *Ninja Kid*, stripped of its anime roots.

The most extreme example, however, has to be *Street Combat*. In the wake of *Street Fighter II*'s popularity, the company Irem licensed the US rights to a Super Nintendo fighting game based on the martial-arts comedy *anime* series *Ranma ½*. But rather than simply releasing the game in the US with a

Screenshots of Ranma ¹/₂ and their counterparts in Street Combat. Note that the characters were changed but the backgrounds remain identical.

basic translation, they took it upon themselves to change all of the characters in the game to ridiculously generic and amateurish character designs that were more "edgy" and "mature" than the comedic, cartoonish cast of the *Ranma* series. Unfortunately for Irem, *anime* fandom was beginning to take hold in America, and fans of the series were not amused. After the backlash, the game's sequel was brought over with the *Ranma* characters intact.

It actually didn't happen with *Street Combat*, but at times the game play—the action, the very heart of the game—is altered. "The balance of a game is essentially arbitrary; it just depends whom you're trying to sell to," wrote J.C. Herz in *Joystick Nation*. "At Nintendo, I'm told that titles arriving from Japan are regularly made slower and easier for their American release. The theory is that Japanese children are more proficient at video games and what they consider challenging fun would simply frustrate and quash American grade-schoolers."[5] Oddly enough, in many cases the opposite is now true; many games end up being easier in their Japanese release, as Dylan Cuthbert recalled about *Blasto*.

But whether harder or easier, the version of the game that comes out second is usually the more *balanced* one, benefiting from longer development time and customer feedback. For the US release of *The Legend of Zelda: The Wind Waker*, Aonuma and Miyamoto went back and polished up a segment of the game that many Japanese users found tiring. The Japanese release of *Metroid Fusion* for the Game Boy Advance, which released after the US version, added two new selectable difficulty levels and multiple ending sequences.

But ultimately, the most time-consuming, difficult, and inescapable change that must be made is to the words; the Japanese language in the game must be translated into English. This requires not only the actual translation of the text but also the game itself must be reprogrammed. This process can be expedited if the original design team thinks ahead and codes the game such that text documents containing translated text can be easily 'plugged in' with minimal effort. In the past, they usually didn't. Today, they do—occasionally.

In the old days of cartridge-based games with limited storage capacity, this was a far more difficult task than it would seem. Perfect translations from the Japanese were mostly impossible, because the Japanese text took up far less space than English. Yes, the pictographic *kanji* characters, about two thousand of which are used in everyday Japanese, took up a fair amount of space when they came into use during the Super Famicom years. But adding them in meant that a full sentence could be made up of far fewer characters, as one *kanji* could represent three or four syllables on its own.

But even if a perfect translation of the Japanese original was possible, it hardly ever happened, for the same reason that crosses continue to be removed from US versions of games. When the onscreen graphics are abstract and far from representational, sometimes changing the onscreen text can transform a potentially offensive situation into a harmless one. It's all about the power of suggestion and context, especially when the graphics are pixilated and abstracted. An inch-tall "stripper" becomes innocuous when renamed a "dancer." In the Japanese version of the game *Chrono Trigger*, the main character is asked to pour a bottle of *sake*, rice wine, over a grave. In the American version, the scene was left intact, but the substance was referred to as soda pop.

Although a great team of translation specialists could strike an adequate compromise, there wasn't much motivation for companies to really polish up their work—a better translation wouldn't necessarily equal more sales. So many games that were written well enough in Japanese were rushed out the door in the US with English text that ranged from awkwardly stilted to embarrassingly poor.

Sometimes the translation hurt the game play. "Secret entrance in the front wall," said an old man in *Milon's Secret Castle*, a two-dimensional game that *had no front walls*. Sometimes a phrase could be grammatically perfect but unintentionally hilarious: "No one can escape from my mighty legs!" said the high-kicking policewoman Chun Li in *Super Street Fighter II*.

Early on in the NES stealth-action title *Metal Gear*, the player-character Solid Snake must sneak around a sentry and jump into a cargo truck. To get through, he must wait until the guard says, "I feel asleep!" and starts to snore. Inside the truck, Snake is surprised: "Uh-oh! The truck have started to move!" The NES title *Pro Wrestling* told a victorious player, "Congratulation—a winner is you."

Some actually entered into the lingo of Internet culture. "BARF!" shouted some defeated enemies in *River City Ransom* for the NES. When an up-dated version of the game was released in 2004 for the Game Boy Advance, the phrase had become so popular among fans of the original that the designers had far more enemies use it in the new version. "All your base are belong to us," said the evil spaceship commander in *Zero Wing* for the Sega Genesis in 1991. Ten years later, as pictures from the once-obscure game were circulated on the Internet, the phrase started appearing on T-shirts, in the comic strip *Fox Trot*, and in an episode of *Futurama*.

These errors, especially when many of them were strung together to form completely inscrutable sentences, used to be called "manglish," "Janglish," or "Japlish," but nowadays—thanks mostly to the popularity of a certain website—they are called "Engrish."

NATION OF IMMIGRANTS

Of course, it took a while before the jokes about "transration" became a staple of the video game fan vocabulary, because it was a while before Japanese video games needed much in the way of localization in the first place. Often, there was little to no actual text in the video games, and it was frequently in English to begin with. This is for a multitude of reasons. The twenty-six capital letters that can be used to spell any English word without ambiguity take up much less of the precious space in early computer memory than the hundred or so phonetic Japanese characters, let alone the two thousand *kanji* in daily use.

And in a variety of contexts, English was even the accepted, standard *lingua franca* in Japan. Walk down a Tokyo street and you might see it more than you see Japanese: on signs, on posters, throughout magazine stands, in advertisements, plastered across

> **English is used to convey a sense of foreignness, but one that is cool and chic, for the same reason a French boutique in New York City might have its name in French.**

T-shirts. English is used to convey a sense of foreignness, but one that is cool and chic, for the same reason a French boutique in New York City might have its name in French.

But this love of English does not extend to actually considering whether the English phrase in question would actually be used or understood in English-speaking countries. This indifference does not correlate with a lack of quality or creator's pride in the product. We have already seen numerous examples of this: a fastidiously neat and well-run video game retailer called Super Potato, an otherwise perfectly designed game called Donkey Kong.

So although the games may not have contained much Japanese at all, there were some linguistic hurdles to overcome. The first two games that Taito licensed to Midway were titled *Speed Race* and *Western Gun*; the former worked in America but the latter did not. While the words *western* and *gun* were perfect for Japanese audiences in that they conveyed the setting and action in as few words as possible, the phrase sounds odd to American ears. The US version was titled *Gun Fight*; this phrase is actually used in English although it does lack a description of the game's setting. Fortunately, this being an arcade game, the cowboys-and-cacti setting could easily be conveyed through the artwork on the game's massive cabinet.

The words *Space Invaders* worked fine in both countries, and the in-game text like "HIGH SCORE" and "GAME OVER" was understandable to all. *Pac-Man* needed a little more help. First, the original name had to be changed, not for linguistic reasons but for cultural ones—*Puck-Man* made just as much (or as little) sense as *Pac-Man*, but American teens were much more likely to vandalize the machine and render *Puck-Man* into something much worse. Don't believe for a second that Japanese teenagers didn't realize what they could change *Puck-Man* into; it's just that they wouldn't ever do it.

So the cabinet art and the attractive title screen in the actual *Pac-Man* game program had to be changed. The names of the ghosts had to be changed as well, and there was actually a level of care taken in coming up with creative names that reflected the personality of each ghost, which showed through in the way that ghost pursued Pac-Man in the maze. *Oikake, Machibuse, Kimagure,* and *Otoboke* became Shadow, Speedy, Bashful, and Pokey. There was less of an attempt to keep the nicknames as descriptive; playing off the fact that one of the ghosts was named Pinky in the Japanese version, the four ghosts became Blinky, Inky, Pinky, and Clyde.

CHARACTER / NICKNAME		CHARACTER / NICKNAME	
OIKAKE · · · · · "AKABEI"		–SHADOW	"BLINKY"
MACHIBUSE · · "PINKY"		–SPEEDY	"PINKY"
KIMAGURE · · · "AOSUKE"		–BASHFUL	"INKY"
OTOBOKE · · · · "GUZUTA"		–POKEY	"CLYDE"

Donkey Kong actually needed less programming work than *Pac-Man*. In fact, since Miyamoto had designed the game for America to begin with, it didn't need any at all. But NOA wanted to print the story of the game as part of the arcade machine's cabinet art, and so the other two main characters, Jumpman and the lady, needed names. The lady was named Pauline after Nintendo of America employee Don James' wife Polly. Jumpman was named Mario after the landlord who ran the business park where the original NOA offices were located. And just like that, Nintendo had named the character that would take them to blockbuster success in the United States.

NOW YOU'RE PLAYING WITH POWER

Every new generation of elementary school children creates a new and specialized vocabulary with which they can communicate with their peers and confound their parents. For the Nintendo generation, many of these words came straight from the pen of Gail Tilden. Tilden joined Nintendo of

America in 1983 as "the entire advertising department." Tilden was single-handedly responsible for "advertising, public relations, marketing, and for naming all the products and games—the entire product line."

To introduce the Famicom to retailers who had taken a bath when the Atari-led US video game industry crashed in 1983, Tilden had to be creative. In fact, strange as it may sound, Nintendo "tried never to call it a video game, because there was lots of dead inventory tied up in two-dollar bargain bins full of 'video games.'" So the Family Computer became the Nintendo Entertainment System (NES), and it didn't play "game cartridges" like the Atari did. A Nintendo game was a "Game Pak." The name and its spelling were Tilden's.

Nintendo wanted to bring an assortment of its hit Famicom games to the US, especially the wonderful games directed by Shigeru Miyamoto. This included arcade classics like *Donkey Kong* and *Ice Climbers*, but also original titles like *Clu Clu Land* and *Excitebike*, as well as the light gun shooting games that had their origins in Nintendo's Beam Gun toys: *Duck Hunt*, *Wild Gunman*, *Hogan's Alley*. There was one problem: the light gun toy sold in Japan was an exact replica of a cowboy's six-shooter, jet-black in color. This was fine in Japan, where actual firearms are practically nonexistent and toy guns are perfect replicas of the real thing.

But in America, where parents are more wary of toys that look like real firearms—and where a police officer might easily mistake a realistic toy gun for a real gun—Nintendo's light gun controller had to be redesigned entirely. The result, which Tilden termed the "Zapper," looked like a futuristic laser gun with its elongated, ultra thin barrel and gray coloring. Years later, as restrictions on what toy guns could look like became even stricter, the Zapper was colored a bright orange.

The Zapper helped differentiate the NES from older video game systems, because it was a unique and interesting method of control. Of course, it lent itself to 'cheating'—rather than standing a distance from the TV set and aiming carefully, children quickly learned to put the gun directly up against the television screen for perfect aim. But the Zapper still helped to prove the point that the NES was more than a 'video game.'

To that end, another peripheral device that was merely a niche product for the Famicom became crucial to the success of the NES. The Family Robot looked like a cross between E.T. and R2-D2 from *Star Wars*, an adorable little plastic robot that stood about a foot tall. It operated on the same electronics as the Zapper gun—the television would flash a signal into the robot's 'eyes,' which were solar sensors, and the robot would send information back to the game system. But unlike the gun, the robot would move around, raise and lower its arms, and grasp things—spinning gyroscopes, stackable plastic blocks.

Thus, in the game called *Robot Gyro*, the player used the standard control pad to move the game's main character through a maze. Red and blue barriers blocked his way, but he couldn't move them—the player had to make the Family Robot pick up a gyro and set it down on a red button that would raise the red barrier.

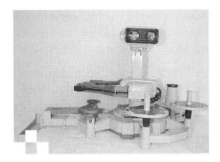

Tilden renamed the Family Robot "R.O.B.," which stood for Robotic Operating Buddy. If the name sounds overly cutesy, know that it could have been far worse: "It was originally going to be OTTO, which was a play on the word *auto*," she recalls. For the launch of the NES, R.O.B. was pushed to the forefront of retail buyers' attention. These weren't video games, Nintendo explained, they were futuristic robot toys. The first NES systems sold in 1985 didn't even include a *Super Mario Bros.* cartridge in the box, but they did include the Zapper, R.O.B., and a game cartridge that worked with each: *Duck Hunt* and the renamed maze game, *Gyromite*.*

★ R.O.B. and the Zapper, having been included with many NES sets, are not difficult to find nowadays. But both of these peripherals were only sold separately in Japan and are consequently very rare finds.

As video game controller peripherals go, R.O.B. was a particularly gimmicky one. Once the novelty of controlling a robot's arms and spinning a glorified top had worn off, usually within days or even hours, R.O.B. got in the way of enjoyment. He required battery replacements too often, and it was immediately apparent that the maze barriers in Gyromite could be turned on and off just as easily by tapping the A and B buttons on a standard controller, which was all that R.O.B.'s complicated motions ended up doing.

R.O.B. was discontinued after only one more game, a now-rare title called *Stack-Up*. But it didn't matter; he was merely a Trojan horse to get NES systems into American homes. The gambit worked like a charm, and nobody missed R.O.B. or the Zapper once players realized that games played with the standard video game controller, like *Super Mario Bros.*, were much more fun.

Like most of the games released in 1985 with the launch of the NES, *Super Mario Bros.* didn't need to be changed at all for its American release. There were no cultural issues with the content, and the few sentences of text in the game were in English from the beginning. The biggest job was to rewrite the game's instruction manual. This was not often an issue with arcade games because they were simple, and they had only the briefest of instructions printed on the machine. But the secrets that *Super Mario Bros.* held and the complexities of its world needed to be spelled out in detail. The instruction book to *Super Mario Bros.*, like most others for Japanese games released on the NES, was a direct translation of the Japanese booklet. Even the illustrations used in the Japanese booklet were carried over to the American one; this practice often provided American children with a brief, flirtatious introduction to *manga*-style artwork.

The Legend of Zelda's instruction manual needed to be translated, of course, but so did all the in-game text that provided clues to the game's many intricate puzzles. It is not clear exactly who did the translation, but it seems to have been done by a Japanese person with a shaky grasp of the English language and an old J-E dictionary. The little old man who gives Link a sword at the beginning of the game says, "It's dangerous to go alone! Take this." While sounding vaguely strange, it's practically Shakespeare compared to some of the things the little old man says later in the game, like:

> *Ones who does not have Triforce can't go in.*
>
> *Eastmost penninsula [sic] is the secret.*
>
> *Eyes of skull has a secret.*

And then, of course, there was "Grumble grumble." Hidden deep inside a dungeon later in the game was a monster that did not attack Link, but merely sat in an otherwise empty room saying, "Grumble grumble." This wasn't very clear in the Japanese original, so it's not surprising that someone struggling with subject-verb agreement would do an inelegant job of clarifying it for Americans. It is actually a pretty literal translation of the original Japanese text, which read *butsu butsu*, the sound of someone murmuring, complaining, grumbling.

Can you solve the puzzle? *Of course not.* The solution, which had to be obtained either through a major epiphany or painstaking trial and error, was to buy a piece of "monster bait" at a store outside the dungeon and use it while standing in front of the monster. It is understandable that Nintendo may have wanted the clues in this intricate puzzle game to be somewhat cryptic, but in this case they may have saved themselves a lot of money on 1-800 help line calls if they'd just had Grumble Grumble say, "Hello. Please put a piece of meat on top of my face to proceed."

Because *The Legend of Zelda* could not be completed in one sitting, it saved the player's progress to the writeable portion of the floppy disc on which it came. But this was not an option in the NES version given that it was a cartridge game. So *The Legend of Zelda* became the first game to feature a long-life lithium battery, like those used in watches, to "save" the game. *Zelda* players were lucky—other Famicom Disk games that came to the US either used a clunky password system requiring the user to write down and re-enter long character strings every time he turned off the system (*Metroid, Kid Icarus*) or simply used no save system at all, making them obnoxiously difficult (*Castlevania*).

Another obnoxiously difficult game released on the Famicom Disk System, called *Super Mario Bros. 2 For Super Players,* was never released on the NES. This sequel was actually a collection of new levels, using the original game's graphics, which ranged from "taxing" in the very beginning to "nearly impossible" toward the end. This was fine for Japan, a country that had been so absorbed in the original game that they had made a book detailing the game's secret worlds into a chart-topping bestseller. And of course, the game was released less than a year after the original title, in 1986, so the graphics weren't outdated.

In 1986 in the United States, however, *Super Mario* didn't need a sequel yet; the original game had only just begun to grow in popularity. In fact, by the time Nintendo of America needed another Mario game, it was already late 1988 and graphics had advanced quite a bit beyond what the original *Super Mario* dished out. Onscreen characters could be more colorful and finely detailed, worlds could 'scroll' left-to-right *and* up-and-down, and the player could even backtrack across terrain already covered. These features were already being built into Miyamoto's *Super Mario Bros. 3*, which would release in Japan that year.

So instead of releasing *Super Mario Bros. 2 For Super Players* in the US, Nintendo had Miyamoto's Mario Team rework another Famicom Disk System game that they had designed. *Doki Doki Panic* was directed by a designer named

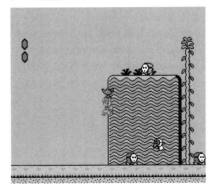

Kensuke Tanabe and was originally created for a summer event that Fuji Television put on in Tokyo called *Yume Koujou* (Dream Factory), a "communication carnival" in which all sorts of new products from the Fuji media group were shown off. The four original characters that starred in *Doki Doki Panic* were replaced with Mario, Luigi, Toad, and Princess Toadstool to make the US version of *Super Mario Bros. 2.*

Because the world of *Doki Doki Panic* was stylistically far different from that of the Mushroom Kingdom, the rewritten storyline was that Mario

and friends had found a mysterious staircase that led to a doorway to a dream world named Sub-Con (standing for *subconscious*). Although the original game featured animated cartoon-like sequences that set up the story, these were axed from the game and replaced with two static screens of text, like *Zelda*'s, that told a very simple version of the longer story in the instruction booklet.

Even with this deletion, *Super Mario Bros. 2* added even more storyline sequences to the Mario formula. The game closed with cinematic scenes depicting the rescue of the kidnapped game characters, a "Cast" sequence (though no credits), and at the very end, a screen-filling graphic showing Mario waking up from his dream as a cursive "The End" was written beneath him.

Some graphical and aural embellishments were made to the game play sequences as well. Because a large NES cartridge could produce better sound quality than the Famicom Disk System, certain sound effects and musical interludes were pepped up. Many objects that were static in *Doki Doki Panic* became animated in *Super Mario Bros. 2*: grass and leaves blew in the wind, potions bubbled. Many

enemy graphics were changed: the Looney Tunes-ish onomatopoetic explosion graphic that read "BOM" in the Japanese version was changed to the better but still not quite right "BOMB"; and certain Super Mario-style items like super mushrooms and Koopa shells were added. An entirely new "boss" enemy, a giant crab named Clawgrip,* was added to the menagerie.

* In the CAST sequence that scrolled by at the end of the game, this character's name was spelled Clawglip. Later editions of the game corrected this error.

The game play was much deeper than that of the original *Super Mario Bros.*: the four different characters had different strengths and weaknesses, and the twenty different levels were gigantic and mazelike, featuring far more hidden paths and secrets than in *Super Mario Bros.* "Even as we were making [*Doki Doki Panic*]," said Miyamoto, "I thought it felt a lot like a Mario game." Ironically, Miyamoto was more involved with *Doki Doki Panic* than he was with the "real" sequel to *Super Mario Bros.* He says he was responsible for "thirty to forty percent" of *Doki Doki Panic* but only ten percent of *Super Mario Bros. 2 For Super Players*.

Later, the US version of the game was released in Japan, on cartridge, as *Super Mario USA*. The game's package contained a brief paragraph explaining what the game was and where it came from. And finally, when Nintendo released an upgraded collection of *Super Mario Bros.* games on the Super NES system in 1993, the original *Super Mario Bros. 2* was finally released in the US under the name *Super Mario Bros.: The Lost Levels*.

■ ■ ■

It wasn't just Nintendo who benefited from the NES boom. The NES was so popular that demand for new games vastly outstripped supply. At first, NOA licensed some games from the computer software publishers who were publishing Famicom games in Japan, but they soon instituted a licensee program much like the one in Japan. The first companies to take advantage of this were, of course, the Japanese publishers who already had partnerships with NCL. For the most part, these companies had already established small subsidiaries in the US to distribute their arcade games.

Their names were already well known to US arcade goers and they would soon be known as the major suppliers of quality NES software: Bandai, Data East, Capcom, Konami, Tecmo, and others. Their early games on the Famicom and NES were generally scaled-down versions of their bigger arcade hits: Capcom's *Gun Smoke*, *1942*, and *Trojan*; Konami's *Contra* and *Life Force*. The NES hardware was quite underpowered compared to the arcade hardware of the time, and sometimes the only thing that the two versions of the game shared in common were their names.

This was especially true of Tecmo's first two NES games, based on two arcade games that hit it big for the company in US arcades and pizza parlors: *Tecmo Bowl* and *Ninja Gaiden* (*Ninja Ryukenden*, or *Legend of the Dragon Sword*, in Japan). *Tecmo Bowl* was a Japanese-designed version of American football that used two monitors placed horizontally to show a larger area of the playfield, and it allowed four players to play simultaneously. It occupied the space of two normal-sized arcade cabinets, but brought in more money because it was so popular.

Creators of sports games generally pride themselves on being big fans of the sport and working hard to deliver an authentic experience. But Dimitri Criona*, then director of sales and marketing for Tecmo USA, believes that Tecmo Bowl's excellent game play came, paradoxically, from the fact that its Japanese designers weren't familiar with football. "The guys who did the game literally sat down with an NFL rulebook and read the rules of football. And because of that, they were able to program a game without bias. If you take an American programmer, he is inherently going to have some biases about the game. But if you take a Japanese programmer, he's going to create a program that follows the rules."

* Criona is currently director of sales in the Electronics (video games) division of Bandai America.

Whether this was true or not, Tecmo Bowl was a smash hit in the arcades and even bigger on the NES. "We would get all these angry letters," recalls Criona, "from parents of kids who had moved away to college, complaining that their kids were now coming home every weekend to play Tecmo Bowl tournaments. The admission fee at that time was $5 and a 12-pack of beer, and you played until someone was the last man standing!"

Tecmo Bowl was designed and programmed in Japan but aimed specifically at the American audience. Later, the game was translated into Japanese and released in Tecmo's homeland. Ninja Gaiden, while designed with both countries in mind, took the opposite route. It was released in Japanese, then translated into English. It was not as big a cultural phenomenon as Tecmo Bowl, but it ended up revolutionizing video games with its courageous, unique, and trailblazing use of cinema scenes.

Between Ninja Gaiden's fast action levels, the cinematic scenes told the story of a young ninja named Ryu Hayabusa, who was investigating the circumstances behind his father's mysterious death and taking revenge on his killers. The story's twists and turns were not merely played out by tiny animated icons, like in early Final Fantasy games. Giant anime-style art filled the top half of the screen while the dialogue was displayed on the bottom. The art style was highly reminiscent of spy thriller manga for grownups, like Lupin III or Golgo 13. The animation was limited—but then, anime television shows had always used techniques of limited animation, so there was not a huge difference.

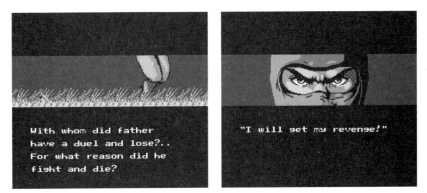

With whom did father
have a duel and lose?..
For what reason did he
fight and die?

"I will get my revenge!"

The original arcade version contained none of these sequences. In fact, although it shared some similar character art and backdrops, the game play was entirely different. The arcade *Ninja Gaiden* was modeled heavily on *Double Dragon*, a popular martial arts beat-em-up game in which the player advanced to the right while pummeling seemingly endless thugs with punches, kicks, and/or the various weapons littering the city streets. The NES version was modeled on Konami's game *Akumajou Dorakyura* (Demon Castle Dracula, or Castlevania in the US), from which it borrowed most of its game play elements, including power-up items that gave Ryu special ninja magic.

Of those four games, the NES *Ninja Gaiden* was the best. Like *Tecmo Bowl*, it was a tremendous hit in the US—even at a time when almost any NES game would sell a huge number of copies, *Ninja Gaiden* was a sales leader.

Another "major difference" between the arcade and home games, says Criona, "was the length of the game and the inclusion of what Tecmo had trademarked 'cinema screens.' The dynamics of the coin-op game industry are very different from the home video games. In a coin-op machine you're looking to motivate the player to keep dropping in quarters, but you're not going to keep him for hours and hours. With a [home] game, the reward structure is very different."

The rewards for home gamers were the lengthy cinema scenes that kept the plot intense. "The cinema screens are there to…lead the player to a finale, the ending. So it's like *Super Mario Bros.*, where the whole idea was to play to the end and find out what happens. The cinema screens were crude, as far as animation goes, but they had text scrolling at the bottom of the screen."

And all that text needed to be translated, the game reprogrammed to fit the English text. This process was handled differently at different companies. At Tecmo, the writers of the Japanese storyline would work up a rough English version of the text, then fax it to the American team, who would "edit it and put it back together, telling the story in a context that an American English speaker would understand. This would go back and forth several times," recalls Criona.

The game would then need to be reprogrammed with the edited English text, which was a laborious process. It wasn't a simple matter of swapping out a text file—far from it, in fact. "You're not bringing up text in ASCII code, as you do in a computer. The text is actually stored as a picture file. And that picture has certain limitations—you don't have unlimited lines of text. You have to say things very clearly and concisely, and sometimes find another word that has the same meaning but fewer characters. Every sentence has to be worked and massaged.

"Nintendo had very specific guidelines about symbols, and about what you could not say. So we also had to make sure that we were in compliance with Nintendo's regulations." Nintendo's NES-era regulations on content were wide-reaching, but specifically targeted at the kinds of offensive material that was bound to be scattered in even the most benign-looking Japanese games. Anything that could be construed as Satanic imagery was a no-no, but also Christian or other religious symbols. Sexual content, including nudity, was out, as were smoking, drinking, and drugs.*

* A complete transcription of Nintendo's early content guidelines is archived at http://www.filibustercartoons.com/Nintendo.php, along with examples of each.

Nintendo of America's playtesters loved the *Ninja Gaiden* games, and the company offered to help Tecmo out with marketing. "At that time, the most powerful publication in the industry was *Nintendo Power* magazine, and they did a lot of promotion. They loved the game and it rated very highly. Besides that, we didn't need to make a super effort to market the game. Demand for product dramatically exceeded the supply. We could sell darn near whatever we could get our hands on, and so promotion was neither as sophisticated nor as necessary as it is today. What did we do to promote *Ninja Gaiden*? Other than *Nintendo Power* magazine, not a heck of a lot."

And yet, although Tecmo knew that *Ninja Gaiden* was going to be a big hit, they didn't know that they had a video game that was going to be extremely influential with its groundbreaking use of cinematics. In 1989 it was unique for an action-oriented game to tell a story between levels; it is now commonplace. The games that tell the grandest, longest stories, though, are still RPGs. And if the translation process for *Ninja Gaiden* was difficult, imagine what it was like to produce an English version of a game that had about a thousand times more text.

RPGS IN AMERICA: THE TWELVE-YEAR OVERNIGHT SUCCESS

The Legend of Zelda did very well in the US, backed by a successful marketing campaign that included television ads and large spreads in the *Nintendo Fun Club News*—a small newsletter that went out to Nintendo's mailing list, it was the predecessor to *Nintendo Power* magazine. *Zelda*'s success proved that, given the right sort of game and an ample amount of coaching and assistance, American gamers would indeed sit down and play massive, lengthy adventures for weeks on end. But would this be the case if the game in question were not action-oriented, like *Zelda*, but a story- and strategy-oriented RPG, like the ones sweeping Japan?

To find out, Nintendo of America looked at *Dragon Quest* and its millions of Japanese sales, and decided that it might work Stateside. Because Enix had no American office, NOA licensed the US rights to *Dragon Quest*, releasing the game in August of 1989. Of course, given that the title was already three years old at the time (in Japan, *Dragon Quest IV* was only months away from release), it needed some upgrades. Some graphics were changed. For example, the sprite that represented the game's main character was redrawn so that he would face the direction he was moving, rather than constantly facing front, as if he was a marker in a board game.

The translation, while grammatically correct and entirely comprehensible, was written in an affected, pseudo-Shakespearian style: "Thy hit points have increased by 1." As would become standard practice at Nintendo, the translation was scrubbed clean of any religious references or risqué humor. Finally, since a pen-and-paper role-playing game company in the US already held the rights to the name "Dragon Quest," Nintendo and Enix renamed the game *Dragon Warrior*.

Nintendo apparently produced what turned out to be an overly optimistic number of copies, because they soon began to give a $50 copy of *Dragon Warrior* away with every $20 subscription to *Nintendo Power*. They netted thousands of new subscribers and caused many current subscribers to renew just to take advantage of the huge bargain. This snowballed NES game sales even more because *Nintendo Power* was essentially a hundred-page monthly ad for Nintendo products. And copies of *Dragon Warrior* were now in the homes of Nintendo's most devoted fans.

Dragon Warrior became a cult hit in the US, allowing Enix to set up shop and release *Dragon Warrior II* through *IV* on their own. Meanwhile, Nintendo looked to create a similar success story in the US by promoting another RPG series that had taken a foothold in Japan by that time: *Final Fantasy*.

Square, unlike Enix, had already published its own games in the US by this time. Although Nintendo had licensed and published *Highway Star* in the US in 1987, calling it *Rad Racer*, Square had published *King's Knight* under their own label in 1989. *King's Knight* failed to take off, but *Rad Racer* was highly popular—popular enough that Square developed and published a sequel, *Rad Racer II*, for the US market in 1990 (it was never released in Japan). Meanwhile, that same year, Nintendo licensed *Final Fantasy* from Square and published it in the US, just as *Final Fantasy III* was ready to be released in Japan.

Despite being three years old, *Final Fantasy* sold well, thanks in part to aggressive cross-promotion with *Nintendo Power*. NOA ran a contest in which four winners would be invited to play a "real-life" game of *Final Fantasy*. A *Final Fantasy* strategy guide went out to all *Nintendo Power* subscribers free of charge, ensuring additional player interest, as well as encouraging them to tackle the difficult game with 'secret' tips in hand.

Nintendo's translation of Final Fantasy was adequate, if sometimes unintentionally humorous in its attempts to match the original exactly. In the original Japanese, Garland says, "The Princess is mine! I won't give her to anybody! You smart-alecky Light Warriors... I, Garland, will kick and scatter you about." It loses a lot in the translation, but he's saying he can easily smack them around. In English, "No one touches my Princess!! LIGHT WARRIORS?? You impertinent fools. I, Garland, will knock you all down!!"

Square hoped to grow the *Final Fantasy* brand in the US. Bringing over a Game Boy RPG called *SaGa* that had no relationship to the series, Square renamed the game *Final Fantasy Legend* and released it on its own. In 1991, Square was ready to introduce the next generation of *Final Fantasy*, sequels to both games. *Final Fantasy Legend II* was eventually released, but for whatever reason, Square decided not to publish *Final Fantasy II* in the US, even though a preliminary translation had been finished and the game had been advertised in a 'sell sheet' for retailers.[*]

Since the Super Famicom was already available in the US by that time (renamed the Super Nintendo Entertainment System), Square decided to release *Final Fantasy IV* in the US, renaming it *Final Fantasy II*. Actually, this isn't entirely accurate. The game that Square released as *Final Fantasy II* in the US was actually called *Final Fantasy IV Easytype* in Japan. It was basically *FFIV* for kids and casual players, with lots of changes made to the game play. For instance, many of the characters had special battle commands; all of them were removed save for one or two that were crucial to the game play. Battles were made to be easier. The item system was simplified.

* A detailed article about the 'lost' US version of Final Fantasy II, and a scanned picture of the 'sell sheet' that advertised its release, can be found at The Lost Levels (http://www.lostlevels.org).

The American game had numerous instances of text censorship: all references to death were removed, the details of Cecil and Rosa's romantic relationship were toned down, and much of the character background was removed. This was mostly necessary, whether to be in compliance with Nintendo's guidelines or simply because of the huge space restrictions on English text.

What weren't necessary, however, were the translation issues in the final product. "My first day on the job," recalls Square's former localization coordinator Ted Woolsey, "I was told to review *FFII*. I started playing the game, and immediately started chuckling at the jumbled English text that I had so often enjoyed on T-shirts in Japan." Rather than being interesting for the player, "the screen text for *FFII* was mostly distracting, with some unintentional poetic lyricism."

This was unacceptable to the series' creator, says Woolsey. "Mr. Sakaguchi was adamant that we raise the bar in this area. He put a lot into the crafting of the Japanese text and the cinematic quality of the game, and had been told that *FFII* was a mess." Perhaps *FFII* was the wake-up call for Sakaguchi.[6]

And so, Ted Woolsey was hired in 1991 as part of an effort to "beef up" the quality of the English versions of Square's games. A Seattle native with a Master's in Japanese literature, Woolsey had lived in Japan on and off over the last ten years, writing textbooks and taking translation jobs as he researched his master's thesis. As a boy, Woolsey would spend hours gazing at the authentic *ukiyo-e* woodblock prints that his grandparents had collected during their travels. He would browse the Japanese grocery and department stores in Seattle, although there was little in the way of *manga* and *anime* available as Woolsey was growing up in the '70s. He was "more into comic books, sci-fi, fantasy, and world literature."

Much like Sakaguchi, Woolsey took what he thought was going to be a brief hiatus from schoolwork, and joined Square for a summer job that ended up lasting half a decade. After reviewing *Final Fantasy II*, he started translating the Game Boy game *Final Fantasy Legend III*. "While I was working on that, I was asked to fly to Tokyo, where it soon became apparent we weren't going to get *FFV*."

Final Fantasy V was deemed too difficult for the American audience. "I knew that this was a great game when I played early versions of it, but the managers felt that the audience might not be ready" for the game's complex character-building system, recalls Woolsey. "Instead, they felt we needed to grow the market in the US, and they pursued development of *Final Fantasy Mystic Quest*, which I helped write and translate. This was, like *FF Legend III*, developed by Square's new Osaka development staff."

Although it was developed in Japan and translated into English, *Final Fantasy Mystic Quest* was aimed directly at the American market.* It was even more simplified than *FFII Easytype*, featuring a bare minimum of characters, options, items, and exploration. Even if *FFV* was indeed too difficult for American gamers, *Mystic Quest* was far too simple compared to *Final Fantasy II*. Contrary to its purpose, *Mystic Quest* failed to light a fire under Square fandom in the US. The game that did was originally intended for the Japanese market, and it was called *Secret of Mana*.

* It was later released as *Final Fantasy USA* in Japan.

The American version of a game called *Seiken Densetsu 2* (Legend of the Holy Sword), *Secret of Mana* was the sequel to a Game Boy title that was released in the US as *Final Fantasy Adventure*. The games were a perfect blend of *Final Fantasy* art, music, and RPG exploration with *The Legend of Zelda*'s action-oriented battling. Even better, although a single player could easily play through the game, up to three friends could take control of the game's three heroes. As *Secret of Mana* owners recruited their friends to come over and play, Square's name recognition and popularity started to grow exponentially.

The translation quality of *Secret of Mana* was quite good, owing to Woolsey's contributions. Woolsey was still faced with as many obstacles as other translators had been, but he had a knack for finding new and creative ways around them while keeping the game experience whole. "I had to translate most games in 30 days, with ongoing re-editing thereafter, so it was hard to get the time I wanted to perfect certain areas.

"Space was continually a problem, because I had a strong understanding of how rich the Japanese versions were, and yet we were only able to squeeze about a quarter of the content into the English versions. Some games, like *Secret of Mana*, were being written and rewritten at night, and I'd come in the next day and have to redo any number of text files. I also had to rewrite SOM, as it turned out to be over the allotted text capacity.

"Also, Nintendo was very, very strict. No scatological humor allowed, no references to religious or other 'hot' topics, pop culture properties or characters, etc." Thus, a lot of the fun of the Japanese versions went away, though some of this wouldn't have made sense to non-Japanese audiences anyway, due to in-jokes, Japanese pop culture references, and the like.

While taxing in its own way, *Secret of Mana* was a lighthearted romp

> **Woolsey's final product is considered to be the best RPG translation to come out of that early era—fitting, for what some consider to be the best RPG of those days and perhaps the best of all time.**

of an adventure game that had far less text and far less potentially problematic content than Woolsey's next translation project. This turned out to be Sakaguchi's cinematic masterpiece of 16-bit gaming, *Final Fantasy VI*, which was going to be renamed *Final Fantasy III* for the American marketplace.

Instantly after playing the Japanese version of the game, Woolsey was captivated. "I immediately felt in touch with the characters. I felt the game played like a movie, which of course is what Saka-guchi-*san* and crew had been trying to achieve."

Woolsey produced what he felt would be a solid translation of the text, and presented it to Sakaguchi and team. Sadly, "in spite of some rudimentary compression techniques, I was told it was over by about 50% of the allotted size. So I sat back and simply tried to hack off as much as I could. When they tested the next set of edited files, I was still over by 15-20%, so it was back to the drawing board, re-editing and rewriting."

Woolsey's final product is considered to be the best RPG translation to come out of that early era—fitting, for what some consider to be the best RPG of those days and perhaps the best of all time. Although a great deal of content had to be sacrificed, the player really couldn't tell that anything was missing; reading *FFVI's* story in English felt entirely natural. Each character's back story felt complete, even if it actually wasn't.

Woolsey was particularly careful with the soon to be famous 'opera scene' (see Chapter 4). "I thought this was one of the most interesting parts of the game. For some reason I knew I had to keep this as lyrical as possible, and try to keep to the meter in the music. I thought having an ode to war and love was a pretty classy thing to insert into a 16-bit video game, and I'm glad people liked that particular section."

Although sales of *Final Fantasy III* did not match the explosive popularity of the Japanese version, it sold well for an RPG in the US and was well received by the growing RPG fan base in the US. Square had this fan base mostly all to its own—Enix was releasing games in America as well, but would not release its Super Famicom versions of *Dragon Quest* due to the amount of translation work they required. Square, meanwhile, would only release two more games on the Super NES before splitting with Nintendo and joining the Sony camp.

One of them was the great collaboration between the *Dragon Quest* and *Final Fantasy* creators, *Chrono Trigger*. Due to the game's time-travel conceit, there were many branching storylines and different endings. It was, according to Woolsey, a "shuffled mess," although he again did an excellent job in the translation.

And the company's final SNES game was again a title aimed specifically at the US market. Even though *Secret of Mana* was very popular in the US, Square decided against releasing the game's sequel, *Seiken Densetsu 3*. There were logistical problems that would have made the game a nightmare to localize; most of the original development team had been quickly placed on a new, important game release, which meant that their crucial support for the American version would not have been possible. There were also rumors that there were bugs and other issues in the game that would not have been easy to fix.

Taking all these issues into consideration, as well as the fact that it was costly in general to send revisions of games back and forth to Japan, "Square Japan decided it made sense to have game development in the US," says Woolsey. And the first and last game from Square's US development studio in Redmond was a pseudo-sequel to *Secret of Mana* called *Secret of Evermore*. Although it featured pretty graphics and a well-written English script, it did not please *Mana* fans because it just didn't feel like a Square game. It had none of the magic of Japanese RPGs.

Woolsey had nothing to do with the creation of *Secret of Evermore*, and indeed he felt it was a bad idea. "I think everyone concerned underestimated the unique product coming out of the Japanese development studios, and didn't understand that it couldn't be replicated abroad," says Woolsey. "We underestimated the *otaku* community here in the US—they are a very vocal minority, the evangelists for these types of games. And it seems they liked the Japanese-made games just fine.

"We launched *Evermore* and *Chrono Trigger* at the tail end of the SNES epoch. They did pretty well, but I think headquarters was less than happy about the quality of the first US-developed SNES product." Worse for the Redmond-based Square USA employees, headquarters was about to have a big falling out with Redmond-based Nintendo. A combination of all these factors led to sweeping changes soon after. "The political fallout was extreme and there were lots of strained relationships in the wake of the PlayStation defection, as it were."

Woolsey was asked to move to Los Angeles, where Square would be setting up shop alongside Sony. He declined for personal reasons—he wanted to keep his new family in the Seattle area where he grew up. So Woolsey split with Square and briefly joined with some other ex-Square employees to form a new game development company, Big Rain, in the Seattle area. Their first game, a PlayStation RPG called *Shadow Madness*, was picked up by Crave Entertainment and shipped in 1997. It failed to sell at retail, mostly because it was competing for attention with *Final Fantasy VII*, which, as luck would have it, was the game that made *Final Fantasy* explode in worldwide popularity.

One can only imagine what Ted Woolsey could have done with *FFVII*'s script, given the virtually unlimited text space afforded by the CD-ROM format. But his absence was truly felt in *FFVII*'s script. In the first hour of the game, one character says, "That man are sick." And at one memorable moment deeper into the game, the player is given a choice between a yes and no answer that was supposed to be phrased thusly: "Of course! / No way!" In the final version of the game, it was spelled like this: "Off course! / No, way!"

Even so, it didn't seem to matter. *Final Fantasy VII* took off like a rocket, eventually selling more copies in the US than it did in Japan. *FFVII* single-handedly took RPGs from "dedicated niche market" to "mainstream" in the US. RPGs could now sell millions, provided, of course, that they were as slick, polished, and full of glamorous full-motion video sequences, as *FFVII* was.

Few were, but other RPGs for the PlayStation followed in its wake, like a strategy game called *Kartia* by a company called Atlus. What made *Kartia* special was that Yoshitaka Amano, who was no longer doing much in the way of design for *Final Fantasy* titles, had done the character designs and illustrations. Dimitri Criona had by then taken over sales and marketing for Atlus, and he made Amano's contributions a key selling point for *Kartia*.

"We knew that the *Final Fantasy* name was very focused. And Atlus had developed a solid reputation among hardcore RPG gamers. We knew there was some crossover with *anime*, and knowledge of the Japanese artists and so on." Amano's involvement and the connection to *Final Fantasy* "certainly helped us make the decision to bring the game over." *Kartia* sold around 60,000 copies, just the number that Atlus was looking for, but a major change from the NES days, when Criona would place orders for *Ninja Gaiden* in *increments* of 60,000.

"*Final Fantasy* was a twelve-year overnight phenomenon," says Criona. "Just like *Teenage Mutant Ninja Turtles* was an eight-year overnight phenomenon." Both seemingly exploded into mainstream popularity overnight, but they had been around for a very long time, just underneath the surface.

MODERN TRANSLATION: GIVING GAMES A VOICE

With the advent of CD-ROM and DVD-ROM technologies, one would think that the jobs of video game translators have become easier. In many senses, they have; text can be stored in ASCII code and swapped out for a new language easily. Storage space for text is virtually unlimited. In one important way, however, translation projects now require much more work, as many creators use the vast storage space of disc media to include voiced dialogue. In Japan, the voiceovers for video games are performed by the same pool of talented actors who record the dialogue for the country's vast output of *anime* films and television shows.

In the US, quality voice acting is never guaranteed. It can be unnatural to the point of unintentional hilarity. The opening scenes of Capcom's original

Resident Evil for the PlayStation are a good example of this. Or it can be absolutely amazing. The fully voice-acted dialogue in *Metal Gear Solid: The Twin Snakes* (see Chapter 10) turned out to be painstakingly professional.

Even the creators of *Final Fantasy* were unable to resist the allure of voice acting, and although they eschewed it entirely during the PlayStation era, they recorded voiceovers for nearly all the major dialogue in *Final Fantasy X* on the PlayStation 2. And although Nintendo still resists using voiceovers for all the dialogue in its *Zelda* series, they were able to add a great deal to the character of Mario by giving him a voice of his own.

That voice came from Charles Martinet, who was oddly enough a classically trained Shakespearian stage actor for ten years out of college before he made a career transition into corporate acting—presentations at trade shows, corporate sales videos, and the like. Martinet was about 35 years old in 1991 when a friend passed along a tip on an audition. "I actually crashed the audition. I'd never done that before in my life, but my friend had said, 'Hey, you should go audition for this…plumber…uh, an Italian guy…for a trade show…that talks to people.' And I was going to be in the neighborhood, so I walked in the door and said, 'Can I please audition?'

"The director had already put his camera away. But he said okay. 'You're an Italian plumber from Brooklyn, and you're going to be talking at trade shows to people. You've got to talk all day, so just make something up. Make up a video game,

> **Hello!**
>
> **It's-a-me,**
>
> **Mario! Woo-hoo!**
>
> **Okie-dokie!**
>
> **You an' me,**
>
> **we gonna**
>
> **make'a da**
>
> **pizza pie!**

talk about video games, whatever. You start talking, and when you stop talking, I'll stop the tape.'

"And I thought to myself…plumber…Brooklyn…and what I heard at first was, of course, *Heeeeeey*, 'ow ya' doin'?, you know,

with a gruff accent and the guy's butt crack is showing. But then I thought that if there were going to be children present, they didn't want to hear somebody abrasive and tough that way.

"I'd done a version of *Taming of the Shrew* at a repertory theatre many years prior, and I played Gremio, who was the oldest Italian man in the world, with this squeaky old voice. And I must have been thinking about that, when all of a sudden the director said 'Action!' and I said, *Hello! It's-a-me, Mario! Woo-hoo! Okie-dokie! You an' me, we gonna make'a da pizza pie!* And I started talking about making a pizza pie until the tape ran out."

Martinet was hired, but his charming and unique voice wouldn't appear in a Mario game for many years. At first, his job was to appear as Mario at trade shows and public appearances: Wal-Mart store openings, game competitions, and the like. To preserve the image of Mario, Nintendo didn't dress up the 6'4" Martinet in a Mario suit. Instead, Martinet sat behind the scenes with a camera where he could see the audience, and his voice was synced up to a computer image of Mario that appeared on a giant monitor.

Martinet's voice was in millions of American homes when Nintendo released *Super Mario 64*. Mario's dialogue was restricted to a few words, but they amplified the experience by making the character that much more life-like. "It fills in the picture," Martinet says, "creates an active place for people's imaginations to go. I think a voice has the ability to be the icing on the cake that really brings joy, and fun, and something people can relate to."

Nintendo makes a lot of different games starring Mario, and Martinet's voice now appears in every one of them, from *Mario Golf* on the GameCube to *Mario vs. Donkey Kong* on the Game Boy Advance. Martinet voices other Nintendo characters like Wario, Luigi, and Baby Mario. Each game takes about a day or two in the studio to record. Nintendo flies Martinet up to Seattle, treats him to an expensive *sushi* lunch, then Martinet and the other actors who play characters like Princess Peach and Toad improvise and "fly off the handle" all day.

Although he had never played Nintendo's games before he auditioned for the part, Martinet has come to be one of Nintendo's and Miyamoto's biggest fans. "Mr. Miyamoto is a genius. He created this sweet, loveable Everyman who has these archetypal qualities—a plumber in love with a princess who spends his life rescuing her. What could be a more enchanting tale than that? He introduced the notion of cinema, a movie, and a plotline in a video game. It's just awesome, and it absolutely changed everybody's lives."

Mario has just as much respect for the man. "*He is-a my Papa!*" says Martinet as Mario. "*I love-a my Papa!*"

THE GAMES THAT DON'T MAKE IT

"In the world of the 1980's," says Gail Tilden, "all the big hits were coming from the Japanese development community, from *Frogger* to *Space Invaders* to *Pac-Man*. We had no real market segmentation between US and Japanese products." But still, says Tilden, there were games even for the Famicom that were "too Japanese," games that American kids would have no interest in. These included, says Tilden, games based on Asian board games like *go*, *shogi*, or *mahjongg*. But it also included other varieties of games.

Even in the earliest days of the NES, one title absolutely could not be released in America. *Devil World* was a *Pac-Man*-styled maze game in which the player controlled a cute little dragon that had to navigate a maze patrolled by monsters. Sound innocuous? Well, the monsters in question were Satanic demons, and instead of picking up Power Pellets, the little dragon had to collect crucifixes and Holy Bibles to defend himself.

This use of Christian symbolism was seen as perfectly innocuous in Japan—and in Europe, where *Devil World* was released along with the NES in 1987—but would be seen as unsettling or even blasphemous in America. So unfortunately, although *Devil World* was a typically ingenious Miyamoto-directed take on the maze genre, with inventive graphics and fun game play, it never made it to US shores. It is the only Miyamoto game never to do so.

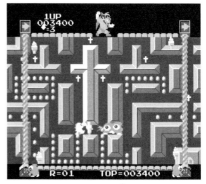

There are even more games that never made it to the United States. In many cases, the games were never that great to begin with and it's not worth losing sleep over. But in many infamous cases, fantastic works of art were never given the green light across the Pacific. Masaya Matsuura's ingenious *Vib Ribbon* never made it, probably due to the game's simple black-and-white graphics. Graphics can be a major concern; a style that works in Japan may not fly at all in America.

Major series have seen major omissions in America. Although *Final Fantasy II* and *Final Fantasy V* were eventually brought to America in remade versions for the PlayStation, *Final Fantasy III* was never released here, and there are currently no plans to bring it over in any form. And what many consider the best game in the *Castlevania* series, *Demon Castle Dracula X: Rondo of Blood* for the NEC PC Engine Duo, was never brought to America.

But besides the games that vast numbers of American gamers actually *want* to play, there are in fact major categories of video game that thrive in Japan that would simply not work in America. It's not as if there haven't been efforts made to release games in the following genres. In fact, many of the types of games mentioned below have seen a handful of American releases. It is doubtful, however, that American game stores will ever have the vast selection of games in these categories that Japanese ones do.

Perhaps the most notorious example of a genre that has remained mostly exclusive to Japan is known here as a "dating game." Fans call them *ren'ai* or romance games. Detractors call them by the derogatory term *gyaru getto ge-mu* (girl get games). They are choose-your-own-adventure games that put the player into the role of a high school boy who attempts to woo the girls at his school, hoping to find true love before graduation. The most famous game in the genre is Konami's *Tokimeki Memorial* ('tokimeki' means 'excitement'), which has appeared on the PC Engine, Super Famicom, Sega Saturn, and PlayStation, among other systems. By the end of 1996, across those four systems Konami had sold 1.1 million games, which was stunning for a dating simulation series. *Tokimemo*, as it was abbreviated, won Japan's Grand Prix award for the best game of 1996.[7]

Unlike some other dating games that had come before, the *Tokimemo* games were not erotic; they were about pure romance. Because this was actually quite similar to the plots of *shoujo* (girls') *manga*, *Tokimemo* caught on with girls and women. Konami finally brought out a game pointed directly at this fan base in 2002 when it released *Tokimeki Girl's Side*, a dating game that put the player in the role of a girl picking between boys. Another PlayStation 2 release called *Kimagure Strawberry Café* ("Kimagure" meaning "capricious," like the pink ghost in *Pac-Man*) put the player in the role of Ichigo (meaning 'strawberry') Mizuhara, a high school senior who runs her parents' café for a year and attempts to get one of the boys who come in to ask her on a date.

Also much like some girls' *manga*, there are dating games that put the female player into the role of a male high school student who goes after other male high school students. One game released by NEC Interchannel, former makers of the PC Engine system, and developed by a company named Spray, is called *Gakuen Heaven: Boys' Love Scramble*. Its box proclaims it a "Love Love Hyper Boys Game."

Another subset of dating games is overtly pornographic, though titles in this genre are generally found only on personal computers. Stores that sell PC games will generally have a large section of pornographic dating games. They proceed very much like *Tokimemo*, but the goal is not true love—it is to get into a sexual situation in which the player's set of action commands becomes a list of unprintable verbs. These are mostly drawn in *manga* style, which allows for a wide range of titles that, like Japanese pornography videos, encompass practically every perversion imaginable.

Not all pornographic titles are adventure games, but they generally feature some obstacle or another between the player and his pornography. There were pornographic games for video game consoles even before the graphics could show anything vaguely stimulating. One of the first games developed by the company Koei was called *Night Life* and was sort of a sex manual, featuring "illustrations of different sexual positions, a rhythm method calculator, and a sex diary." The title of another early Koei game translated roughly to "Tempting Housewife In The Building."[8]

Such games even appeared on early video game systems, unauthorized by the hardware makers, of course. A company called Hacker released adult-oriented versions of parlor games for the Famicom and Famicom Disk System: strip *mahjongg*, strip pachinko, strip poker, even strip *hanafuda*. Some of these games were actually released in the US, again unauthorized, by a company called Panesian, who gave them names like *Hot Slots* and *Peek-A-Boo Poker*. An array of unlicensed adult games for the PC Engine system in Japan got even more creative in their use of genre; one fighting game featuring nearly nude women was called *Strip Fighter*.

The non-strip varieties of games based on the *pachinko* and *pachisuro* gambling games are also quite popular. By design, they are extremely simple. In *pachinko*, the player repeatedly presses a lever to flip tiny metal balls to the top of what looks like a small, vertical pinball machine, attempting to aim the balls into holes that pay out more balls, which can be played again or cashed in. *Pachisuro* machines are like standard slot machines but the player stops each wheel individually. Since gambling games of pure luck are banned in Japan, these machines provide just enough "control" over the outcome to qualify as legal games of skill. But in reality, they are so difficult to control that the outcome might as well be random.

> **As of this writing, the Fist of the North Star pachisuro game has racked up more sales than Grand Theft Auto: Vice City in Japan.**

And yet…they *are* controllable, hence the popularity of *pachinko* and *pachisuro* simulations for every major console from the Famicom to the PlayStation 2. With enough practice at home, one can learn to beat the machine and pocket big bucks. This is aided by the fact that the very same pachinko manufacturers, like Sammy and Aruze, produce video game versions of their hottest machines. And just like a *Street Fighter* addict will buy a special arcade style joystick for home use, so too are authentic arcade-style pachinko and pachisuro controllers available at premium prices.

And the games really do sell. To name a recent example, two pachislo games, *Jissen Pachisuro: Fist of the North Star* and *Pachisuro Tokondensho: Inoki Festival*, held strong places on the Japanese Top Ten sales charts for the months of May and June, outselling games like Nintendo's *Mario vs. Donkey Kong* and *Pikmin 2*.[9] As of this writing, the *Fist of the North Star* pachisuro game has racked up more sales than *Grand Theft Auto: Vice City* in Japan.

Another popular genre in Japan also revolves around a form of gambling: horse breeding/racing simulators. In games like *Derby Stallion* and *Gallop Racer*, the player breeds and trains a championship horse, and then races it. Players don't control their horses during the race, though—they just watch and cross their fingers as in real life. Sega introduced an elaborate arcade version of these games, called *Derby Owners Club*, in 2000. Eight individual playing areas are seated around a giant monitor that shows the races. Players can save their horses onto a credit-card-like magnetic device and bring them back to any machine to continue training and racing them. Some players, mostly middle-aged salary men, spend hours and hours at the machines, sometimes eating meals there.[10]

In fact, many massive arcade simulation games seem to be most popular with adult men. Rather than concentrating on fast action and unreal scenarios, some arcade games replicate a mundane real-life experience as closely as possible. This allows the player to fantasize about living a different life, an alluring concept in a country where lifetime employment with one company is the norm and career change is very rare. The most popular is *Densha de Go!* (Let's Go By Train!). The player sits on a stool in front of a bank of controls identical to the ones that control the train lines all over the country. Likewise, the train lines in the game replicate the actual train lines that commuters ride around Tokyo every day.

There is just too much of a cultural knowledge gap for titles like *Densha de Go!* to be released in America, because the enjoyment of playing them comes from the familiarity of the train line. Previous knowledge of another facet of the culture is required to enjoy the game. This also holds true for some games produced as tie-in products to *anime* series. Though the situation has drastically improved over the days of the NES, when companies swapped out *anime* heroes and replaced them with generic characters, publishers are still wary of bringing over any game, no matter how good, if the *anime* itself is not available in the US.

This situation is not all bad. Firstly, *anime* tie-in games can often turn out to be, much like American-made games based on Hollywood movies, not very good. And some of the games fall into strange genres that make little sense in America: the *Fist of the North Star* pachisuro game is one, and so are the "soccer adventure" games that Tecmo produced for the Famicom, based on the *anime Captain Tsubasa*. These games weren't your typical version of video soccer; rather than controlling the action directly, you watch animated sequences play out until the star player on the team gets into a pinch. Then, you select what you want him to do, and see if you made the right choice.

In a sense, the *Captain Tsubasa* titles are 'dating games' for the middle school set, less actual sports simulator and more drama. These games have never really caught on with Americans, and perhaps they never will. Even American *otaku*, lovers of *anime* as they are, aren't really sure why these sorts of adventure games are appealing. I'm not even sure myself.

A HISTORY OF ONGOING CHANGE

"The whole process has evolved," says Criona. "It's evolved from translations, to grammatical translations, to what I would call 'reculturalization.' What they did at Atlus and what we do here at Bandai is a many-step process. Step one: translation. Step two: clean that up as best you can. Step three: rewrite and manipulate it to be culturally acceptable. Many of the people here at Bandai are not only bilingual, they're bicultural. And that's very important."

Nowadays, knee-jerk censorship for censorship's sake has been mostly eliminated. From region to region, the player's experience is more consistent than it has ever been. But there will always be a need for "localization" as well as translation, because, just as Americans are shocked and surprised over what the Japanese consider acceptable, so too does the average Japanese have no way of knowing innately what Americans find offensive.

And yet, says *Gitaroo-Man*'s designer Keiichi Yano, "with the game industry as it is right now, most games have to be designed with the thought that it will be international." And indeed, Yano's game ended up selling more copies in the United States than in Japan. "I thought that was very interesting," he says, noting that it made him think about how America as a whole has progressed. "It's started to seek more different, more unique points of Japanese culture than it used to. When I lived in LA, eating sushi got the reaction, '*Oh my God, you're eating raw fish?*' And now, everybody eats sushi. In the ten years that I've been away from LA, times have really changed over there."

Yano sees Japan, also, as an ever-changing nation. "The history of Japan has been a history of ongoing change. Japanese people love new things: new culture, new identities, new foods. Every year there's a new fad. That's why we wanted to use 326 as our illustrator for *Gitaroo-Man*—we wanted somebody who was popular now, and unique.

"But you know, I thought that in America, that choice was not going to fly at all. Just like I thought *Pokémon* wouldn't fly at all. And boy, was I wrong about that."

▨　▨　▨

CHAPTER 9

POKéMON: SHIKAKU SEDAI NO SEKAI SHÔHIN

"I was told...that this kind of thing would never appeal to American audiences."

—Shigeru Miyamoto[1]

What is there to say about *Pokémon* that hasn't already been said? And yet, it would be almost irresponsible to write a book on Japanese video games that did not contain at least a cursory overview of the phenomenon. As a worldwide multimedia juggernaut, it is without equal. As a video game, it is stellar. And as an instructive example of practically everything that has been discussed in this book, it is priceless.

Japanese are proud of *Pokémon*, the most successful export of Japanese popular culture ever. Nonetheless, had Japanese societal norms had their way, *Pokémon* would have never been born, its creator not given the freedom to follow his own path. Designer Satoshi Tajiri was one of the original game *otaku*—born in 1965, he was thirteen when *Space Invaders* was released, and spent most of his time from then on in arcades. He refused to follow the accepted path of society; he wouldn't go to college, but spent two years at a technical school. His father got him a job as an electrical technician. He refused to take it.[2] "The nail that sticks up gets pounded down," goes the Japanese maxim. Tajiri continued to elude the hammer.

In 1982, at seventeen, Tajiri started making a *doujinshi*, or fanzine, dedicated to video gaming. Tajiri would document all of the secret tips and tricks he found in the popular arcade games of the time. An *otaku* named Ken Sugimori saw the first issue of Tajiri's fanzine, called *GameFreak*, in a *doujinshi* store in Shinjuku. Recognizing a kindred spirit, he wrote to Tajiri and included some of his illustrations, asking if he could write for *GameFreak*. The two became fast friends, and eventually started experimenting with game design.

Tajiri had long thought about designing his own games. He submitted design concepts to various game idea contests; in 1981 he won first prize in a Sega-sponsored one.[3] When the Famicom was released in 1983, Tajiri tooled around with *Family BASIC*, a cartridge that included a full-size keyboard and let the user program rudimentary games in the BASIC programming language. Once he understood the rudiments of how the system worked, he pieced together his own Famicom development system using spare parts that he bought in Akihabara.[4]

After five years of work, Tajiri and Sugimori had finished a Famicom game, which they called *Quinty*. Although it was released in 1989, two years after *Final Fantasy*, it was a fond look back at the classic arcade game style that Tajiri and Sugimori loved, with simple, easy-to-learn game play and beautifully animated graphics. The guidebook for the Tokyo Metropolitan Museum of

Photography's 2003 exhibit of Famicom software called it "The End Result of the *Otaku* Culture of the '80s" and noted that its single-screen nature and simple controls were decidedly old school.[5]

Because of his great admiration for the company, Tajiri took *Game-Freak*'s first title to Namco. He could not imagine any company except Namco publishing his title—the Namco game *Xevious* was his favorite—he had devoted entire issues of his fanzine to *Xevious* strategy. And *Quinty*'s design was most reminiscent of Namco's colorful, cute arcade games like *Pac-Man*. Namco published *Quinty* on June 26, 1989; it was a success.

Tajiri believed that he could sell the game in the US as well. So he flew to California, rented a car, and "drove all over the West Coast" showing off the game to NES licensees. Even though demand for NES games still exceeded supply, publishers were becoming a little more discerning. *Quinty* was rejected for being 'too cute' by most of them.[6] Finally, the US arm of Hudson Soft picked up the game and released it as *Mendel Palace* in the US, altering the title screen and package art so that the game's characters, while still *anime*-styled, were more realistically proportioned and less cute. The actual in-game graphic style was unchanged.

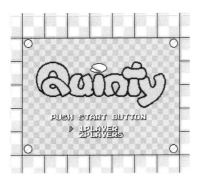

Mendel Palace sold about 60,000 copies in the US[7], but the experience made Tajiri wonder what he had to do in order to create a game that would be equally appealing to both markets. By 1990, Nintendo's portable handheld gaming system, Game Boy, was becoming a phenomenon all its own, selling millions of units worldwide and bringing with it a brand new way of playing video games—anytime, anywhere. A cable that was included in the box allowed two Game Boys to link up and share data. It was used for two-player contests, mostly for head-to-head games of *Tetris* and other puzzle games.

Tajiri had what he believed to be the seeds of a better idea. It was based on the childhood activity that consumed his free time before video arcades came along: bug collecting. Tajiri would explore all around his town as a young boy, collecting insects, especially beetles. He was fascinated by all the different creatures that could be found if only one looked. "If I put my hand in a river, I would get a crayfish. Put a stick underwater and make a hole, look for bubbles and there were more creatures."[8] Little Satoshi wanted to be an entomologist when he grew up; his elementary school friends called him "Dr. Bug."[9]

Later, after *Pokémon*'s success, Tajiri would write a book on game design in which he advanced his personal theory that "masterpieces are created from new verbs."[10] That is, a great game can be designed around a single word. Of course he knew, as many Japanese did, that *Pac-Man* was designed around the verb *taberu*, to eat. *Quinty* was designed around the verb *mekuru*, to flip over. And Tajiri's next game was designed around the verb *koukan suru*, to trade.

Tajiri envisioned a game that would let the player collect all sorts of mythical creatures. But he had bigger plans for the link cable. "I imagined an insect moving back and forth across the cable. That's what inspired me."[11] Tajiri took his inspiration to Nintendo, who was impressed enough with *Quinty* that they contracted him to design the game, which Tajiri was calling *Capsule Monsters*, for them to publish.

It took Tajiri, Sugimori, and the rest of the staff at *GameFreak* nearly six years to finish *Pocket Monsters*, as it soon became known. Toward the end of the project, Tajiri "barely had enough money to pay his employees." Five of them actually quit when they found out how bad things were. Finally, Nintendo released *Pocket Monsters* in 1996, but did not have high hopes for its success.[12]

Cynics believe that Nintendo planned the *Pokémon* onslaught from the beginning, carefully coordinating the various properties to maximize their profits and brainwash legions of children. This is not quite the case. The games—two versions, *Red* and *Green*, which contained different Pokémon to encourage trading—were released in Japan on February 27, 1996 to little fanfare. A weekly comic series was begun in the popular children's magazine

Koro Koro Comic, but that was it as far as tie-in product. And *Pokémon* didn't exactly explode onto the sales charts.

The unique thing about *Pokémon* was that after the first few weeks, when most games in Japan sell the vast majority of the copies they're going to sell, *Pokémon* kept selling. Nintendo was not pushing the game hard, but word of mouth caused sales to snowball, growing exponentially. By the end of 1997 Nintendo had sold four million copies, more than Square's *Final Fantasy VII*, and more than Konami's *Metal Gear Solid*.[13]

When Nintendo realized how big *Pokémon* was becoming, they moved fast, licensing toys and other related products. *Pokémon's* adorable characters tapped into the ever-growing Japanese affinity for *kawaisa*—cuteness—which Duke University professor Anne Allison calls Japan's main millennial product. *Kawaisa* came into vogue with the ultra-popular Hello Kitty products that swept Japan in the 1970s, and nowadays, notes Allison, cute characters are "omnipresent in the landscape of urban, millennial Japan," appearing on "T-shirts, book bags, lunch boxes, pencils, hair ribbons, hand towels, rice bowls, bath soap, cooking pans, calendars, and erasers."[14]

And of course, besides this sort of merchandise licensing, Nintendo worked again with the media group Shogakukan to produce more *Pokémon* *manga* in KoroKoro Comic but also to produce an animated version of the show. It became the country's top-rated children's program.

While the original *manga* featured the pink puffball Pokémon Pippi (Clefairy in the US version) as its mascot character, Shogakukan chose another of Sugimori's 150 monster designs to be the central character of its animated show. It was an electric rat named after the Japanese onomatopoeic words for the sparkle of lightning and the sound of a mouse's squeak: *pika* and *chu*.

■　▨　▨

But we're getting ahead of ourselves by discussing the success of the *Pokémon* cartoon. First, let us ask what was so appealing about *Pokémon*, the piece of software? Again, cynics complain that the game is ruthlessly commercial, that it programs children to be consumers of anything and everything *Pokémon*. But as Shigeru Miyamoto said, "Mr. Tajiri didn't start this project intending to make something which would become very popular. He just wanted to make something he wanted to play himself. There was no business sense involved, only his love involved in the creation. Somehow, what he wanted to create for himself was appreciated by others in this country and is shared by people in other countries."[15]

What Tajiri created was an RPG in the style of *Dragon Quest*, simplified in some aspects, less so in others. The player assumed the role of a young boy who lived in a world where wild Pocket Monsters roamed. Boys and girls would leave their homes at adolescence to venture out into the world and become Pokémon trainers, capturing and taming Pokémon, then pitting them in battle against the Pokémon held by other trainers, in a quest to be the world's great master.

Much like *Dragon Quest*, when the player ventured outside the safe confines of the towns and into the wilderness he would be attacked, either by wild Pokémon or by rival trainers looking for a fight. Battles were strictly one-on-one and turn-based, although the player could swap out his Pokémon for another one during the battle, losing a turn in the process. He could carry six Pokémon at once. Any single Pokémon could have up to four abilities, far more limited than the characters in most RPGs. These abilities would inflict damage to the opponent's Pokémon or affect their status: lower their attack or defensive power, or confuse them, paralyze them, poison them, and so on. Pokémon never died, but if they suffered too much damage they would "faint" and the player would have to bring them back to the PokéCenter—similar to 'inns' in traditional RPGs—where they would be healed back to full stamina.

Of course, two players could always link up and battle with their Pokémon teams. But they could also link up to trade Pokémon, and if they wanted a complete collection of 150, they would have to. The *Red* and *Green* versions of the game contained different sets of Pokémon right from the outset, so even the youngest beginner players had some bargaining chips. In this way, *Pokémon* was what its producer Tsunekazu Ishihara called a "not-closed" product. "Take film: we see a beginning, an end, and finally, the credits rolling. That is a 'closed' product— *Pokémon* also has a beginning and an end, and even credits. But for the player, this hardly means that the game is over."[16]

> **Pokémon also has a beginning and an end, and even credits. But for the player, this hardly means that the game is over.**

Indeed, most studies of *Pokémon* have noted how the game's design bucks popular industry trends. "Far from aspiring to ever greater three-dimensional filmic realism, in the manner of contemporary console games, *Pokémon* is a two-dimensional puzzle game," wrote the authors of one essay contained in *Pikachu's Global Adventure*, a collection of scholarly papers on *Pokémon*. "Although it creates a complete fictional world in the manner of role-playing games aimed at older players (such as the *Legend of Zelda* and *Final Fantasy* series), it effectively leaves children to imagine much of that world themselves."[17]

Pokémon games "were not based around cutting-edge technology," noted another scholar. "Rather…their game worlds were rendered in 2-D, in four shades of grey, with limited animation, and with music and sound effects reminiscent of that emanating from 1970s' consoles and home computers. Yet *Pokémon*…[speaks] of the way in which the experience transcends the apparent limitations of the host platform." *Pokémon*, he concluded, "undermines the efficacy of attempts to understand video games simply as audio-visual spectacles."[18]

Even to adults, *Pokémon* can be addicting. I began my first play-through of *Pokémon* earlier this year, as part of the research for this chapter, with an almost clinical, detached attitude. Not an hour into the game I was furiously attempting to raise my Metapod to level 10, so that he would evolve into the more powerful Butterfree, an air-type Pokémon that would be powerful against the ground-type rock Pokémon held by another trainer, who I had to beat in order to proceed through the game. I didn't know all this at the time, of course. I had to ask my thirteen-year-old cousin, who, although he has outgrown the game, will probably forever be a virtual encyclopedia of Pokétrivia, just like I can still remember the names of all the Masters of the Universe action figures.

Everybody during *Pokémon*'s heyday had a younger cousin, a sibling, a nephew or niece, or two, or three, or four, who were certified Pokémaniacs. And they might have been immersed in more than one form of the game; in America they might have been hopelessly addicted to the collectible trading card game, which like the game and TV show became the best selling and most popular game of its kind, beating out the teen-oriented fantasy game *Magic: The Gathering*. This was of little concern to *Magic*'s publisher, Wizards of the Coast, as they produced the *Pokémon* game as well. Much like *Pokémon* was a scaled-down version of traditional RPGs, the card game was crafted to be as balanced and as addictive as, but easier to learn than, its big brother.

The cross-platform nature of *Pokémon* in the US came from the fact that the game was only introduced here after its wild success in Japan as an *anime*, *manga*, game, toy, and licensed merchandise phenomenon. Nintendo of America knew that they had a potential blockbuster, so their launch was carefully coordinated for maximum impact across all platforms.

To head up its *Pokémon* invasion, NOA tapped NES marketing master-mind Gail Tilden, pulling her away from her previous job at *Nintendo Power* magazine. "When we started *Pokémon*, my sentiment was this: because it was such a complicated property, Nintendo needed to have a separate group doing the whole thing, and that if I was going to do this I would need a larger area of responsibility.

"At the same time, and I'm a little embarrassed to say this now, but I didn't think it was going to be enough of a challenge. I knew it meant I had to interface and coordinate with Japan, but I didn't expect it to be that big."

Almost a year away from the scheduled US rollout of *Pokémon*, Tilden was thrown a major challenge. On December 16, 1997, the thirty-eighth episode of the *Pokémon* TV series in Japan, titled "Dennô Senshi Porigon" (Electric Senshi Porigon), was broadcast. Toward the episode's climax, Pikachu defends against an exploding bomb by using a lightning blast. When the flashing effects of both attacks were combined in the final animated product, the resulting light burst caused epileptic seizures in roughly seven hundred Japanese children. Most recovered quickly, but some had to be hospitalized overnight. The government investigated. Shogakukan shut down production of the show for four months.

Once the cause of the seizures had been found, the news exploded around the world and was all over American media in particular. Besides countless news articles and TV reports, the episode was lampooned in popular culture. In an episode of *The Simpsons* where Bart and family go to Japan, they watch a show on TV called "Seizure Robots," which promptly causes the entire clan to have an epileptic fit on the floor of their hotel room.

"'CARTOON MONSTER ATTACKS KIDS' was the first headline Americans read about *Pokémon*. It was not a good omen," noted *Time* magazine two years later.[19] Of course, what *Time* got wrong was that none of those articles referred to anything called *Pokémon*; the title of the Japanese game and TV show was *Pocket Monsters*. But the Japanese have an affinity for shortening to three syl-lables any especially lengthy construction, so just as 'Family Computer' became *Famicom*, Pocket Monsters became *pokemon*. But the only thing Americans knew was that a Japanese TV cartoon called Pocket Monsters was the culprit. Thus, rather than call the US product "Pocket Monsters," it was renamed *Pokémon*—the accent over the 'e' was intended to help consumers pronounce it correctly.*

★ It didn't work in some cases; as often as I've heard parents say "Po-kay-mon," I've heard "Pocky-mon," which is excusa-ble, and "Pokey-man," which is not.

Also presenting a potential stumbling block was that the game itself had to be entirely reprogrammed for the US market. It's not that many changes had to be made, but the original game, having been in development over six years, was in such a fragile state that any changes to the code, even altering the text, would render the program useless. So Nintendo had to start from scratch and rewrite the game program entirely.

Being a Game Boy game, *Pokémon* didn't have much in the way of lengthy dialogue sequences that needed to be translated. But it did pose a unique linguistic problem, because it contained 150 monsters, most of which had very Japanese names. Just as Tilden was very careful about the names given to the US versions of NES games and related products, she and the *Pokémon* division took a great deal of care in renaming the pocket monsters for their US debut, choosing names that were easy to remember, clever, and logical. "The names," notes Joseph Tobin, "are both rich in cute puns and in a pseudo-Linnean attention to family and genus. For example, the little lizard with fire on its tail [known as Hitokage or "shadow" in Japan] in English is Charmander; his more evolved version is called Charmeleon, and his most evolved version is Charizard."[20]

The human characters' names had to be changed as well, which eliminated a clever joke. In the Japanese version, the main character is named Satoshi. His rival, who follows him, taunts him, and keeps him on his toes throughout the entire game, is named (what else?) Shigeru. Their names became Ash and Gary in the US. Other names, as well, reflected subtly the original meaning or sound of the Japanese name. "Kasumi" (meaning "mist") became "Misty." "Professor Okido" became "Professor Oak."

And Tilden had concerns about the very nature of the game play. RPGs were not yet popular in the US, especially not on the Game Boy system. And they tended to have Japanese themes, which was one reason that Shigesato Itoi's original *Mother* went unreleased in America. Tilden attributed it to the "different play behavior of Japanese kids. They would sit for hours in front of the TV, and we didn't think American kids would do that. We went into *Pokémon* with that theory, and found out we were mistaken. Whether that had been the case all along or whether it had changed, we don't know."

These concerns were what caused NOA to craft a completely different debut for *Pokémon* in the US. Rather than unveiling the game and, if it was successful, localizing the *anime*, Tilden decided that the US needed a simultaneous rollout of the various *Pokémon* properties. If it worked, in large part the *anime* would be what attracted children to the game.

And so Warner Bros. licensed the animated cartoon for their Saturday morning WB Kids lineup. Shogakukan's US subsidiary, Viz, would help with the localization and later release the videos and DVDs in partnership with Pioneer. Further damaging the Nintendo-as-evil-mastermind theory, Joseph Tobin notes that although Nintendo has made "quite a bit of money" through *Pokémon* licensing, "they made some mistakes, including underestimating the value of the rights to the TV show… As a result, during the height of the *Pokémon* craze much of the money was made by companies other than Nintendo."[21]

Localizing the *anime* presented the biggest problems of all. It wasn't because the action took place in Japan—*Pokémon*'s world was entirely fictional and mostly fantastic. It was as *mukokuseki,* free of nationality, as any *anime* could reasonably be expected to be. Indeed, argues Koichi Iwabuchi, "Even if Japanese animators do not consciously draw *mukokuseki* characters in order to appeal to international consumers, they always have the global market in the back if not the front of their minds, and they are well aware that the non-Japaneseness of their animated characters works to their advantage in the global market… The producers and creators of game software *intentionally* make the characters of computer games look non-Japanese because they are clearly conscious that their market is global."[22]

> **The producers and creators of game software *intentionally* make the characters of computer games look non-Japanese because they are clearly conscious that their market is global.**

And yet, it is clear that what comes out of Japan, despite artists' attempts to make it *mukokuseki,* is clearly identifiable as Japanese in origin. *Pokémon*'s characters might not look like Japanese people, but they are highly influenced by standard *anime* style, which differs vastly from that of traditional Ameri-can Saturday morning fare. *Pokémon*'s animation style is also identifiably Japanese; its animation techniques incorporate lots of camera pans across still frames, facial close-ups with limited mouth movement, and repeated frames. This is necessary to crank out daily, sequential episodes in a timely fashion. If you watch half an hour of Looney Tunes, it doesn't matter what Bugs Bunny was doing yesterday or last Saturday. But *Pokémon* is a continuing serial, a lengthy drama that builds up to a conclusion every season. This, too, was very different.

And there were "distinctively Japanese elements" to *Pokémon* that were left in the show even as it was considered to be appropriately *mukokuseki.*

Tobin notes the "*sensei-deishi* (master-disciple) relationship" between the main character and the old Pokémon professor. He points out that although *Pokémon's* world is mostly fantastic, on occasion the characters sit down to eat rice and noodles with chopsticks in restaurants with signs painted in *kanji* characters.[23] Patrick Drazen points out that some of the Pokémon draw on elements of Asian culture, like the twelve animals of the Zodiac. And in one episode, the characters meet up with a band of Pokémon that are dressed like a traditional Japanese fire brigade.[24]

But there were elements in *Pokémon* that, although perfectly acceptable for children's entertainment in Japan, just wouldn't work in a show directed at American children. NOA removed scenes containing fistfights. Any vaguely scatological humor had to go. Religious references, too. No guns, either.

Some episodes were simply not shown in the US. One was the seizure-inducing Porigon episode. Another was not shown because—as difficult as this is to believe about an episode of a children's cartoon series—it was riddled with sexual humor. Called "Ao Puruko no Kyûjitsu" ("Holiday in Blue Pulco"), the episode centers around a bikini contest at a seaside resort for Pokémon trainers. Seconds into the episode, twelve-year-old Kasumi (Misty) appears in a bikini to the wide-eyed stares of Satoshi and fellow trainer Takeshi (Brock). They meet a dirty old man who stares at her breasts and comments that he'd like to see her in eight years.

What's interesting about this old man is that he actually turns out to be a sympathetic character; Kasumi enters the bikini contest only to help the old lecher save his beachside restaurant. But she is in danger of losing the contest to the evil Team Rocket—not merely Musashi (Jesse), the team's voluptuous female, but also Kojiro (James), the male half of the team, who is dressed in drag and wearing a magical bikini that gives him breasts larger than Musashi's. He teases Kasumi relentlessly over her small chest: "You're ten years too young."

So yeah…that had to go.

As is apparent now, Nintendo of America's tireless preparations, alterations, and marketing—$20 million to start—paid off. The Game Boy titles *Pokémon Red* and *Pokémon Blue* were released on September 27, 1998. They became the fastest-selling Game Boy titles ever, selling a combined 200,000 copies in the first *two weeks* of their availability. By the end of 1998 they had sold four million units in the US alone across three versions. In Japan, across four versions the game had sold nearly 12 million copies.

The release of *Pokémon Yellow*, a remix of the original game that included more elements from the *anime*, such as a Pikachu that followed the player around, set US sales records for first-week availability on *any* system when it sold 600,000 copies in its first seven days. In late 2000, the Game Boy Color sequels, *Pokémon Gold* and *Pokémon Silver*, broke *that* record by selling 1.4 million copies in their first seven days.[25] By that time, *Pokémon* had already appeared on the cover of *Time* magazine, featured in an article that called the series "a multimedia and interactive barrage like no other before it."[26]

The first *Pokémon* theatrical movie, *Mewtwo Strikes Back*, opened on November 12, 1999. It took in $25 million in its opening weekend. Hasbro paid $325 million for the rights to *Pokémon* toys; it was a sound investment to say the least. *Pokémon* is "endlessly expandable," notes Anne Allison; it can easily be transplanted into other media. In lengthy articles examining the phenomenon, *Time* and *Electronic Gaming Monthly* noted how far the transplants had gone; *Time* ironically juxtaposed *Pokémon* candy and toothbrushes, EGM highlighted unbelievable Japanese *Pokémon* goods, such as a toy *Pokémon* airplane—unbelievable because it replicated a *real* plane that All Nippon Airways painted with *Pokémon* characters.

▪ ▫ ▪

So what does all this mean? Iwabuchi paints *Pokémon* as what the Japanese call a *sekai shôhin* or "global commodity," defined as something of "universal or trans-cultural appeal that bear[s] the creative imprint of the originality of a producing nation."[27] That is, even though *Pokémon* is *mukokuseki* in some ways, it is identifiably Japanese in others. *Pokémon*, then, is the ultimate *sekai shôhin* of the *shikaku sedai*. It is the product by which the *manga* style, so prized by the "visual generation," has become popular around the world. Anne Allison notes the impact:

> As for American children themselves, all whom I interviewed knew that *Pokémon* came originally from Japan. And while none linked this fact to their reasons for liking the product ("I don't like *Pokémon because* it's Japanese"), many said that they have developed an interest in Japan *as a result of Pokémon* and other "cool" Japanese goods. A number said that they now wanted to study Japanese and travel there one day. When I then asked what image they had of the country, a number answered that Japan was the producer of "cool" products. In the words of one ten-year-old boy,

"I like Japan. It's a good place because they make cool things for us like Nintendo game systems, Sony Walkman, and now *Pokémon*." In the minds of these young American kids, Japan has a positive association directly linked to its production of play technology.[28]

Through their experience with localized Japanese *anime*, Japan becomes appealing to American *otaku*. "[I]n the West the term *otaku* connotes something stunning and attractive, so much so that *anime* and *manga* products elicit in Westerners a sense of yearning for 'Japan,'"[29] is the way of thinking of some Japanese media critics. Iwabuchi addresses this theory then refutes its importance, asserting that the "yearning for another culture…is inevitably illusory, as this yearning lacks concern for and understanding of the complexity of processes by which popular cultural artifacts are produced."[30]

And indeed, *Pokémon* is not even so appealing to American *otaku* after a while; after all, it's a children's show. Although it might have more depth and excitement than American cartoons, *Pokémon* by design can never show the riveting imagery of Hayao Miyazaki's films like *Princess Mononoke* or *Spirited Away*, nor can it possess any of the gravitas of dramatic works such as *Akira* or *Perfect Blue*. But it doesn't matter, because nobody is mistaking *Pokémon* for Japan. It is, like *Super Mario Bros.*, a gateway. It opens a door on Japanese culture. It is a meeting halfway—no easier to *translate* than live-action film, but easier to *localize*.

And if that "number" of children in Allison's study group *do* study Japanese and *do* travel there one day, it won't matter what their first impression of Japan was. What will matter is that they will have started down the road to an actual understanding of Japan and Japanese culture. *Pokémon* will have started the ball rolling, even if they've long grown out of Pokémania.

And the editors of *Pikachu's Global Adventure: The Fall And Rise of Pokémon* take pains to point out that as a nation, America has indeed grown out of Pokémania. Although the games continue to be incredibly high sellers in both markets—the *Ruby* and *Sapphire* versions on Game Boy Advance sold unbelievable amounts in Japan and the US, and the US launch of *Fire Red* and *Leaf Green* this fall is hotly anticipated—making *Pokémon* cards, toys, and movies is no longer the license to print money it once was. It's still profitable, but the insanity is over.

What does this mean for Pikachu and pals? To find the answer, look at the last Nintendo craze that swept the nation: Mario and the NES. Mario's mug appeared on every kind of product that Pikachu ever did, from breakfast cereals to underwear. There was a Mario comic series, a daily Mario cartoon show. After a few years, the Mario fad ended, but the games lived on. At the 2004 E3, Nintendo showed off _Paper Mario 2_, _Mario Tennis_, _Mario Pinball_, _Donkey Konga_, _Donkey Kong Jungle Beat_, _DK: King of Swing_, _Mario Party Advance_, _Wario Ware DS_, _Super Mario 64x4_, and _New Super Mario Bros. DS_. Clearly, Nintendo knows how to keep its franchise characters around—clearly, rumors of Pikachu's death have been greatly exaggerated.

■ ■ ■

CHAPTER 10

FUTURE GAMES

What does the future hold for the cinematic Japanese video game? Designers like Shigeru Miyamoto, Hironobu Sakaguchi, and Masaya Matsuura have already left a lasting mark, changing video games forever. In the preceding chapters we heard from some up-and-coming designers, artists and musicians who just might leave an equally lasting mark in the years to come. In this chapter we talk to three more such gentlemen: a designer whose one and only video game thus far is considered one of the best ever created; the formerly anonymous designer to whom one of the world's most famous and groundbreaking video game series has been entrusted; and a North American game designer who strives to learn from and emulate the Japanese method.

"THE BASIC TONE IS A LITTLE BIT EROTIC"
— FUMITO UEDA

To gain a better understanding of ICO, one of the most critically beloved and commercially unsuccessful games of 2001, one might go back to the Taisho period (1911-1925). There you will find Japanese filmmakers of the time involved in what they called *jun'eigageki undo*: the Pure Film Movement. In very simple terms[*], they felt that the cinema of the time was too theatrical; the films themselves were like recorded plays—extended long shots that looked like a static camera filming a theater performance from the twentieth row. The proponents of the Pure Film Movement wanted to do things with film that could be done only with film; close-ups and careful editing are just two examples. Using such techniques the movement strove to advance the legitimacy and uniqueness of the medium. And indeed, the films that came out of this movement, though still rough around the edges, look much more similar to contemporary movies.

They were still art house films, however, and ICO is still an art house game. It won rave reviews from nearly every journalist who touched it and became an intensely personal experience for nearly every player who happened to buy it. But not enough players bought it, and it plummeted in price, unsold, faster than nearly every other PlayStation 2 game released that year.[†] This was a surprise, as a Sony team internally developed ICO.

A young designer named Fumito Ueda headed that team. Born in 1970 in an area of Japan that he remembers as being "not too rural, but not too metropolitan—somewhere in between," Ueda "wasn't very interested in video games—I didn't want to spend money on something where you didn't really own anything or have anything physical to show for your efforts. I was more interested in fishing and catching, collecting fish and collecting the items used to catch fish. I made my own fishing rods."

[*] The only terms I feel comfortable using. I took only two classes in Japanese film as an undergraduate, so I apologize to anyone reading who actually *is* an expert in this matter.

[†] New copies were selling for $12.99 less than a year after its release in certain video game specialty stores. Its original price was around $40.

Ueda aspired to be a *manga* artist as a child, but didn't end up studying *manga* at university. Instead, he chose to study fine arts and majored in oil painting. Eventually, though, he found his way back to commercial *manga*-style art, hired by Sony to produce animation for video game opening sequences. "I wanted to make CG sequences to *open* games, but as soon as I was hired, my boss said, 'why don't you just make games?'"

Asked to design a game, Ueda recalled a childhood fascination with "the mechanical things of rural areas—seeing a giant farm machine out in the middle of nowhere." So the world he created for *ICO* was an abandoned,

dilapidated, castle filled with massive, broken-down (but entirely fictional, Ueda stresses) machinery. Once-massive staircases lay in rubble, dizzyingly tall towers held secrets at their pinnacles, courtyards overgrew with grass and weeds. *ICO*'s castle looked simultaneously surreal and *too* real, dreamlike yet totally lacking the plastic artificiality of most game worlds.

Ueda put nothing else on the screen to obscure his designs. In fact, *ICO* was deliberately stripped of gaming's artificial trappings. There were no score counters, life meters, menus, maps, and lengthy text boxes full of dialogue. "I don't like games that are too complicated," says Ueda. "That's one reason why I did that. Another reason is that, as an artist, when I flip through game magazines and see the screenshots of my own games next to other people's, I wanted to show the difference between my game and RPGs."

Providing some insight onto why *ICO* sold poorly, Ueda reflected on his design choices: "Eliminating conventional items, such as the menu bar, is actually a minus point for the users and for people in the industry since it's something that's never been seen before. I was anxious about what the players were going to think. But in the end, after the game was released, I was happy to get a positive response. Instead of feeling that they were playing a game, the players said that they felt a real emotional response. They were attached emotionally to the characters, more so than in other games."

The characters and setting were certainly nothing like what typically sold in the US. The main character was Ico, a 13-year-old boy with horns growing from the top of his head. His companion was Yorda, a 16-year-old, apparently blind girl. The strange thing about *ICO*'s story, or about the player's reaction

* The Japanese release of *ICO* was released a bit later than the US version, but included a hidden option to subtitle Yorda's dialogue into Japanese.

to it, is that the player is actually told very little story. The characters barely talk to each other, there are precious few dialogue sequences, and all of Yorda's dialogue is spoken in an undecipherable, untranslated foreign tongue.* "You're given a lot of hints," says Ueda, "but what specifically happens is left up to the imagination of the player."

Thus, the player must become attached to Ico and Yorda in other ways. "Interaction between the character and the player is why I chose video games as a medium," says Ueda. Ico and Yorda are cartoonish in appearance, but the character animation is key; their movements are so fluid and so human-like as to actually bring out their personalities. Ico's jerky movements make him noticeably awkward and impulsive. Yorda's calm, methodical movements make her clearly brave but hesitant. As befits the bare-bones game design, Ico's athletic abilities are few and Yorda's fewer—they can jump and climb to a limited extent. They have to fix and use the machines to make it through the castle. At times, evil shadows emerge from the ground and attempt to capture Yorda. Ico must fight them off with his only inventory item: a stick. If she is taken, both die.

ICO flipped on its head the stereotypical video game notion of the strong man saving the helpless woman. In fact, not only is Yorda older than Ico, she must also save his neck multiple times in the course of the game. "When I was a child," says Ueda, "the popular *anime*, like *Galaxy Express 999*, featured older women and younger boys. And I always thought that was artistically perfect, putting together a younger boy and a tall, older woman. You don't even have to think about who she is, or who the boy is—just having them there together has meaning, is artistically desirable. But nowadays, this aesthetic has disappeared from *anime*. And I felt that I should bring it back.

"Having the reverse, having the older man and younger woman, would lead to some—other thoughts..." Ueda laughs. "The basic tone is still a little bit erotic. But having a taller woman and a younger boy makes it a little milder, not too direct. Initially I was thinking of having the boy be 11 and the girl be 19. But when you actually think of what might happen between them, I couldn't really visualize a happy ending there. So I brought their ages closer together, 13 and 16."

Because the player had direct control of Ico, a direct attachment to him came much more easily. Getting the player to feel emotionally attached to

Yorda, however, was the difficult part. "Since the beginning," says Ueda, "I wanted to make this a game where both characters collaborate with each other to achieve something. But since the girl was run by computer artificial intelligence, we had to bring the computer level up so she was able to be more active in the game."

Early in the game, Yorda needs help in almost every case. If you want her to climb up a small step, you must first get Ico up it, then have him turn around and reach his hand down to her. And you get so used to doing this that eventually you do it without thinking. But about halfway through the game, just as you are ready to turn around and help her up, Yorda leaps up on her own. "Some users are shocked when she does that," says Ueda.

Another repeated action that you must undertake to get Yorda across some otherwise impassable gaps is to get at the very edge of the precipice, then extend Ico's hand out to her. She will run to the opposite edge and take a leap of faith, catching the tips of Ico's fingers, dangling over the other side of the cliff as he pulls her to safety.

This situation is repeated a few times in the game, and it plays into one of the final climactic moments. Just as Ico and Yorda reach the exit of the castle, the evil Queen, who wants to kidnap Yorda, catches them, sealing off the castle and retracting the bridge that leads to safety. Separated from Yorda by the ever-growing gap, the player first tries to leave the castle (he cannot), find a hidden pathway under the bridge (there is none), and finally entice Yorda to jump the gap (she will not). Eventually, the player realizes that he must rely on Yorda the same way she has relied on him the entire game—on blind faith alone. He jumps out directly over the gap, and she catches him with the tips of her fingers.

The realistic setting and lifelike characters combine to form a heretofore-unseen level of emotional involvement. You identify with Ico and Yorda the way you identify with your favorite characters from a book or movie, perhaps even more so, because you really are in *control* of their actions. Your actions end up reflecting your personality, or the personality you choose to give to Ico: you can drag Yorda around by the hand, or let her follow you independently. After a narrow escape, you might stand on a ledge with Yorda, simply holding her hand and looking at the scenery, just because you feel so drained.

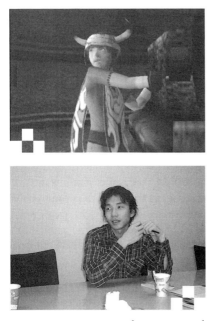

"A lot of designers are limited to the world of gaming. But by eliminating the stereotypical trappings, I wanted to prove that it isn't just a 'video game'—it's entertainment. The notion of 'video game' is too limited in people's minds. Better to have people see it as entertainment that just happens to be controlled by a Dual Shock controller.

"I'm glad to hear about it when parents watch their children play *ICO*. I think that's very important too. I always have my mother in mind when I create games; I don't think I'm able to have my mother approve *everything* in the game, but I think it's important to have some things that she can appreciate. It's important to attract to the game people who are usually *not* interested in games. Other games that were like this are *Parappa The Rapper* and *Virtua Fighter*, the first one. As one of the first 3-D games, it had the power to attract people who usually don't play games.

Perhaps decades from now, *ICO* will be seen as the first step in a Pure Games Movement, where instead of trying to replicate Japanese *anime* style or Hollywood movies with lengthy, uncontrollable cinematic scenes and volumes of dialogue, video games started to tell stories. And in so doing, reach a comparable level of emotional involvement, by emphasizing the things that only video games can deliver. There is a reason why gaming enthusiasts are holding their collective breath in anticipation of Fumito Ueda's second game.

"Something With Volume" — Eiji Aonuma

The Electronics Entertainment Expo, or E3, is the great video game trade show. For three summer days each year, tens of thousands of attendees—everybody who is anybody in the video game industry—pack into the Los Angeles Convention Center to do business, have fun, and play early demonstrations of games that are months, sometimes years, away from commercial release. Attendees come from the four corners of the globe, filling downtown hotels and paying eight-dollars-plus for bland convention-center hamburgers, all to be a part of the great spectacle.

Nintendo's E3 booth is the largest on the show floor. Surrounded by makeshift walls, covered with projection screens that suspend from the ceiling, and featuring numerous attractions and games, it is almost like a miniature show in and of itself. Some attendees voluntarily spend all three days in the Nintendo booth and *still* don't manage to play every game on display. At the 2003 E3, held from May 14-16, Nintendo's booth spotlighted titles that required players to connect their Game Boy Advance portable systems to the Nintendo GameCube. This was not a brand-new concept, but the titles on display exploited the technology more than ever before.

Two titles were especially unusual in that they were multiplayer games that required *all four* players to connect a Game Boy Advance to one GameCube.

This would be a decidedly pricey setup, but the games were worth it; they were the latest additions to the *Zelda no Densetsu* series. *Tetra's Trackers* and *Four Swords* were four-player competitive games during which the action switched between the shared TV screen and the individual Game Boy screens. Had any of the players been able to tear themselves away from the action and look behind them, they might have caught a glimpse of Eiji Aonuma—the newly anointed producer of the *Zelda* games, heir to the job long held by Shigeru Miyamoto—standing right behind them, carefully observing their reactions.

Shigeru Miyamoto is simply too recognizable, too famous to walk the show floor. He would be hounded by autograph seekers at every step, unable to do business. In contrast, Eiji Aonuma, in 2003, had rarely if ever been featured at press conferences or in interviews. But he was about to enter the public eye, as the director of *Majora's Mask* and *The Wind Waker* he was the one to whom the precious *Zelda* series had been passed.

Going by the numbers, Eiji Aonuma is not a young man; at forty, he is only ten years younger than Miyamoto. But Aonuma, with hair cut stylishly and dyed *chapatsu* brown like that of most young Japanese, stands in stark contrast to Miyamoto with his shaggy salt-and-pepper locks. He is businesslike and serious throughout our interview, laughing only when I produce my trusty Irish whistle from my bag and play him an awful rendition of *Wind Waker*'s opening title theme.

Born in Nagano prefecture, Aonuma was offered admission to the General Design program of Tokyo National University of Fine Arts and Music, a prestigious school founded in 1887. In that program, students get an all-around education in various aspects of design. They learn the history of design and practice their drawing, model-making, and communication skills. Through this general education they discover their own areas of special interest, finally drawing upon their accumulated knowledge for a final graduation project.

"Initially," Aonuma says, "I didn't think about designing games, because they weren't as popular as they are now. I wanted to do advertising design at first. But in the process of my studies I discovered that I was more interested in three-dimensional art, something with volume." For his final project, Aonuma created his own *karakuri ningyou*, Japanese traditional mechanical dolls that date back to the 18th century. *Karakuri ningyou* are fitted with intricate clockwork mechanisms that make the dolls move, turning somersaults, performing magic tricks, serving tea. They were the expensive playthings of the feudal lords and rich merchant class.

Aonuma interviewed with Nintendo right out of college and brought his dolls to show Miyamoto, unknowingly replicating Miyamoto's own interview experience in which he brought his whimsical toys and creations to Yamauchi's office and was hired based on that talent. "Miyamoto really liked them," says Aonuma. "In fact, that might be the reason I was hired." Miyamoto and Aonuma soon discovered another shared love: music. Aonuma is a percussionist, Miyamoto plays guitar. "If you listen to that *Wind Waker* title music," Aonuma tells me, "you can hear Miyamoto's own mandolin." One imagines late-night jam sessions during game deadlines—or perhaps not, because Aonuma is also as serious about his work as Miyamoto.

Having learned two-dimensional design at school, Aonuma was set to draw the dot-graphics for some lesser-known Nintendo titles. The first was *Mario Open Golf* for the Famicom; Aonuma drew the main character animations for computer and player characters. His first project as a director was an adventure game called *Marvelous: Another Treasure Island** for the Super Famicom. An adventure game with action elements and a Tom Sawyer-inspired cast, *Marvelous* was never released in the US. After that, he was assigned to assist international third parties on their Nintendo 64 projects, while he directed the enemy and dungeon design for *Zelda: Ocarina of Time* on that system.

* Marvelous: Mou hitotsu no takarajima, for the Japanese-inclined among you. Aonuma told me, "It was never released in America so you've probably never heard of it." He was wrong, at least in my case.

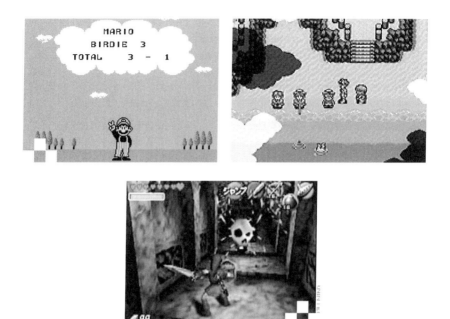

Ocarina would be Miyamoto's final project as a director. That meant he would serve as producer on all future titles, still working closely with the directors to shape the games but taking a more hands-off approach the game's levels. For the next Zelda project, Majora's Mask, Aonuma became the overall director. He worked with Yoshiaki Koizumi, who would later direct Super Mario Sunshine, to determine the game's overall look and feel: the three-day repeating system, the dark, gothic aesthetic flavor. "We needed to establish a sense of urgency, a sense of fear in the player. We needed to let him know that at the end of those three days, that's the end of everything."

Majora's Mask was perhaps the darkest, scariest game released on the Nintendo 64 and a true departure from Miyamoto's cheery worlds. When Link donned the various masks that transformed him into anthropomorphic forms with new powers, the cinematic scene that accompanied these transformations was chilling; the mask attached itself to Link's face as he screamed in pain, his body contorting and twisting into its new shape against a dark, lightning-filled sky.

Character-based scenes in the new game could be just as unsettling, especially if Link visited some people at the end of the third day, as the world was about to end. If Link had failed to save a farm, run by two sisters, from invaders, he found the youngest sister mute with shock, huddled in a corner of the farmhouse. Even if he managed to help them, of course, the world would still end, casting a tangible pathos over their happy ending.

The next console *Zelda* game, *The Wind Waker*, was directed by Aonuma but turned out to be a much brighter affair. "It's not like we establish a mood beforehand. But with *Wind Waker*, because it takes place on the sea, and you see the blue of the ocean set against the blue of the sky, the game had a bright, sunny feeling."

Are there times during game development that Miyamoto steps in and says, "I don't think you should do it this way," and Aonuma has to fight for his design choices? "Never," he says. "There are very few times when Miyamoto-san doesn't like what we decide, and even then we always come to an agreement.

"Miyamoto is still a producer, and our relationship has not fundamentally changed; he is still in the position of giving feedback on the direction of the *Zelda* games. But I now go between Miyamoto and the games' directors. Just because my title has changed does not mean that my day-to-day duties will change, but I will now work more with the game directors and less with the full creative team.

"*Zelda no Densetsu*, of course, is Miyamoto's creation. I feel a responsibility to stay true to the series, to Miyamoto, but I do try to add my own flavor. There isn't a clear distinction between Miyamoto's style and mine; in fact, I often ask myself, 'What would Miyamoto-san do in this situation?' But over the years, I've gradually gained the confidence to add my own little Aonuma-esque touches along with the Miyamoto-esque touches. And in general, Miyamoto likes these.

"In the process of developing a game, I will often come to a sticking point and won't know where to go. It is times like these that I lean on Miyamoto-san.

"Also," he adds with a smile, "when I want to implement something in a game that my team doesn't like, that's when I say, 'Oh, but Miyamoto-san wants this in there...'"

"We Learned So Much" —Denis Dyack

"Denis Dyack is an author. We're working to give him the business opportunity to make the games that he wants to, to support him and help him realize his dream."

—Shigeru Miyamoto

Can Japanese game design merge with Western game aesthetics? Denis Dyack certainly believes so. Dyack is president of Silicon Knights, a game developer located just south of Toronto that, between the months of May 2000 and April 2004, was the beneficiary of a "strategic equity investment"

care of Nintendo. That is to say, they became a Nintendo-exclusive developer, one of only a handful of Western companies ever given such an honor. This close relationship with Kyoto has resulted in games that are perhaps the perfect merging of East and West: a truly American atmosphere with an underlying game play that is Japanese through and through.

Like most other extraordinary game designers profiled in this volume, Denis Dyack never intended to become a game designer. "I started my undergraduate degree in physical education at Brock University, which is ten minutes away from Niagara Falls. I was there primarily to become a varsity wrestler. I was very interested in martial arts too; I was the Canadian Tae Kwon Do champion one year.

"But as I was doing this, I realized that I didn't want to be a gym teacher. I had always wanted to make video games, but I didn't feel confident enough. So I finished my phys ed degree and started again in computer science. I got my undergrad in CS, then went to Guelph University, which is also around the Toronto area, and got my masters in CS. So I ended up being in university for eleven years."[1]

At Brock, Dyack and a friend began working on a PC game. By the time he was at Guelph, Silicon Knights was formed. Their first game was called *Cyber Empires*, which was published by Electronic Arts in Europe and Strategic Simulations in the US, on the Atari ST, Amiga, and IBM PC, in

March 1992. After that first publishing deal, Silicon Knights incorporated.

After further success in the PC market with two more simulation titles, *Dungeons and Dragons: Fantasy Empires* [October 1993] and *Dark Legions* [April 1994], Silicon Knights moved to the world of video game consoles. "Our first console game was *Blood Omen: Legacy of Kain*. This was where we started to think seriously about storylines, thinking that they were the future of video game entertainment." *Blood Omen* was a *Zelda*-style adventure game, but a decidedly unpolished one with some serious game play issues. Simply moving the main character around and navigating the game's menus was a chore. But the storyline was promising; told in narrative voiceovers and the occasional graphical cut scene, it was clear that Silicon Knights was attempt-

ing to tell a unique story, one about a vampire hell-bent on revenge.

Blood Omen's storytelling showed that the company had potential. It was clear that they needed game play guidance, and they were about to get it. "And then, after *Kain*, we started looking for other projects... That's when we bumped into Nintendo. Back in those days, we had an agency that represented us. And they knew some people at Nintendo. I'd played Nintendo games, but honestly I didn't really understand their background as a company, what they were about. But after we stated talking, I realized that they were just like us. When we first started Silicon Knights, there were very few games out there that we felt were worthwhile. We wanted to be the knights in shining armor for the games industry. We wanted people to relate Silicon Knights to quality, always. And we soon found out that that was Nintendo's entire mantra: quality, quality, quality."

Silicon Knights' first collaboration with Nintendo was called *Eternal Darkness: Sanity's Requiem*, which was released for the Nintendo GameCube

in the summer of 2001. *Eternal Darkness* was a rarity for Nintendo: a Mature-rated game set around a psychological horror/thriller story that borrowed heavily on Poe and Lovecraft. *Eternal Darkness* was the story of the Ancients, a species of creature bound by neither space nor time, transcending the physical world. Long before the rise of the human race, the Ancients were imprisoned deep within the Earth, but their time had come again, and in 26 B.C. they begin their two-thousand-year journey back to power.[2]

The story picks up in the year 2000 with Alexandra Roivas, a young, blonde, ponytailed college student who, while investigating her grandfather's mysterious and violent death, discovers an ancient book hidden in the Roivas family mansion in Rhode Island. It is the Tome of Eternal Darkness, and in it are the stories of those who came to combat the Ancients, ordinary people caught in humanity's greatest struggles: the horror in Cambodia, the Spanish Inquisition, World War I. As Alexandra finds each new page of the Tome, she opens up new stories, and the player takes on these new roles one by one.

Dyack, a history buff, went to great lengths to ensure that *Eternal Darkness* was historically accurate down to the smallest details. When he discovered that a level set in a cathedral featuring stained-glass windows was staged fifty years prior to the invention of stained-glass windows, the team went through the laborious process of removing them. (Because that stage's story was shaped around the historical French leader Charlemagne, the date and time could not be altered to accommodate stained-glass windows.)

"History," says Dyack, "is creative enough on its own. Doing things like the Spanish Inquisition…that was really fun! Of course, we had to hold back, because you don't want to show *everything* they really did. Historical facts are really chilling when you think about them; working them into a story is really fun."

Like many of Nintendo's high-profile titles, *Eternal Darkness* was in development for over three years. It began its life as a Nintendo 64 title, but the decision was made late in the development process, after the game had been shown off at E3 twice, to move it to the GameCube. "We don't like to talk about development times," says Dyack, "but you can guess how long it took us. *Eternal Darkness* was never intended to have a long development cycle, but we had to switch platforms. And going from the N64 to the GameCube is a pretty significant switch. And we were almost finished too. We don't want to develop a game that takes that long again, but it's beyond our control."

Clearly, Silicon Knights thought along the same lines as Nintendo with regard to taking as much time as necessary to make the game as good as it could be. "We've worked with a lot of people in the industry, and they're all about making deadlines, et cetera. Nintendo's all about quality. With other publishers, we'd have to push *them* to let us work on the game more; they'd say, 'no, no, no...ship it.' With Nintendo, we'd say, 'we'd like to work on this more,' and they'd say, 'yes, we'd like you to work on this more, too.'"

Eternal Darkness' game play was inextricably tied to the story concept. Superficially, the game play was a cross between *Zelda*-style action/adventure, with numerous labyrinths to explore, and item-based puzzle solving in the manner of the *King's Quest* computer games. Where it broke from all other previous game designs was the addition of a *sanity meter*. Onscreen were three gauges: As in *Zelda*, the player had life and magic meters whose readings were obvious, but the sanity meter, which decreased whenever the player saw a horrifying creature, could wreak all sorts of havoc if it dipped too low. The screen might go black. A message might appear that the game controller was unplugged—while zombies mauled your helpless avatar. A realistic shadow of a very large spider might crawl quickly across the screen and then disappear with no indication that it was only in the game world.

Such *sanity effects*, you will notice, mostly affected the game player. Indeed, in Japan, the game was subtitled *Norowareta Juusan-nin*: thirteen cursed (or 'fated') people. There were only twelve characters in the game; the thirteenth was the player himself.

How much did Nintendo's Japanese designers improve Silicon Knights' work? "So much. Inherently, the heart of the game play was Nintendo's doing. We learned so much, so much during that development cycle. They helped us with the feel of the game play, and the color-coordinated game play elements. We combined elements of this game play with the story... Also, the boss fights felt, to me, very Nintendo.

"Working with Shigeru Miyamoto is like working with Aristotle, like working with one of the great masters. Game play is his ocean, and he navigates it like no one else. He has a talent, an insight, a vision, and a conceptual understanding of game play like no one else I've ever met. He will sit there and play the game for a long time, and he refuses to make any comments until he's finished. And when he finally comments, he will say something that is so deep, it literally takes weeks to understand totally what he means. And you have to go back and say later, is this what you meant? And he'll say, yes, now you understand. And I'll feel like Grasshopper from Kung Fu.

"For example, at one point, he said to us that it would be really great if we could do something to make the characters seem…real and not stiff, to have them react naturally to the environment as a person would.[3] And I thought about it for several weeks. And we created the *Reactive Animation System* in which the characters' eyes would follow things, snap and move around. And so with this in place, regardless of whether you were moving the controller or not, the characters would move a little; they would seem alive."

"And if you're thinking about it as Miyamoto playing the game every four months or so and making comments, that's not how it happens. It's all-the-time communication. We have videoconferences. We often fly to Kyoto, groups of us… He is very easy to talk to and get along with. Sometimes it is shocking how he presents groundbreaking ideas in a casual and relaxed manner. There are times when I have wanted to jump up in a meeting and say, 'That is pure genius!' After several meetings I began to think that I would start to sound like a broken record if I did this."[4]

But aren't there bound to be some style conflicts between Hollywood-style design and Nintendo's legendary conservatism? *Eternal Darkness*, for example, boasted a professional voice cast whereas previous Nintendo titles like *Super Mario 64* and *Mischief Makers* featured the voices of untrained Nintendo staffers (*Nintendo Power* magazine editor Leslie Swan, for example, provided the voice of Princess Peach). If there are any, Dyack downplays them with conviction. "A lot of people like to make things very dramatic and say that there's always internal conflict working with Nintendo. Well, it's not like that. There's always a collaboration of doing what's best for the game. And if it's something as obvious as, say, using professional voice actors for a complicated script, what they'll say is, 'Okay, when do we start? How do we organize it?'"

Silicon Knights' next project is the latest in a video game series that perhaps comes closest to rivaling *Eternal Darkness*' complex dialogue and fully cinematic presentation. *Metal Gear Solid: The Twin Snakes* is a GameCube-exclusive remake of the seminal 1997 PlayStation action espionage game *Metal Gear Solid*, which won critical acclaim and commercial success worldwide. The brainchild of Konami designer Hideo Kojima, *Metal Gear Solid* was the long awaited third entry in the *Metal Gear* series, which got its start on the MSX personal computer but found cult popularity when it was converted to the Famicom in 1987.

Kojima designed *Metal Gear*'s game play to be substantially different from practically every other Famicom game that starred a man with a gun. As covert operative Solid Snake, the player's goal was to *avoid* enemy combat as much as possible by sneaking around guards and disabling security systems. As the game progressed and Snake got further and further into the enemy compound, the plot twisted and turned, mostly through Snake's radio communication with the outside. A localized version released in 1988 for the NES failed to capture the attention of more than a small cult following; in large part, the adult audience for whom the game was intended did not yet see video games as a delivery medium for mature storytelling (the laughable English translation didn't help either), and the children and early teens were more interested in Konami's *Teenage Mutant Ninja Turtles* games.

Ten years later, on the PlayStation, *Metal Gear Solid* kept the same game play concept but had finally found the sophisticated graphics and cinematic storytelling techniques that would help it attract the attention of an older audience. The labyrinthine plot was conveyed not only through static radio-communication screens but also with film-like cut scenes. Every line of dialogue was recorded with professional voice actors. The voice of Solid Snake, actor and screenwriter David Hayter, went from virtual anonymity to national recognition when his name appeared in the game's opening credits. He went from bit parts in obscure *anime* dubs to writing the screenplays for the Hollywood blockbusters *X-Men* and *The Scorpion King* (as well as appearing in *Eternal Darkness* as a Roman legionnaire and a Cambodian temple guard).

Armed with far more advanced techniques for avoiding guards, the 'tactical espionage action' gameplay became easier to understand and more fun. *Metal Gear* went from being cult-classic to mainstream, one of the crown jewels in Sony's PlayStation lineup. A 2001 sequel, *Metal Gear Solid 2: Sons Of Liberty* was one of the most anticipated titles for the PlayStation 2, putting attention back on Sony's system even as Nintendo and Microsoft were launching their new hardware.

So, as Silicon Knights were wrapping up *Eternal Darkness* in early 2002, Dyack found himself in Kyoto, talking with Shigeru Miyamoto about the future. "So," said Miyamoto. "How about *Metal Gear Solid?*" At first, Dyack wasn't sure what his *sensei* meant—wasn't *Metal Gear Solid* a PlayStation series? But as Miyamoto explained the first beginnings of a partnership that would remain top-secret for another year and a half, Dyack leapt at the opportunity to become involved.

"And *the next day*," says Dyack, "Hideo Kojima took the bullet train down from Tokyo. And we all had this meeting and decided that we were going to do it. We started that first day, looking at the original *Metal Gear Solid* and talking about what we could do to make this remake a unique GameCube experience. We talked about what Kojima's vision of the project was, and of course what Silicon Knights could bring to the table."

And what *did* Silicon Knights bring to the table? "We're bringing our technical experience with the GameCube, adding new graphic features like bump mapping and shine mapping. The voice acting is being entirely redone. And we're combining all of this as it comes together. We're the final gatekeeper, making sure that it's all together and all finished," said Dyack before the game's release.

It is clear that Nintendo and Konami know how best to enhance the game play experience. They refined *The Twin Snakes* by not only expanding the things that the character can do, giving the player a greater degree of control, but also by working with a film director, a personal friend of Kojima's, to rework the game's cinematic scenes. "It's going to stay true to the original story," said Dyack, "but look for significant game play enhancements."

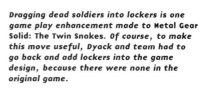

Dragging dead soldiers into lockers is one game play enhancement made to Metal Gear Solid: The Twin Snakes. Of course, to make this move useful, Dyack and team had to go back and add lockers into the game design, because there were none in the original game.

Denis Dyack has much to say about the development of video games as a medium. "If you look at the movie industry back in the nineteen-thirties, all the people with the cool technical tricks ruled the industry. But once they standardized the camera, the people who talked about serious *content* came to the forefront, and they're still the major players today—the people who *told the best stories*. That's where our industry needs to go now. We're going to reach a perceptual threshold where people won't be able to tell the difference anymore as the graphic quality leaps up. And that's when the people who focus on content are going to emerge. Kojima, Miyamoto, and I all feel that way. And we're working toward that.

"There's so much to be admired about Japanese culture; there's so much to learn from it. Our game design philosophy is based on Miyamoto Musashi's

The Book of Five Rings, and we were working from that *years* before we met Nintendo!" As a former tae kwon do champion, Dyack recalls how his martial arts training influenced his game design philosophy: "I was involved in martial arts for a long time, and so a lot of the philosophies that make sense to me have Japanese roots. *The Book of Five Rings* was very influential in my life, in martial arts and in general.

"We've studied [the importance of control] a lot, in our research and development. It's basically a further level of immersion into the story. The part of our development that comes from *The Book of Five Rings* is called 'engagement theory.' This stems from psychological studies on a phenomenon called 'flow.' Flow, or immersion, is a state in which you are having a perfect aesthetic experience, where you lose track of time. And what we think is that you have to combine all of the elements—story, gameplay, graphics, art, technology—until it's seamless." Musashi, he elaborates, spoke of perfect harmony between the five elements: earth, wind, fire, water, the void. "Some games achieve it very well. The ones that don't are missing the point."

Some would argue that *Metal Gear Solid: The Twin Snakes,* as a remake of an old game, is not worth making much of a fuss over. Some, however, see *Twin Snakes* as the small tip of a giant iceberg, an indicator of things to come— the beginning of a future in which Western and Japanese game designers work together, learn from each other, and develop games that appeal to both Western *and* Japanese sensibilities in equal proportion. And although Silicon Knights is no longer a Nintendo-exclusive developer, it's clear that Denis Dyack and his team might be some of the people who help to bring about this future.

■ ▨ ▨

CONCLUSION

THANK YOU, MARIO (BUT OUR PROFITS ARE IN ANOTHER COUNTRY)

As succeeding generations emerge unscathed from the experience of playing computer games without being transformed into gibbering idiots, attitudes might begin to change, but at present the computer game is the pariah of fictional forms.

-Barry Atkins, *More Than A Game*

In the days leading up to the Electronics Entertainment Expo each year, the industry's major players hold press conferences that pack the largest theaters and soundstages in the greater Los Angeles area. At these invitation-only gatherings, Nintendo, Sony, Microsoft et al debut their brand new, top secret software and hardware on giant movie screens while parading their top developers and executives across the stage to wild applause and the pops of flash photography. They are spectacle at its finest, which is perhaps why they are referred to as "media events" rather than "press conferences."

Nintendo's 2003 press conference played host to a groundbreaking moment in video game history, although few in attendance truly grasped its significance. At the close of the event, Shigeru Miyamoto stepped to the podium and announced that he had something special to show off. Many assumed that he was talking about a new *Super Mario* game that had been kept in secret, but to everyone's surprise Miyamoto instead invited onstage Toru Iwatani, the creator of *Pac-Man*.

Miyamoto and Iwatani shook hands for the cameras, then announced that they had worked together to create a multiplayer *Pac-Man* game for the GameCube titled *Pac-Man vs*. This was a doubly amazing event. It represented a closer relationship for Nintendo and Namco than ever before, *and* it was the first time that these legendary designers, these two men who had created video games that had passed into pop culture iconography, had ever worked together.

For Iwatani, it was also the first video game he had worked on in over twenty years. The last game he designed was *Libble Rabble* in 1983. Some say he quit designing games in protest after being awarded a piddling $3000 bonus check for *Pac-Man* after Iwatani's ingenuity had put Namco on the map.

Miyamoto, meanwhile, had always thought of Iwatani in the same way that other game designers think of, well, Shigeru Miyamoto. Iwatani was the idol of the idol, the creator of Miyamoto's favorite game. Miyamoto loved *Pac-Man* so much that when he began to experiment with "connectivity" titles that let the GameCube and Game Boy Advance link up to play games that used both the GBA screen and TV screen in sync, he fashioned a multiplayer *Pac-Man* game on his own. He then brought the prototype to Iwatani at Namco, asking him to help finish the design. Iwatani accepted, and thus *Pac-Man vs*. marked the return to game development of an exiled master.

And practically nobody cared. In fact, most of the audience sat in near-shock—*this* was Nintendo's next generation surprise? *Pac-Man*? Never mind the fact that it was a damned fine game or that Nintendo planned to give it away practically for free. Instead of being recognized as the historical event that it was—and the focal point of a Namco/Nintendo collaboration that would extend to three more high-profile games—the teaming of Miyamoto and Iwatani was used as evidence that Nintendo had lost their marbles. *Pac-Man* wasn't worth playing anymore—eating dots was out, killing hookers was in.

■   ■   ■

As games like *Grand Theft Auto* and *Halo* gradually continue to overshadow Nintendo's efforts in the public eye, in the mindshare of teenagers, and on sales charts, some dismiss Shigeru Miyamoto as irrelevant to modern game design. And yet it is impossible to imagine where we would be without him. Miyamoto's first game changed the world, because it simultaneously broke new ground in nearly every area possible: character, game play, music, graphics, narrative, and cinematic. Mario would achieve such international superstardom that, in 1990, the 'Q' ratings, an American poll that measures the popularity of politicians, movie stars, and characters, found that Mario was more recognized than *Mickey Mouse* among American children.

As of late, Nintendo has had trouble creating another Mario. As of late, Miyamoto has been more deeply involved in the creation of a handful of important games. And yet the fact that other games are beginning to compare more favorably to Nintendo's should not be read as evidence that Miyamoto has 'lost the touch.' On the contrary, it could easily be argued that an increasing number of Nintendo's competitors are simply beginning to see the value of spending a Miyamoto-like length of time polishing their games.

Hironobu Sakaguchi has also had his ups and downs. He learned the hard way that a decade and a half of directing video games that he and his staff felt were "like little movies" did not guarantee success with an actual theatrical film. Looking at the sheer volume of critical praise and retail sales that *Final Fantasy* games have received worldwide, one could make the argument that Hironobu Sakaguchi is the master of the story game, a man who brought full-scale cinematic scenes and deep, complex narrative to console games long before their time. As the catalog for a twentieth anniversary exhibition of Famicom software at the Tokyo Metropolitan Museum of Photography put it, "Every time a new piece of '*Final Fantasy*' series was released, progressive elements were crammed into it…the epoch-making technique of beginning the actual game after having finished one episode gave the player the impression that this was going to be a 'grand story.'" It was, as the catalog described, created to be an *eigatekina gēmu*—a 'motion-picture-like game.'

Sakaguchi's characters were loved and his stories devoured by millions of *Final Fantasy* enthusiasts worldwide. And yet it was apparent, after the box office disappointment of *The Spirits Within*, that some felt Sakaguchi, too, had 'lost his touch.' It's difficult to imagine how this could be possible, however.

Why single out Miyamoto and Sakaguchi for special recognition? Clearly, nothing happens in a vacuum and there were indeed many other game designers around the world making important breakthroughs. But consider what these two men added, and whether your favorite video games would be the same without them:

The Beginning/Middle/End Narrative: Prior to *Donkey Kong*, there were *zero* video games with this narrative structure. There were games with the slightest hint of a story and with identifiable, original characters, but *Donkey Kong* was leaps and bounds ahead of them all. *Donkey Kong*'s influence on video games is profoundly felt today; recall from Chapter 1 that, of *Electronic Gaming Monthly*'s 2001 list of the 100 best video games, 78 had storyline elements and another eight at least had recognizable, distinct characters.

Cut Scenes: The term 'cinema scene' began to enter the gaming fan's vocabulary around the time that *Ninja Gaiden* was released (1989 in the US), mostly because these scenes looked so different from the game play. But as a percentage of total game time, *Donkey Kong* featured even more of them; only the fact that they ran nearly seamlessly into the game play kept players from giving them a special name. *Final Fantasy VII* featured hours of digital video rendered with high-powered computers, but scenes in the six earlier games served the same purpose.

Fully Fleshed-Out Characters: *Final Fantasy II* was the first RPG, and perhaps the first video game, to put the player in control of three characters playing out a *ningen dorama*. RPG players were used to creating their own characters and giving them their own personality, and early titles like the original *Dragon Quest* and *Final Fantasy* let them do the same in video games. Sakaguchi reverted back to this original form with *Final Fantasy III*, but the *ningen dorama* concept was so popular that all future *Final Fantasy* games—and many, many imitators—stuck with creating original characters whose personal conflicts were 'resolved' by the game player.

Film-Styled Presentation: Between cinema scenes with their dynamic camera angles, character development, and dramatic music, these games were already beginning to resemble films. But the innovative addition of opening scenes, staff rolls, 'cast' lists, and elaborate "The End" screens only served to heighten the experience and add to the perceived legitimacy of video games as a storytelling medium not unlike movies.

We should discuss one other important factor before we can fully understand the appeal of story games and of Japanese video games in general: that is the element of **control**. This is what separates video game narrative from stories told through books or movies. It is one of the reasons why Miyamoto is the world's great master of video game design. He understands and prioritizes the importance of control. When I interviewed him for the first time in late 2002, I wanted to talk about stories; he wanted to talk about interface. Months later I realized they were one and the same.

As I wrote in Chapter 3, near the beginning of our conversation, he described his job as *ningen kougaku*. I didn't know what he meant at first, so I looked it up on my electronic Japanese-English translator, which I had bought in Akihabara two months before. Not having any luck, Miyamoto took the device from me and brought the definition up in seconds: *human engineering*.

Miyamoto explained that this was the art of creating an intuitive and fun control scheme. "The first and most important part of creating a game should be creating the interface. A good game has to be fun to play." Graphics, music, even characters and story mean little, he explained, if the play control isn't interesting and fun.

He went on to explain that he believes that finally people outside of Nintendo, outside of Japan, are beginning to get it, that Western game designers "are slowly beginning to understand how important it is to spend a lot of effort polishing the game. But still," he chuckles, "sometimes they spend eighty to ninety percent of their energy creating other things—making storyboards, implementing Dolby 5.1 Surround Sound—and then only 10% of their time creating the interface. We *start* with the interface."

Although Miyamoto would go on to confess a dislike of RPGs in general, it is clear that polishing control and interface also helped Sakaguchi's games. While it was true that you couldn't directly manipulate the *Final Fantasy* warriors in battle, only select their commands from a text menu, the fact that that text menu interface was streamlined and easy to understand worked wonders. Not to mention the fact that a certain level of control can more fully immerse the 'reader' into the story. Film directors use subtle, but very specific, techniques to draw the viewer's attention deeply into the story. The video game can use these, but **control** is something it can call its own.

■ ■ ■

When I started to research this book, I was sure that I knew exactly what it was that made Japanese games so impressive. Now that I'm nearly done with it, I'm filled with more questions than answers. I don't intend this book to be the definitive word on the subject. Quite the opposite, I hope that this will be the jumping-off point that gets other writers, academics, and designers researching their own theories and conclusions. Before drawing the curtain on this book, then, I would like to present some of the questions that I've been turning over in my head in the hopes of starting new discussions and perhaps getting closer to an answer.

HOW MUCH CONTROL IS TOO MUCH?

Miyamoto, in any of the numerous articles written about him or in books like David Sheff's *Game Over*, is often praised for his creation of "open-ended" worlds filled with "exploration." I would argue that this is *not* what Miyamoto creates—although the fact that people mention it is testament to how well he does his job. In fact, Miyamoto is the master of leading players exactly where he wants them to go *while always making them feel like they are exploring on their own.*

When Miyamoto talks about the importance of interface, he doesn't mean that the interface should allow as much freedom as possible to the player. He means that there should be a balance on what the machine does for you and what you control, and that the player should feel like he is in control of what the machine is doing for him.

So how does this apply to narrative? In my opinion, the chase after "open-ended" or "nonlinear" storylines in video games—"interactive storytelling," as the buzzword went a decade ago—leads down a dead-end alleyway. The video game stories that have been most effective in recent years, like *Eternal Darkness*, *ICO*, or *Prince of Persia: The Sands of Time*, have been perfectly linear, told while the player interacts with something else; the *illusion* of control in this case is preferable to the real thing.

Or, as Steven Poole put it in his book *Trigger Happy*, "If everyone wanted to make up their own story, why would they buy so many novels and cinema tickets? We like stories in general because they're *not* interactive."[1] So the optimal solution is not to *actually* strive to create an open-ended, nonlinear story. It is to make the player *think* and *feel* that he is in control of the narrative. Whether this is done with optional "side quests" or various orders in which the player can accomplish certain goals, as seen in *Final Fantasy*, or is simply done through mastery of interface and level design, as seen in *Prince of Persia*, is up to the designer and still dependent on the game's genre.

ARE JAPANESE GAMES, OR STORY GAMES, THE BRIDGE ACROSS THE 'GENDER GAP?'

When I taught my video game history course at Tufts University, I devoted the final few classes of the semester to hot-button topics like violent video games and the issue of the 'gender gap'—that is, why more boys play video games than girls. I had the class read some of the essays in *From Barbie To Mortal Kombat*, but to balance out the book's feminist-activist tone I included, among other pieces, an article penned by Joyce Worley, who, along with her husband Arnie Katz, became one of the first video game journalists.

In the article, titled *The Gender Phallacy*, Worley took pains to point out the game design philosophies that had traditionally attracted female players. Women "don't like to spend hours on unsolvable problems," she wrote, and "don't like to look foolish. They seldom enjoy any game that requires them to fail over and over in the learning process. The arcade games women liked were instant-learners: Anyone could make at least some headway with *Pac-Man*... *Tetris* and *Shanghai* charmed women... *King's Quest* drew them into Roberta Williams' magical fairy tale..."[2]

As it turns out, Worley was right on the money. Nearly a decade later, a *Wall Street Journal* news story summed everything up in its headline, "Where the Girls Are: They're Online, Solving Puzzles, And Making Up Characters In Narrative-Driven Games."[3] For the record, Worley went three-for-three with the *Journal*: she also predicted in her article that online gaming would eventually bring in more women.

What part does Japan play in this? "It seems that Japanese developers create more games that women like to play," writes Poole.[4] "Demographics are to some extent determined by aesthetics," he notes, mentioning that Japanese women seem to prefer cartoon-like games like *Parappa The Rapper*, *Super Mario*, or *Crash Bandicoot*, as well as *Pokémon*. Worley agreed, noting, "girls like games with pretty graphics. They...won't get too involved in play without something attractive on screen to look at."[5] But we should be reassured, says Poole, by the fact that, ultimately, "quality will out—that 'gender' differences are dissolved in the face of a truly great game, such as *Mario 64* or *Final Fantasy VII*."[6]

IS THE JAPANESE GAME INDUSTRY DUE FOR A SHAKEOUT?

In the spring of my Fulbright year I wrote an article for the website Tokyopia as part of their series "What's Wrong With the Japanese Games Industry?"[7] In the piece, I set down to paper for the first time some of the things that had been worrying me since I started the research for this book. There was a time, I knew, when games from Nintendo and other Japanese publishers were the best selling software worldwide, and console games by Western publishers could only be found far down the sales charts. Watching the US sales charts month-by-month, sometimes this is the case: highly anticipated Japanese games like *The Legend of Zelda: The Wind Waker* or *Pokémon Ruby* and *Sapphire* fly off the shelves anywhere in the world.

But more and more, Western-developed games are taking over the Western sales charts, especially when titles like *Grand Theft Auto: Vice City* or *Enter The Matrix* are released. *Vice City* was by far the top-selling game for all of 2002, followed in a close second by its forerunner, *Grand Theft Auto 3*. This is especially impressive when you consider that *Vice City* was available for less than three months out of that year and that GTA3 had been released in the year *2001*.

And it's not just in sales. Western-developed games are capturing the hearts and minds of console game enthusiasts. Remember from Chapter 1 that when the editors of *Electronic Gaming Monthly* voted for their top one hundred games of all time, ninety-three of said games were Japanese in origin? Well, when those same editors voted for their top games of the year 2002, ten of them were Western-developed compared to only five from Japan.

Does this bring my thesis crumbling to its very foundations? At first glance, yes. But count the *nominated* games for each award and the ratio is 38 West, 35 East—a little better, but still a loss, and nowhere near the 7-93 that Japan had pulled in the past decade and a half. It used to be that Japanese games would sell in the West because they were simply made better. It's not necessarily the case anymore, and it could be argued that Western developers are catching up because they're paying attention to the things Japan has known about for years. (Phew—my thesis is safe).

So although Japanese games can still sell well in the USA, they're not the steamrollers they once were. And they're not even guaranteed to do well in their own country anymore. But it's certainly not because more Japanese are turning to Western games. Western games perform terribly in Japan.[*] And some Japanese games aren't doing that great either. As the American industry grows each year, from $4.4 billion in 1997 to $6.9 billion in 2002, the Japanese industry as a whole is experiencing a massive, steady drop in revenues, from ¥758,167 million in 1997 to ¥501,372 million in 2002.[8] How far this will go, whether this will be a shakeout as seen in America is anyone's guess.

> [*] Even *Grand Theft Auto: Vice City*, which sold millions and millions of copies worldwide, could only manage a few hundred thousand in Japan. And this was considered a victory.

The American games industry has had two shakeouts, maybe three, depending on if the person you're asking has ever lost his job. In 1983, profits dropped dramatically and large companies like Mattel and Magnavox pulled out of the games business as smaller companies folded up entirely. The industry revived when Nintendo and its Japanese licensee companies came in two years later. In 1994, all sorts of companies went out of business or posted losses after the next generation console revolution turned out to be a few years away; Sony came in later with the PlayStation and did the job right.

These shakeouts were, in the long run, positive for the industry because they shook out the stuff that shouldn't have been there. In both cases, the market had become thoroughly glutted with low-quality software that prevented consumers from playing or buying the good stuff.

This is happening in Japan as well. But it's not just that; as Internet surfing and cell phones become more popular, *Dragon Quest* producer Yuji Horii explained to me, video games become less necessary. Games are great time killers, but the Internet and cell phones are better time killers. So many gaming companies in Japan are pursuing online games and cell-phone gaming; they think they need a foothold in those markets.

But for the time being, the American market grows as the Japanese market shrinks. So, much like Nintendo strives to create *mukokuseki* entertainment that will pull in big sales numbers worldwide, some think other Japanese developers should try to design their games to appeal to Americans. Steven Kent quotes ex-Sega boss Peter Moore, now of Microsoft, as saying, "They need to fish where the fish are biting."[9]

ARE EAST-WEST COLLABORATIONS THE ANSWER?

Speaking of which, it's probably no coincidence that the Nintendo software on the GameCube rated highest by American game journalists have been collaborative efforts between Nintendo's Japanese designers and North American game studios. There was *Eternal Darkness*, of course, but even more widely praised was *Metroid Prime*, produced by the Austin, Texas-based Retro Studios under the supervision of Miyamoto and team. Western designers are more in tune with the cultural wants and needs of their home audience, but Japanese designers know more about how to polish the game play. Working together they can achieve the best of both worlds.

But crossovers shouldn't go too far, argues Keiichi Yano: "I think Japanese designers should try to make 'Japanese games,' and I think American designers should try to make 'American games' because that's what they make the best, that's what they've grown up with. We should try to do what we do well." Collaborations have worked, but perhaps Japanese should not strive, on their own, to create games that will appeal to a Western audience specifically...

...And yet Shigeru Miyamoto's breakthrough game *Donkey Kong* was designed for America. But the Japanese view of America is skewed. "American culture" as seen in Japan is viewed through a funhouse mirror. Look at what passes for American: thin-crusted pizza topped with corn, potato, and mayonnaise, Teriyaki McBurgers with a curry pie for dessert at McDonald's, T-shirts with bizarre English language slogans like "SNOOPY IS THE WORLD FAMOUS BEAGLE AND BEST FRIEND OF CHARLIE BROWN."

That is the image of the West, along with Starbucks and Prada, that the Japanese find appealing. They don't like *Metroid Prime* or *Eternal Darkness*, though—both games sold poorly in Japan. Yes, they were programmed and designed in part by the premier Japanese software publisher. But it didn't matter. They had that western 'cultural odor.' They were far from *mukokuseki*. And this is to say nothing of games designed entirely by Americans, which the abysmal sales of Microsoft's Xbox system in Japan illustrate. Two friends of mine from the game enthusiast club at the university I attended in Kyoto are interested in Western games and want to buy an Xbox to play *Halo*. But, they cautioned me, they were on the fringe even of Japanese game enthusiast club members.

IS SIMPLER BETTER?

In a now-infamous interview with *Time Asia*, Nintendo president Satoru Iwata asserted a long-held belief at Nintendo that what the game industry needs are "simpler, more accessible" games.[10] The interviewer, clearly not impressed, dismissed Iwata as trying to create "thumb candy for dummies."

He didn't get it. Was *Tetris*, the industry's great all-time best-selling game, for "dummies?" Not in the least, although it was "simple" and, perhaps most importantly, "accessible." More adults are video game players than will admit it or even know it. How many intelligent adults while away their lunch breaks on *Solitare* or *Minesweeper*? Deep adventure games with complex controls are thrilling, but only to *game enthusiasts*. If the game industry is to reach out beyond that core group, it needs pick-up-and-play entertainment.

But it doesn't stop with simple puzzle game time-killers. The fact is that twenty years ago, Mom and Dad used to join right in with Junior and Sis playing *Super Mario Bros.* on the NES. Sometimes Dad would stay up late trying to beat *Dragon Quest*. But these days it's hard to imagine, no matter how much "better" video games are today, anyone's mother familiarizing herself with the complexities of even *Super Mario Sunshine*, much less *Splinter Cell: Pandora Tomorrow*.

To put it another way, when a video-game-related event or program, from the hardcore game industry to the mainstream, needs instantly recognizable, eye-catching, meaningful imagery for their advertisements, they don't use Sam Fisher, Lara Croft or even Mario. They use a little Space Invader. *Space Invaders*, *Pac-Man*, *Frogger*… these are the characters that entered American pop culture. These are all, not coincidentally, Japanese games.

And if Japan leads the industry in creative breakthroughs, establishing the trends that will spread worldwide years later, then the simple-games revolution is coming. Nintendo leads the pack with a hugely popular series called *Famicom Mini*, a collection of Famicom software playable on the Game Boy Advance. Sure, there's the pure nostalgia factor: the games come in deluxe collectible packaging that appeals to nostalgic twenty- and thirty-somethings who remember playing the Famicom as kids. But there's still something appealing about a game that uses one control pad and two buttons, a game that you don't have to read a giant instruction book just to be able to start playing.

And besides that, sometimes older games really are more fun, better designed. Film scholar Mark J.P. Wolf spelled out why in his book *The Medium of the Video Game*. Video game programmers working on earlier hardware, wrote Wolf, "were forced to compress their ideas. But that compression had a creative edge—it functioned much in the way a sonnet necessitates a compression of language and an economy of metaphor."[11] Now that game designers are able to do practically anything with advanced hardware and DVD storage, there's much less pressure to pare their ideas down to only the best ones.

Nintendo isn't the only company catching on to the fact that old games will sell; companies like Namco, Hudson, and Taito are reviving their old franchises with both straight Game Boy Advance ports and graphically updated remakes for home systems. But you can only drive so far on re-treaded tires. What about brand new, but accessible, game designs? They're slow in coming, but they're coming. Nintendo's new handheld system, codenamed the Nintendo DS, promises a whole new way to play video games with its dual screens and touch-input devices. Early games shown for the system are easy to understand and captivatingly fun; players use a stylus to control the on-screen action intuitively.

And new hardware isn't always necessary. It took a little convincing, but my parents sat down for a game of *Pac-Man vs.* after I assured them they could handle it. Finally, it is worth mentioning that music games like *Samba De Amigo* and *Dance Dance Revolution* are the only games that my parents ask *me* if I would please play with them.

■ ■ ■

Over the course of my research, there was one final question that I needed to answer: was I right about all this being *important*, not just for the games industry but in terms of a greater understanding between the US and Japan? Was I reaching a bit too far when I wondered if video games have been a bridge of cultural understanding between two wildly different societies? Was my personal experience, from video games to *anime* to a more general study of Japan and the Japanese language, reflective of a larger phenomenon?

"Sure," said Keiichi Yano; video games were "the big can opener" that led to a broader sharing of culture. "After the Atari shock, who would have thought a video game system from *Japan* would have succeeded? And I know a lot of guys who came in from video games and went to *anime*. And a lot of people actually learned Japanese through that.

"If you look at [legendary *manga* creator] Osamu Tezuka's early works, he was very influenced by Disney. And now the tables are turned with Disney copying him; *The Lion King* was just like his *Jungle Emperor Leo*. And I think that's a great thing. I think between American and Japanese culture, there's always been this artistic fascination that goes both ways. And today, Hayao Miyazaki and Pixar have a very good relationship. It's on the artistic level that we most influence each other."

Toward the end of the first interview I ever had with Shigeru Miyamoto in October 2002, he turned the tables on me and began to ask the questions. "You write for *Animerica*," he said. "So what *manga* do you read? As for me, I like Shotaro Ishinomori." I immediately recognized the name—Ishinomori was the celebrated creator of such legendary *manga* as *Kamen Rider*, *Skull Man*, *Japan Inc.*, and...

"*The Legend of Zelda manga* in Nintendo Power," I said excitedly. In 1991, when Nintendo released *The Legend of Zelda: A Link To The Past* for the Super Nintendo, their in-house magazine *Nintendo Power*, then hugely popular among most gamers, ran a series of lengthy, episodic *manga*-style comics based on the *Super Mario* and *Zelda* series. The *Zelda* comic had been penned by Ishinomori, although I'd only realized that later as I became a *manga* fan.

"When I first read those," I told Miyamoto, "there wasn't very much *manga* in America, so it was amazing. Right after that, I started to become interested in *manga*, and *anime*, and Japan. I was about 11 or 12 years old."

"And that was your first *manga* experience?" Miyamoto asked. "After that, you got interested in *manga*?"

"Yes."

"You know, Ishinomori-*san* has already passed away. But he would have been very happy to hear that. He wanted Americans to read Japanese *manga* very much, and he thought this would be a great opportunity. So he drew the *Zelda manga* for *Nintendo Power*. He was a legend in the world of *manga*, so we were excited to have him do this."

I wondered how many others like me were studying in Japan right then because of Miyamoto and Ishinomori. I thought about how amazing it was to be sitting there in Nintendo's conference room. And right then, I realized that I had once again taken the very path that Miyamoto had led me down, without knowing he was pulling the strings. But this time, instead of leading me to a super mushroom, he had led me to the other side of the world.

■ ▪ ■

BIBLIOGRAPHY

BOOKS

Atkins, Barry. *More Than A Game: The Computer Game As Fictional Form*. Manchester: Manchester University Press, 2003.

Birnbaum, Alfred. *Monkey Brain Sushi: New Tastes In Japanese Fiction*. Tokyo: Kodansha, 1991.

Bloom, Steven. *Video Invaders*. New York: Arco Publishing, 1982.

Bordwell, David, and Kristin Thompson. *Film Art: An Introduction*. New York: McGraw-Hill, 2001.

Burnham, Van. *Supercade*. Cambridge: MIT Press, 2001.

Buruma, Ian. *A Japanese Mirror: Heroes and Villains in Japanese Culture*. London: Phoenix, 2001.

Cassell, Justine, and Henry Jenkins, eds. *From Barbie to Mortal Kombat*. Cambridge: MIT Press, 1999.

Cohen, Scott. *Zap!: The Rise and Fall of Atari*. New York: McGraw-Hill, 1984 (Reprints available from Xlibris Corporation, www.xlibris.com).

Cross, Gary. *Kids' Stuff: Toys and the Changing World of American Childhood*. Cambridge: Harvard University Press, 1997.

DeMaria, Rusel, and Johnny L. Wilson. *High Score!: The Illustrated History of Electronic Games, 2nd Edition*. New York: McGraw-Hill/Osbourne, 2004.

Desser, David. "*Ikiru*: Narration as a Moral Act" in *Reframing Japanese Cinema* (Arthur Nolletti, Jr. and David Desser, eds.) Bloomington: Indiana University Press, 1992.

Drazen, Patrick. *Anime Explosion!* Berkeley: Stone Bridge Press, 2003.

Furniss, Maureen. *Art In Motion: Animation Aesthetics*. Sydney: John Libbey & Company Ltd., 1998.

G-Trance and Battei. *Sou da, gêmu myûjikku wo kikou!* (OK, Let's Hear The Game Music!). Tokyo: Micro Magazine, 2002.

Hatakeyama Kenji and Kubo Masakazu. *Pokémon Story*. Tokyo: Kadokawa, 2002. p. 55.

Herman, Leonard. *Phoenix: The Fall and Rise of Videogames*. New Jersey: Rolenta Press, 2001.

Herz, J.C. *Joystick Nation: How Videogames Ate Our Quarters, Won Our Hearts, and Rewired Our Minds*. Boston: Little, Brown and Company, 1997.

Kent, Steven. *The Ultimate History of Video Games*. New York: Prima Publishing, 2001.

Kerr, Alex. *Dogs and Demons: The Fall of Modern Japan*. London: Penguin, 2001.

Kinder, Marsha. *Playing With Power In Movies, Television, and Video Games*. Berkeley: University of California Press, 1991.

King, Lucien, ed. *Game On: The History and Culture of Videogames*. London: Laurence King, 2002.

Kinsella, Sharon. *Adult Manga: Culture and Power In Contemporary Japanese Society*. Honolulu: University of Hawaii Press, 2000.

Kubey, Craig. *The Winners' Book of Video Games*. New York: Warner Books, 1982.

Kusano Tsuyoshi. *Credit 00: I Love Game Graphics*. Hong Kong: All Rights Reserved, 2004.

Levi, Antonia. *Samurai From Outer Space: Understanding Japanese Animation*. Chicago: Open Court, 1996.

McCloud, Scott. *Understanding Comics: The Invisible Art*. New York: HarperCollins, 1994.

McCloud, Scott. *Reinventing Comics*. New York: Harper Collins, 2000.

Mizusaki, Hikaru. *Electronic Game 70's and 80's Collection*. Tokyo: Ohara Press, 2000.

Napier, Susan J. *Anime from Akira to Princess Mononoke*. New York: Palgrave, 2001.

Newman, James. *Videogames*. London: Routledge, 2004.

Poole, Steven. *Trigger Happy: Videogames and the Entertainment Revolution*. New York: Arcade Publishing, 2000.

Provenzo Jr., Eugene F. *Video Kids: Making Sense of Nintendo*. Cambridge: Harvard University Press, 1991.

Schilling, Mark. *The Encyclopedia of Japanese Pop Culture*. New York: Weatherhill, 1997.

Schodt, Frederick L. *Dreamland Japan: Writings on Modern Manga*. Berkeley: Stone Bridge Press, 1996.

Schodt, Frederick L. *Manga! Manga! The World of Japanese Comics*. Tokyo: Kodansha International Ltd., 1983.

Sellers, John. *Arcade Fever: The Fan's Guide to the Golden Age of Video Games*. Philadelphia: Running Press, 2001.

Sheff, David. *Game Over*. Wilton, CT: CyberActive Publishing, 1999.

Shida Hidekuni and Matsui Yuuki. *Gêmu maesutoro Vol. 1: purodyûsâ/direkutâ hen* (Game Maestro Vol. 1: Producers/Directors). Tokyo: Mainichi Communications, 2000.

Sullivan, George. *Screen Play: The Story of Video Games*. New York: Frederick Warne & Co., 1983.

Tilden, Gail, ed. *Mario Mania*. Redmond (Washington): Nintendo of America, 1991.

Tobin, Joseph, ed. *Pikachu's Global Adventure: The Rise and Fall of Pokémon*. Durham: Duke University Press, 2004.

Tokyo Metropolitan Museum of Photography. *Family Computer 1983-1994*. Tokyo: Ohta Publishing/Level X, 2003.

Wolf, Mark J.P., ed. *The Medium of the Video Game*. Austin: University of Texas Press, 2001.

ARTICLES

"20th Century Game Soft Museum." *Weekly Famitsu* 11/17/2000. pp. 85-101.

Borow, Zev. "The Godfather." *WIRED* January 2003, p. 145.

Chua-Eoan, Howard, and Tim Larimer. "Beware of the Poké-mania." *Time* November 22,1999. p. 83.

Gliatto, Tom, and Kimberly Aylward. "Master of the Games." *Time* 6/14/93, pp. 129-130.

Jenkins, Henry, and Mary Fuller. "Nintendo and New World Travel Writing." *Cybersociety: Computer-Mediated Communication and Community*, ed. Steven G. Jones (Thousand Oaks: Sage Publications, 1995): 57-72. [Reprinted in full online at <http://www.stanford.edu/class/history34q/readings/Cyberspace/FullerJenkins_Nintendo.html> Last accessed 22 July 2004.]

Kent, Steven. "The Top Bananas." *Electronic Games* May 1995. pp. 48-52.

Kohler, Chris. "AV Import Interview: Yasunori Mitsuda." *Animerica* 11-4. pp. 86-87.

"Pokémon." *Electronic Gaming Monthly* November 1999, p. 172.

Porcorobba, Janet. "Freedom Within Bounds: A Conversation With Donald Richie." *Kyoto Journal* 41, pp. 8-20.

"Why Are Shigeru Miyamoto's Games So Damn Good?" *NEXT Generation* February 1995. pp. 6-11.

WEB SITES

"Biography" at Amano's World. <http://www.amanosworld.com/html/bio.html> Last accessed 22 July 2004.

Center For Advanced Research on Intellectual Property. "Japan's Supreme Court Decision on the Sales of Used TV Game Software." *CASRIP Newsletter* August 2002.

<http://www.law.washington.edu/casrip/newsletter/newsv9i3jp2.PDF> Last accessed 22 July 2004.

"Choosing a DDR Machine." <http://www.ddrfreak.com/library/buying-machine.php> Last accessed 22 July 2004.

Collette, Chris. "Spotlight: Final Fantasy II." *Lost Levels.* <http://www.lostlevels.org/200312/200312-ffan2.shtml> Last accessed 22 July 2004.

"Derby Owners Club – Press Release." <http://expertdoc.flex.com/specsDX.htm> Last accessed 22 July 2004.

"Final Fantasy VII Reunion Tracks." (Liner notes translation.) <http://www.ffmusic.info/ff7reunionliner.html> Last accessed 22 July 2004.

"Final Fantasy: The Spirits Within Interview, Part One" at *Gamers.com.* <www.gamers.com/news/488302> Last accessed 28 April 2002.

Gifford, Kevin, trans. "Miyamoto's Tokyo University Lecture." Video-Fenky. <http://www.video-fenky.com/features/miyamoto.html> Last accessed 22 July 2004.

"History." *The Dragon's Den.* <http://www.woodus.com/den/general/history.php>. Last accessed 22 July 2004.

"Interview With Shigeru Miyamoto" at *Gaming Infinity.* <www.gaminginfinity.com/news/100742852592649.html>. Last accessed 28 April 2002.

"Interview With Hironobu Sakaguchi" at *The Gaming Intelligence Agency.* <www.thegia.com/features/f011004.html> Last accessed 28 April 2002.

"Interviews" at *NobuoUematsu.com* <www.nobuouematsu.com> Last accessed 28 April 2002.

Maragos, Nich. "Final Fantasy: The Spirits Within" at *The Gaming Intelligence Agency.* <www.thegia.com/movies/ffmovie/ffmovie.html> Last accessed 28 April 2002.

"Mastiff Responds on La Pucelle Localization." <http://www.1up.com/article2/0,2053,1574354,00.asp>

Mottram, James. "BBC – Films – Interviews - Hironobu Sakaguchi." <www.bbc.co.uk/films/2001/08/01/hironobu_sakaguchi_final_fantasy_2001_interview.shtml> Last accessed 22 July 2004.

"Regrets – Square has a few." *Planet Gamecube.* <http://www.planetgamecube.com/news.cfm?action=item&id=2261> Last accessed 22 July 2004.

"Tokusyuu: Square Enix." <http://www.geocities.co.jp/CollegeLife-Club/1665/kure03_2_tokusyuu.htm> Last accessed 22 July 2004.

Whipple, Charles T. "Words of Wisdom."
<http://www.charlest.whipple.net/itoi.html> Last accessed 22 July 2004.

Yukino Yoshi. "My Sweet Valentine."
<http://www.freetype.net/features/games/tokimemo/p2.html> Last accessed 22 July 2004.

ENDNOTES BY CHAPTER

CHAPTER 1

1. Steven Kent, *The Ultimate History of Video games* (New York: Prima Publishing, 2001) p. 193.

2. Justine Cassell and Henry Jenkins, eds., *From Barbie To Mortal Kombat* (Cambridge: MIT Press, 1999) p. 263.

3. Cassell and Jenkins, p. 278-279.

4. Cassell and Jenkins, p. 274.

5. Steven Bloom, *Video Invaders* (New York: Arco Publishing, 1982) p. 39.

6. Bloom, p. 181.

7. Alex Kerr, *Dogs And Demons: The Fall Of Modern Japan* (London: Penguin Books, 2001) p. 349.

8. Frederick L. Schodt, *Manga! Manga! The World of Japanese Comics* (Tokyo: Kodansha International Ltd., 1983) pp. 148-149.

9. Scott McCloud. *Understanding Comics*(New York: Harper Collins, 1993).

10. J.C. Herz. *Joystick Nation.* (Boston: Little, Brown and Company, 1997) p. 162.

11. Koichi Iwabuchi, "How Japanese is Pokémon?" in *Pikachu's Global Adventure*, Joseph Tobin, ed. (Durham: Duke University Press, 2004) p. 58.

12. Schodt, p. 149.

13. Bloom, pp. 42-43.

14. Leonard Herman, *Phoenix: The Fall and Rise of Video games, 3rd Edition* (New Jersey: Rolenta Press, 2001) p. 97.

15. Eugene F. Provenzo, Jr, *Video Kids: Making Sense of Nintendo* (Cambridge: Harvard University Press, 1991) p. 140.

16. Kent, p. 470.

17. Kent, p. 472.

18. Provenzo, p. 126.

19. Antonia Levi, *Samurai From Outer Space: Understanding Japanese Animation* (Chicago: Open Court, 1996) p. 2.

20. Levi, p. 137.

21. Schodt, p. 158.

22. "Nintendo and New World Travel Writing." An essay by Henry Jenkins and Mary Fuller, originally published in **Cybersociety: Computer-Mediated Communication and Community**, ed. Steven G. Jones (Thousand Oaks: Sage Publications, 1995): 57-72. Reprinted in full online at http://www.stanford.edu/class/history34q/readings/Cyberspace/FullerJenkins_Nintendo.html

CHAPTER 2

1. Kent, p. 18. The PDP-1 was one of those large, double-refrigerator-sized computers that saved data on strips of punched paper.

2. Kent, p. 43.

3. Hideyuki Shida and Yuuki Matsui. **Game Maestro Volume 1: Producers and Directors** (Tokyo: Mainichi Communications, 2000) p. 15.

4. Shida and Matsui, p. 17.

5. Kent, p. 63.

6. Shida and Matsui, p. 18.

7. John Sellers, **Arcade Fever** (Philadelphia: Running Press, 2001) pp. 36-37.

8. Kent, p. 117.

9. Kent, p. 118.

10. Scott Cohen, **Zap! The Rise and Fall of Atari** (McGraw-Hill, 1984) pp. 71-72.

11. Sellers, p. 58.

12. Sellers, p. 60.

13. Shida and Matsui, p. 38.

14. Shida and Matsui, p. 41.

15. Kent, p. 141.

16. Shida and Matsui, p. 42.

17. Shida and Matsui, p. 42.

CHAPTER 3

1. David Sheff, **Game Over** (Wilton, CT: CyberActive Publishing, 1999) p. 44.

2. Steven Kent. "The Top Bananas." **Electronic Games**, May 1995. pp. 48-52.

3. Tom Gliatto and Kimberly Aylward. "Master of the Games." **Time**, 6/14/93. p. 130.

4. Shida and Matsui, p.103-105.

5. Sheff, p. 45.

6. Sheff, p. 45.

7. Sheff, p. 45.

8. Kent, p. 157.

9. Shida and Matsui, p. 105.

10. Sheff, p. 45.

11. Kent, p. 157.

12. Shida and Matsui, p. 105.

13. Shida and Matsui, p. 105.

14. Sheff, p. 15.

15. Sheff, pp 19-20.

16. Kent, p. 94.

17. Sheff, p. 46.

18. Shida and Matsui, p. 101.

19. Unless otherwise noted, all quotes are from this personal interview, 14 July 2003.

20. Kent, p. 157.

21. Kent, p. 157.

22. Van Burnham, *Supercade* (Cambridge: MIT Press, 2001) p. 227.

23. Kent, pp. 156-157.

24. Video of the speech is available online at Gamasutra (www.gamasutra.com).

25. Sheff, p. 51.

26. Sheff, p. 47.

27. Gliatto and Aylward, p. 129.

28. Marsha Kinder, *Playing With Power In Movies, Television, and Video Games* (Berkeley: University of California Press, 1991) p. 105.

29. Ian Buruma, *A Japanese Mirror: Heroes and Villains in Japanese Culture* (London: Phoenix, 2001) p. 209.

30. Shida and Matsui, p. 101.

31. Interview with Shigeru Miyamoto. *Gaming Infinity*. *www.gaminginfinity.com/news/100742852592649.html* Last accessed 28 April 2002. URL now redirects to a different website.

32. From the 1999 GDC keynote.

33. David Bordwell and Kristin Thompson, *Film Art: An Introduction* (New York: McGraw-Hill, 2001) p. 60.

34. Maureen Furniss, *Art In Motion: Animation Aesthetics* (Sydney: John Libbey & Company Ltd., 1998) p. 98.

35. Gary Cross, **Kids' Stuff: Toys And The Changing World of American Childhood** (Cambridge: Harvard University Press, 1997) p. 109.

36. Kinder, p. 105.

37. Kinder, p. 204.

38. Scott McCloud, **Reinventing Comics** (New York: Perennial, 2000) p. 118.

39. Cassell and Jenkins, p. 263.

40. Janet Porcorobba. "Freedom Within Bounds: A Conversation With Donald Richie." Kyoto Journal 41, pp. 8-20.

41. **New Horizon English Course 1** (Tokyo: Tokyo Shoseki Co., 1997) p. 36.

42. Hitaru Mizusaki, **Electronic Game 70's and 80's Collection** (Tokyo: Okara Press, 2000) pp. 14-41.

43. Shida and Matsui, pp. 108-019.

44. David Desser, "**Ikiru**: Narration as a Moral Act" in **Reframing Japanese Cinema,** Arthur Nolletti, Jr. and David Desser, eds. (Bloomington: Indiana University Press, 1992) p. 57.

45. "Miyamoto's Tokyo University Lecture," trans. Kevin Gifford on Video-Fenky (website). <http://www.video-fenky.com/features/miyamoto.html> Last accessed 22 July 2004.

46. Personal interview, 14 July 2003.

47. Kent, p. 354.

48. "Why Are Shigeru Miyamoto's Games So Damn Good?" **NEXT Generation**, February 1995. pp. 10-11.

49. Zev Borow. "The Godfather." WIRED, January 2003, p. 145.

50. Gail Tilden, ed. **Mario Mania** (Redmond, Washington: Nintendo of America, 1991) p. 31.

CHAPTER 4

1. "Tokusyuu: Square Enix." <http://www.geocities.co.jp/CollegeLife-Club/1665/kure03_2_tokusyuu.htm> Last accessed 22 July 2004.

2. Sharon Kinsella. **Adult Manga: Culture and Power In Contemporary Japanese Society** (Honolulu: University of Hawai'i Press, 2000) p. 52.

3. Shida and Matsui p. 136.

4. Shida and Matsui p. 138.

5. Sheff, p. 69.

6. This and other examples of Dragon Quest's mainstream popularity in Japan are collected in "History" <http://www.woodus.com/den/genenral/history.php>. Last accessed 22 July 2004.

7. Charles T. Whipple. "Words of Wisdom."
   <http://www.charlest.whipple.net/itoi.html> Last accessed 22 July 2004.

8. Tokyo Metropolitan Museum of Photography. *Family Computer 1993-1994* (Tokyo: Ohta Books, 2003) p. 59.

9. Tokyo Museum, p. 60.

10. Tokyo Museum, p. 60.

11. Quoted on www.nobuouematsu.com, an unofficial (fan-created) Web site. Last accessed 28 April 2002.

12. Sakaguchi's early years are recounted in Shida and Matsui pp. 140-187.

13. Shida and Matsui, p. 163.

14. Kent, p. 540.

15. Biography on "Amano's World," Amano's official website. <http://www.amanos-world.com/html/bio.html> Last accessed 22 July 2004.

16. From the liner notes to Uematsu's CD "Final Fantasy VII Reunion Tracks." Translated at <http://www.ffmusic.info/ff7reunionliner.html> Last accessed 22 July 2004.

17. Kent, p. 540.

18. Interview conducted by Yoichi Shibuya for Digicube. Translated and reproduced on www.nobuouematsu.com. Last accessed 28 April 2002.

19. I am not entirely sure if this is true, since it is entirely possible that a Japanese-only Famicom game slipped under my radar. There were quite a few of them, after all.

20. Interview conducted by Yoshitake Maeda for Digicube. Translated and reproduced on www.nobuouematsu.com. Last accessed 28 April 2002.

21. For more on the Famicom version of *Final Fantasy IV* that never was, see the article and magazine scan at http://www.lostlevels.org.

22. "20th Century Game Soft Museum." *Weekly Famitsu*. 11/17/2000. p. 100.

23. Kent, p. 542.

24. *Regrets – Square has a few*.
    <http://www.planetgamecube.com/news.cfm?action=item&id=2261> Last accessed 22 July 2004.

25. Kent, p. 542.

26. James Mottram. "Interview: Hironobu Sakaguchi."
    <www.bbc.co.uk/films/2001/08/01/hironobu_sakaguchi_final_fantasy_2001_interview.shtml> Last accessed 22 July 2004.

27. "Final Fantasy: The Spirits Within Interview, Part One." *Gamers.com.* <www.gamers.com/news/488302> Last accessed 28 April 2002. URL now invalid.

28. Personal interview. 28 November 2002.

29. Maragos, Nich. "Final Fantasy: The Spirits Within." *The Gaming Intelligence Agency.* <www.thegia.com/movies/ffmovie/ffmovie.html> Last accessed 28 April 2002. URL now invalid: The Gaming Intelligence Agency went offline on 30 April 2002, but much of its content is archived on various mirror sites.

30. "Interview With Hironobu Sakaguchi," *The Gaming Intelligence Agency.* <www.thegia.com/features/f011004.html> Last accessed 28 April 2002. See above footnote.

CHAPTER 5

1. Numbers, facts, and dates in this section are compiled from *Sou Da, Game Music wo Kikou (OK, Let's Hear The Game Music!)* (Tokyo: Micro Magazine, 2002).

2. J.C. Herz. **Joystick Nation** (Boston: Little, Brown and Company, 1997) pp 109-110.

3. An earlier version of this section originally appeared in *Animerica*, Volume 11, no. 4, pp. 86-87.

4. Maureen Furniss. (**Art In Motion: Animation Aesthetics** (London: John Libbey and Company, 1998) p. 85.

CHAPTER 7

1. "Mainichi Daily News Tokyo City Guide – Akihabara 'electric town.'" <http://mdn.mainichi.co.jp/cityguide/tokyo/akihabara/> Last accessed 22 July 2004.

2. For information on how to reach all Mandarake stores, visit their homepage (English available) at http://www.mandarake.co.jp.

3. Center For Advanced Research on Intellectual Property (CASRIP). "Japan's Supreme Court Decision on the Sales of Used TV Game Software." *CASRIP Newsletter* August 2002. <http://www.law.washington.edu/casrip/newsletter/newsv9i3jp2.PDF> Last accessed 22 July 2004.

4. CASRIP.

CHAPTER 8

1. Berkeley: Stone Bridge Press, 2003. p. 142.

2. p. 144.

3. "Mastiff Responds on La Pucelle Localization." <http://www.1up.com/article2/0,2053,1574354,00.asp> URL now invalid.

4. p. 184.

5. p. 119.

6. Chris Collette. "Spotlight: Final Fantasy II." <http://www.lostlevels.org/200312/200312-ffan2.shtml> Last accessed 22 July 2004.

7. Yukino Yoshi. "My Sweet Valentine." <http://www.freetype.net/features/games/tokimemo/p2.html> Last accessed 22 July 2004.

8. Rusel DeMaria and Johnny L. Wilson, **High Score!** (New York: McGraw-Hill, 2004) p. 371.

9. "Media Create Software Sales 7-13 June." <http://game-science.com/news/000632.html> Last accessed 22 July 2004.

10. "Derby Owners Club – Press Release." <http://expertdoc.flex.com/specsDX.htm> Last accessed 22 July 2004.

CHAPTER 9

1. Electronic Gaming Monthly, November 1999, p. 172.

2. Howard Chua-Eoan and Tim Larimer. "Beware of the Poké-mania." *Time* November 22,1999. p. 83.

3. *Electronic Gaming Monthly* November 1999. p.168.

4. Tokyo Museum, p. 171.

5. Tokyo Museum, p. 120.

6. Tokyo Museum, p. 172.

7. Hatakeyama Kenji and Kubo Masakazu. **Pokémon Story**. Tokyo: Kadokawa, 2002. p. 55.

8. Chua-Eoan, p. 84.

9. Chua-Eoan, p. 86.

10. Quoted in Tokyo Museum, p. 120. The book is called *Shin Gêmu Dezain* (New Game Design) and is published by Enix.

11. Chua-Eoan, p. 84.

12. Chua-Eoan, p. 86.

13. *Electronic Gaming Monthly* November 1999, p. 168.

14. Anne Allison. "Cuteness as Japan's Millennial Product." Included in **Pikachu's Global Adventure: The Rise and Fall of Pokémon** (Joseph Tobin, ed.) Durham: Duke University Press, 2004. p. 40.

15. *Electronic Gaming Monthly* November 1999, p. 171.

16. Lucien King, ed. *Game On: The History and Culture of Videogames.* p. 41.

17. David Buckingham and Julian Sefton-Green. "Structure, Agency, and Pedagogy in Children's Media Culture." Included in *Pikachu's Global Adventure: The Rise and Fall of Pokémon* (Joseph Tobin, ed.). Durham: Duke University Press, 2004. p. 15.

18. James Newman. *Videogames.* London: Routledge, 2004. p. 164.

19. Chua-Eoan, p. 86.

20. Tobin, p. 267.

21. Tobin, p. 10.

22. Koichi Iwabuchi, "How 'Japanese' Is Pokémon?" In *Pikachu's Global Adventure.* p. 67.

23. Tobin, pp. 262-263.

24. Drazen, pp. 321-322.

25. "Pokemon Sets Sales Record, Again." *Gamespot.* 10/23/00. http://www.gamespot.com/gbc/rpg/pokemongold/news_2643751.html

26. Chua-Eoan, p. 81.

27. Iwabuchi 54.

28. From an unpublished draft of the paper printed in Tobin.

29. Iwabuchi 60.

30. Iwabuchi 62.

CHAPTER 10

1. Quotes in the Aonuma and Dyack sections, unless otherwise noted, were from personal interviews conducted at E3 2003. Parts have been published in question-and-answer format on www.gamespy.com.

2. Certain paragraphs here were taken and revised from my Eternal Darkness review that originally ran in Animerica.

3. E-mail interview with WIRED magazine (unpublished, conducted by Chris Baker), 2002.

4. Ibid.

CONCLUSION

1. Stephen Poole. *Trigger Happy* (New York: Arcade Publishing, 2000) p. 109.

2. Joyce Worley. "The Gender Phallacy." *Electronic Games*, August 1994, p. 42.

3. http://online.wsj.com/article/0,,SB106729313030890700,00.html?mod=todays%25 5Fus%255Fmarketplace%255Fhs> Requires subscription.

4. Poole, p. 143.

5. Worley, p. 42.

6. Poole, p. 147.

7. Chris Kohler. "What's Wrong With The Japanese Games Industry: The Historian's View." <http://www.tokyopia.com/articles.asp?articlesid=45> Last accessed 22 July 2004.

8. American Numbers courtesy of the ESA: <http://www.theesa.com/industrysales.html> Japanese Numbers: Kent, Steven. "Lessons Learned In Japan." <http://www.gamespy.com/articles/506/506473p2.html> Last accessed 22 July 2004.

9. "Lessons Learned In Japan."

10. Jim Frederick. *The Console Wars: Game On*. Time Asia, Dec. 15, 2003. <http://www.time.com/time/asia/magazine/article/0,13673,501031215-557120,00.html> Last accessed 22 July 2004.

11. Mark J.P. Wolf. **The Medium of the Video Game** (Austin: University of Texas Press, 2001) p. 139.

INDEX

How Japanese Video Games Gave the World an Extra Life

By Chris Kohler

©2005 Pearson Education

BradyGAMES® is a registered trademark of Pearson Education, Inc.

All rights reserved, including the right of reproduction in whole or in part in any form.

BradyGAMES® Publishing

An Imprint of Pearson Education
800 East 96th Street, Third Floor
Indianapolis, Indiana 46240

ISBN: 0-7440-0424-1

Library of Congress Catalog No.: 2004110354

Printing Code: The rightmost double-digit number is the year of the book's printing; the rightmost single-digit number is the number of the book's printing. For example, 04-1 shows that the first printing of the book occurred in 2004.

07 06 05 04   4 3 2 1

Manufactured in the United States of America.

BRADYGAMES STAFF

Publisher . . . . .David Waybright

Editor-In-Chief . . . . .H. Leigh Davis

Licensing Manager . . . . .Mike Degler

Creative Director . . . . .Robin Lasek

Director of Marketing . . . . . .Steve Escalante

Marketing Manager . . . . . .Janet Eshenour

Assistant Marketing Manager . .Susie Nieman

Team Coordinator . . . . .Stacey Beheler

CREDITS

Title Manager . . . . .Tim Fitzpatrick

Screenshot Editor . . . . .Michael Owen

Book Designer . . . . .Kurt Owens

Production Designer . . . . .Amy Hassos

ABOUT THE AUTHOR

Chris Kohler completed the research for *Power-Up* as a Fulbright scholar to Kyoto, Japan. Kohler was Phi Beta Kappa at Tufts University, where he graduated *summa cum laude*. As an undergraduate, Kohler designed and taught a full-credit course on the history of the video game industry and served as the teaching assistant for the school's first ever course covering Japanese animation. His graduation thesis, titled *The Cinematic Japanese Video Game*, received highest honors.

Kohler has covered the Japanese video game industry since 1996 and contributes regularly to *Wired News*, *Animerica*, and *Nintendo Official Magazine UK*. His work has appeared in *Wired*, *GameSpy*, *Shonen Jump*, *Games Domain*, *IGN*, and *Kyoto Journal* among numerous other publications. He has been the subject of an interview in the *Boston Globe*, and has contributed to such books as **High Score!: The Illustrated History of Electronic Games, Second Edition** (McGraw-Hill), **Phoenix: The Fall and Rise of Videogames, Third Edition** (Rolenta Press), and the upcoming **Gaming Hacks** (O'Reilly). He lives in Northford, Connecticut. This is his first book.

CHRIS KOHLER'S ACKNOWLEDGMENTS

Playing video games and writing about them is a lot of fun. But like most fun, it comes at someone's expense, so I'd like to thank all the people who made it possible. Charles Shiro Inouye at Tufts University was the first person to ever read parts of this book back when it was called *The Cinematic Japanese Video Game*; had he been anything less than enthusiastic about my writing a graduation thesis on video games it is doubtful you would be reading this. His mentorship and insight into Japanese culture were one of the best things about my four years at Tufts.

Also invaluable during my Tufts education were Hosea Hirata, Gary Leupp, Mitsuyo Wada-Marciano, Kiyomi Kagawa, Mayumi Lincicome, and Kiyoko Morita. Robyn Gittleman of the Experimental College let me teach a class on video game history—twice. Bert Reuss of the Geology department took us to fascinating geological sites in the Boston area, and then wrote me a recommendation for *summa cum laude* honors—I have never read it, but it apparently worked.

At the Tufts In Japan program at Kanazawa, Sonoko Matsuda and Takao Okazawa were instrumental in my adjustment to the culture and school life. At the Japan-US Educational Commission (Fulbright) office in Tokyo, Sam Shepherd and Miyuki Ito, as well as the rest of the staff, were infinitely helpful and approachable. My fellow Fulbrighters also tended to be very nice people who were surprisingly willing to talk about video games even as they researched far more important subjects. In Kyoto, Ken Rodgers and the international division of Kyoto Seika University were exceptional, and my friends in the gaming club were amazingly accepting and accommodating to my strange foreign mannerisms.

And this is not even mentioning the amazing people in the video game industry. Although Japanese companies are not used to working with freelancers, especially American freelancers, the people at Nintendo Co, Ltd. were helpful and amazingly patient. Extra special thanks to Shigeru Miyamoto, Eiji Aonuma, and Yasuhiro Minagawa. At Nintendo of America, thanks go out to Perrin Kaplan, Gail Tilden, Anka Dolecki, Beth Llewellyn, Tom Harlin, and Bill Trinen. At Golin/Harris, Chris Olmstead, Eileen Tanner, and Glenn Mandel.

At Sony Computer Entertainment Interactive, thanks to Fumito Ueda and Nanako Kato. Very special thanks to designer Kenji Kaido for introducing me to the manga *Bobobôbo Bôbobo*. At Nana-On-Sha, Masaya Matsuura and Akiko Ogawa welcomed me into their studio for an enlightening discussion on music games. PR representatives for Sony Computer Entertainment America, John Rafacz and Norma Kelly, also deserve thanks, not least for putting me on an airplane with Sheryl Crow.

There are too many more people to thank. At Silicon Knights, Denis Dyack and Ross Lillo. At Q-Games, Dylan Cuthbert; at Vitei, Giles Goddard. At INIS, Keiichi Yano, Arka Roy, and Masako Harada. At Bandai, Linda "Linda" Shannon, Dimitri Criona, and Daisuke Uchiyama. At Procyon Studio, Yasunori Mitsuda and Matt Washimi.

Thanks also to Kahori Ezaki, who brought me as an invited guest to Motoi Sakuraba's live concert in Tokyo. If you ever purchase Japanese video game music CDs and DVDs, make absolutely sure to buy them from Ezaki-san at www.cocoebiz.com. Thanks also to Stephen Kennedy and everyone from Project Majestic Mix, Ted Woolsey, and Charles Martinet.

I would not have ever imagined **Power-Up** had other writers not blazed the trail. Leonard Herman and Steven Kent have written exceptional histories of the industry, which I have referred back to time and time again. They have been very, very willing to help with this project. Rusel DeMaria let me advertise my book in his book, which is pretty cool if you think about it, and went above and beyond the call of duty to find me some great pictures that appear here. Other books I found to be helpful as well as inspirational were David Sheff's amazing **Game Over** and J.C. Herz' personal and insightful **Joystick Nation**.

Pioneering video game journalists Arnie Katz, Bill Kunkel, and Joyce Worley are incredible people who gave me one of my first freelance gigs years and years ago; for that reason Jason Thompson at *Viz* and Chris Baker at *Wired* deserve credit as well. Thanks to Urian Brown and the *Animerica* crew for letting me reprint bits of my articles and columns in this volume. Thanks also to *Gamespy* and *Wired News* for the same reason. And huge thanks to Dean Scott and the rest of the crew at *Nintendo Official Magazine UK* for letting me drag down the quality of their fine magazine with my inscrutable American slang.

Other game journalists who deserve thanks include but are not limited to Jess Ragan, John Ricciardi, Andrew Vestal, Jeremy Parish, Justin Keeling and the rest of *Tokyopia*, Jonathan Metts and everyone at *Planet Gamecube*, Dean Scott, James Mielke, and probably a whole lot of people who in their infinite generosity and grace will forgive me for forgetting to put their names down. My Tokyo journalist friend

Kunio Muto arranged some great interviews for me, including one with Yuji Horii, which I think made me only the third foreigner to ever interview him at the Enix office in Tokyo. Dan Dormer came up with a bit of the subtitle.

And of course, thanks to the people at BradyGAMES. Their enthusiasm for this project stunned me, but not as much as their dedication and desire to make it as good as it could be. Thanks to David Waybright for his initial interest in the project; to Leigh Davis for her camaraderie and support; to Tim Cox and Tim Fitzpatrick for staying on top of all the things I could never be expected to; and to Janet Eshenour and the marketing team for coming up with ways to actually get you, the reader, to buy this.

You can't play video games without friends, or at least you shouldn't. At Kanazawa, Monbusho scholars Josh Glover and Matthew Penney, both of whom know more *kanji* than me, were always ready to debate game industry theory or throw down at *Soul Calibur*. In Nara, JETs Robert Ota Dietrich (who knows more *kanji* than Josh) and Carol Van Epps were exceptionally talented at shopping and karaoke as well as video games.

At Tufts, a huge amount of credit is due to the thirty or so brave students who actually took my classes on video game history despite the fact that the reading load was ridiculous. They constantly engaged me in a classroom dialogue that forced me to think through and then rethink everything I thought I knew about the games industry. Jon Fried, Tal Dibner, and the rest of the Strategic Gaming Society would occasionally put down their twenty-sided dice and pick up a GameCube controller. Josh Martino, Megan Liotta, Sam Dangremond, and the rest of the gang at THE PRIMARY SOURCE helped learn me how to write, as well as how to argue my way out of or into pretty much any debate. Josh and Megan currently live in Brooklyn and let me sleep on their couch whenever I feel like going to NYC. Cici Chao in Los Angeles did the same thing for me for nearly a week, for which I am not sure how to repay her.

Closer to home, Matt DelGiudice; Nick Civitello; Patrick C.[1] Baer, Esq.; Helena Leschuk; James Abbatello; Al Riccitelli and their families put up with me for many years, mostly because I promised I would put their names in this section. Speaking of families putting up with me, my long-suffering parents Chris and Pam and brother Dan must be given their due. Thank you for your constant, unconditional love, support, and money; you will always get at least two of those back for sure.

AND...

YOU

---

[1] Caramello.